THE MERCURIAL EMPEROR

The Magic Circle of Rudolf II in Renaissance Prague

PETER MARSHALL

First published under the title
The Theatre of the World

PIMLICO

Published by Pimlico 2007

4 6 8 10 9 7 5 3

Copyright © Peter Marshall 2006

Peter Marshall has asserted his right
under the Copyright, Designs and Patents Act 1988
to be identified as the author of this work

This book is a work of non-fiction. The author has
stated to the publishers that the contents of this book are true.

First published in Great Britain in 2006 under the title
The Theatre of the World by
Harvill Secker

Pimlico edition 2007
Pimlico
Random House, 20 Vauxhall Bridge Road,
London SW1V 2SA

www.randomhouse.co.uk

Addresses for companies within The Random House Group Limited can be found at:
www.randomhouse.co.uk/offices.htm

The Random House Group Limited Reg. No. 954009

A CIP catalogue record for this book
is available from the British Library

ISBN 9781844135370

The Random House Group Limited supports the Forest Stewardship
Council® (FSC®), the leading international forest certification organisation.
All our titles that are printed on Greenpeace approved FSC® certified paper
carry the FSC® logo. Our paper procurement policy can be found at
www.randomhouse.co.uk/environment

Printed and bound in the UK by CPI Antony Rowe, Chippenham, Wiltshire

FOR

Elizabeth

ACKNOWLEDGEMENTS

This book, set in one of the finest cities of Europe at a pivotal moment in the history of Western civilisation, has been a delight to research and write. I would first like to thank warmly my friends in the Czech Republic: Bohumil Vurm, author and director of exhibitions, for giving me leads; Gerik Císař, translator and theatre director, for discussions of Czech history and culture; and Vladislav Zadrobílek, author and publisher, for conversations about alchemy and the occult in central Europe.

Back at home, I am grateful to Robin Waterfield for making translations from Latin and Eloïse Sentito, from Italian. Robin Waterfield also kindly read the entire manuscript.

My warm thanks also to Geoff Mulligan, Publishing Director at Harvill Secker (London), and George Gibson, Publisher at Walker & Co. (New York), for taking on the book so enthusiastically. I am particularly indebted in London to Stuart Williams for expertly editing the text, to Becky Toyne for making useful suggestions and for organising the illustrations, and to Anne Wegner for her careful copy-editing. I much appreciate the careful work of Rosalind Porter in editing the paperback for Pimlico. In New York, editor Michele Lee Amundsen made many perceptive comments. My agent Bill Hamilton of A.M. Heath & Co. continues to be a fount of good counsel and steady encouragement.

Above all, I would like to thank Elizabeth Ashton Hill who joined me in my travels to Prague and the Czech Republic. She has supported me magnificently throughout my research and writing and helped greatly with the illustrations. My children Emily and Dylan have, as always, greatly inspired me on the way.

My website is at www.petermarshall.net. I welcome any readers' comments.

Peter Marshall
Little Oaks, Devon
Summer solstice, 2005

Contents

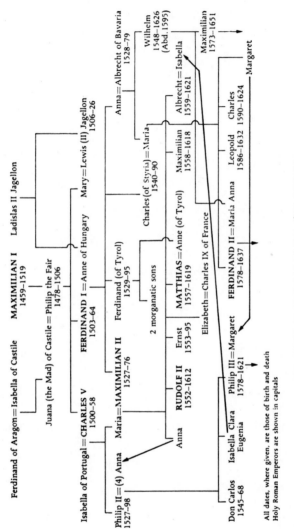

Ferdinand of Aragon=Isabella of Castile   MAXIMILIAN I   Ladislas II Jagellon
                                           1459–1519

Juana (the Mad) of Castile=Philip the Fair
                           1478–1506

Isabella of Portugal=CHARLES V   FERDINAND I=Anne of Hungary   Mary=Lewis (II) Jagellon
                      1500–58   1503–64   1506–26

Philip II=(4) Anna   Maria=MAXIMILIAN II   Ferdinand (of Tyrol)   Anna=Albrecht of Bavaria
1527–98   1527–76   1529–95   1528–79

                      Anna   Wilhelm
                                                                           1548–1626
                                                                           (Abd.1595)

                                   2 morganatic sons   Charles (of Styria)=Maria
                                                               1540–90

RUDOLF II   Ernst   MATTHIAS=Anne (of Tyrol)   Maximilian   Albrecht=Isabella   Maximilian
1552–1612   1553–95 1557–1619   1558–1618   1559–1621   1573–1651

Isabella Clara   Philip III=Margaret   Elizabeth=Charles IX of France   Leopold   Charles
Eugenia   1578–1621   1586–1632   1590–1624

Don Carlos   FERDINAND II=Maria Anna   Margaret
1545–68   1578–1637

All dates, where given, are those of birth and death
Holy Roman Emperors are shown in capitals

THE HOUSE OF HABSBURG IN THE 16TH CENTURY

Boundary of Holy Roman Empire

Lands of direct rule by Austrian Habsburg

0   50 100 150 200 km

UNITED PROVINCES

Amsterdam
The Hague
Utrecht

Oldenburg

Stadthagen
Bückeburg
Wolfenbüttel
Cassel

BRANDENBURG

Warsaw

POLAND

Leipzig UPPER LOWER
LUSATIA

Breslau (Wrocław, Vratislav)

Dresden LOWER UPPER
SILESIA

Krakow

SAXONY

Cologne

Frankfurt am Main

Bamberg

Nuremberg

HESSE

Antwerp

SPANISH NETHERLANDS

Trier Mainz

PALATINATE

Nancy

Strasbourg

Freiburg im Breisgau

Basel

Berne

SWISS CONFEDERATION

Neuburg

BAVARIA

Augsburg

Munich

Innsbruck
Ambras

TYROL

Trent

Prague

BOHEMIA MORAVIA

Brno (Brünn)

LOWER
AUSTRIA

Vienna

UPPER

Salzburg

Graz

STYRIA

CARINTHIA

CARNIOLA

VENETO

Venice

Presburg (Pozsony,
Bratislava)

Raab (Győr)

Tisza

Tisztergom (Gran)

Buda (Ofen)

HUNGARY

TRANSYLVANIA

Maros

OTTOMAN EMPIRE

LOMBARDY

Milan

Parma

Florence

TUSCANY

Po

Paris

Fontainebleau

FRANCE

Seine

Rhône

Rhine

Danube

Meuse

Vistula

Oder

Elbe

ILLUSTRATIONS

INTRODUCTION

Rudolf II, the Holy Roman Emperor, paced agitatedly up and down the long corridor of his *Kunstkammer*, his Chamber of Art, in the cold and draughty castle on Hradčany hill overlooking Prague. He was dressed as usual in black, in the style of the Spanish court. He was in his own *theatrum mundi*, his theatre of the world, designed for his personal pleasure and enlightenment. Since he never travelled, he made the world come to him. Few were privileged enough to be invited into his inner sanctum. The paintings were not hung on the walls but placed upright on the floor, on a bench or a plinth. The ceiling too was covered with canvases, mostly in the

The Feast of the Rosary (*1505*) by *Albrecht Dürer, brought from Venice and over the Alps by Rudolf's agents. Kneeling on the right is Rudolf's great-great-grandfather Maximilian I*

Mannerist style of the late Renaissance. Chests of drawers were stuffed with rare manuscripts, priceless works of art and bizarre objects from all over the known world.

The year was 1606, towards the end of Rudolf's reign. At fifty-four, he was prematurely aged, his eyes rheumy and hooded and his receding hair and sparse beard flecked with grey. His long nose, thick lower lip and jutting jaw betrayed his Habsburg lineage. Years of sensual living, with an excess of food, wine and women combined with a lack of exercise, had left his body soft and fleshy.

We can imagine him walking through his gallery without a glance at the most impressive art collection in Europe. He might have paused briefly in front of an empty space and shaken his head, and then, with a determined step, marched along the dark corridors until he reached the Old Royal Palace. From there he would have had a grand view of the red-tiled roofs of the splendid mansions of the Malá Strana (Lesser Town) under the castle walls and then across the wide River Vltava he would have seen the spires and steeples of the Old Town. Clearly visible below was the solid stone bridge, built in 1357 by his illustrious ancestor Charles IV.

And then the long-expected cavalcade appeared. Guards brandishing halberds strode out in front clearing the way and others brought up the rear. In the middle of the throng were four powerful young men, carrying a large, flat, rectangular packing case suspended from a long rod. Inside the waxed canvas was a painting. Rudolf had been waiting for it impatiently for months and had coveted it for years. Its name was *The Feast of the Rosary*.

The German community in Venice had commissioned Albrecht Dürer a hundred years earlier to paint it as a panel for the altar of their church of San Bartolomeo near the Fondaco dei Tedeschi. The painting had been carried with immense care in a vertical position, passed from hand to hand in a relay throughout the long and arduous journey from Venice over the Alps to Prague Castle. Rudolf's agents had only managed to acquire the painting after lengthy and complicated negotiations. Before it was released from the Church of San Bartolomeo, they had to pay 900 ducats (nine times the original price) as well as to commission a new altarpiece by the German painter Hans Rottenhammer who was living in Venice at the time.

Rudolf knew of the painting through his great-great-grandfather, Emperor Maximilian I, who had been Dürer's generous patron and was one of the central figures in *The Feast of the Rosary*. Rudolf had it brought immediately into his *Kunstkammer*. After his court artists had unpacked the monumental painting, first removing the canvas, then the soft carpets and finally the cotton wool, it was placed in the most favourable position to catch the northern light. At such moments, Rudolf liked to be left alone. After all those months of anxious waiting and trepidation, he had at last in his exclusive possession the fabled work of art by one of his favourite artists.

It depicts the Madonna as a stunning Renaissance beauty. She is wearing a flowing blue robe, and is crowning, with a garland of roses, Rudolf's great-great-grandfather, the kneeling Emperor Maximilian. The naked baby Jesus in her lap offers a similar garland to the Pope, probably Julian II. St Dominic gives out the garlands and crowns a bishop. Dürer had painted himself into the retinue as a long-haired and bearded figure leaning against a tree, the only figure turning his gaze to the spectator. A vellum held in his hand gives his name, to which he added 'Germanus' to distinguish himself from other Venetian painters, along with the time he took to paint the work – five months. The complex allegory symbolises the divine blessing on Church and King, a theme close to Rudolf's heart, as he still cherished the vision of abso-lute monarchy despite the growing democratic demands of the Reformation and individualism of the Renaissance.

Rudolf's men had fortunately not stumbled in their journey over the Alps. Unknown to them, they had carried all those miles a great masterpiece which not only marked a turning point in Dürer's development but was to earn a prominent place in the history of European art.

As was his wont, Rudolf spent hours alone with his beloved painting. The contemplation of art was one of the few remaining pleasures in his troubled life. But it was only a temporary calm before a gathering storm – a storm which would ruin his life and then tear apart his empire in the ensuing Thirty Years' War.

Thanks to the Holy Roman Emperor Rudolf II (1552–1612), *Dominus Mundi*, King of Bohemia, Hungary, Germany and the Romans, a remarkable and unparalleled meeting of minds took place in Prague at the end of the European Renaissance. The seat of his power was Prague Castle, at the centre of Bohemia, at the centre of Europe, at the centre of the known world. Here he established a magic circle into which he invited some of the most creative, original and subversive minds of the day.

Rudolf's English contemporary Francis Bacon, a pioneer of the modern scientific method, wrote in his *Religious Meditations* (1597) that 'knowledge is power'. But it was not political influence that Rudolf sought – he was already the most powerful man in Christendom – but rather power over nature, and power over life and death. Like Christopher Marlowe's Faust, he was prepared to risk his soul in his headlong search to understand the deepest secrets of nature and the riddle of existence. Exposed, moreover, like Hamlet to the new humanist learning, Rudolf questioned the old certainties, saw both sides of any question, and found it difficult to decide and to act.

More than any other contemporary monarch, Rudolf exemplifies the Renaissance drive to obtain power through knowledge, both in its positive and negative aspects. Ready to believe almost anything, however fanciful and absurd, he became obsessed by the alchemists' dream of discovering the Philosopher's Stone which would allegedly turn base metal into gold and prolong life indefinitely. He was seduced by the astrologers' promise to understand and predict the influence of heavenly bodies on human character and worldly affairs. He was captivated by the practitioners of natural magic who were pushing back the frontiers of science and claimed to be able to manipulate the hidden forces of nature. And when alchemy, astrology and magic failed, he was increasingly drawn to use the black arts of sorcery and necromancy to achieve his ends.

As the Holy Roman Emperor, Rudolf was responsible for upholding the temporal power of the Catholic Church. But by tolerating Protestants and Jews and by encouraging freedom of thought and expression, Rudolf would not be able to avoid a head-on clash with both the Vatican and the forces of the Inquisition and Counter Reformation who sought complete control over thinking and learning. Anyone crossing the boundaries laid down by the Vatican was accused of having contact with the devil. In the view of the Inquisition, the unbridled pursuit of truth did not lead to enlightenment but rather to damnation. Nevertheless, Rudolf dared to defy the dictates of the Church, and thereby earned an important and intriguing place for himself in the cultural history of the Renaissance.

Rudolf pursued his search for miraculous knowledge relentlessly. Often unable to distinguish between fact and fantasy, between reason and wishful thinking, and quite incapable of learning from past mistakes, his fragile sanity in the end was seriously threatened. Prone from early childhood to bouts of elation and melancholy – what today would be diagnosed as manic depression – he would, during his tortured reign, increasingly withdraw from the world and abandon the affairs of state. While his all-consuming drive to penetrate to the essence of nature ended in failure, both for himself and for his empire, it nevertheless turned out to be a truly heroic failure.

During the slow process of his personal disintegration, Rudolf presided in his theatre of the world in Prague over an extraordinary flowering of late Renaissance science and art which marked a crucial phase in the history of Western thought. Among his puffers and charlatans, there were some undeniable geniuses. His generous patronage of alchemists, physicians and astrologers from all over Europe inadvertently laid the foundations of the Scientific Revolution of the seventeenth century. He provided an island of intellectual security at a time of growing religious conflict, especially between Catholics and Protestants. By encouraging religious tolerance and the freedom of enquiry, he helped lay the foundations of the Rosicrucian Enlightenment, as well as the Age of Reason which eventually forced it underground. In his mystical aspirations, his obsession with occult learning, and his ceaseless pursuit of truth, the first glimmerings of modern philosophy and science can be found.

So while destroying himself and his empire, Rudolf played a key role in the transition from the medieval world view to the modern outlook in the Western world. How all this happened will now be revealed.

THE MAKING OF THE HOLY ROMAN EMPEROR

Our sovereign the noble Emperor Rudolf, may his glory be exalted,
eminent in science, wisdom and knowledge, learned in astronomy, a
lover of wise men and a great patron of scholars.

David Gans, *Nechmead ve-N'Maim*

Rudolf's ancestry could not have been more illustrious. Born in Vienna
on 18 July 1552 at 6.45 p.m. according to the Julian calendar, he was
the third child and eldest surviving son of Emperor Maximilian II and
Maria, daughter of Charles V of Spain and Isabella of Portugal. Rudolf was
raised at the heart of the Habsburg dynasty which lasted from 1438 to 1740,
and with its Austrian and Spanish branches formed the most powerful empire
in Europe at the time. The empire reached its zenith under Rudolf's
grandfather Charles V with lands that stretched from Madrid to Vienna,
Naples to Brussels, Prague to Mexico. Only France and England stood outside
the Habsburgs' grasp.

To hold their sprawling empire together the Habsburgs realised the
importance of maintaining the mystique and power of the monarchy. To
unite their disparate nations and peoples, they used every means possible,
from developing a cult of ancestors (among them Julius Caesar) to
encouraging Christian solidarity against the Islamic Turks of the Ottoman
Empire. To create a symbolic charisma, chivalric organisations such as the
Order of St George and the Order of the Golden Fleece were founded.

But the medieval trappings could not hide the new vigour of the
Renaissance and the Reformation which brought democratic demands and
the cult of the individual.

This was an age of transformation and contradiction. The generation which recovered the learning of the ancients also allowed the Inquisition: Erasmus was a contemporary of the Grand Inquisitor Tomás de Torquemada. Enlightened humanists observed the spread of religious fanaticism and war: Leonardo da Vinci not only painted the *Last Supper* but had also drawn designs for machine guns. The Moors in Spain may have been defeated but the Islamic Ottoman Empire was constantly threatening the eastern and southern borders of Europe. Never since the fall of the Roman Empire in the sixth century AD had life been so turbulent and uncertain.

Not only was the Habsburg constitution highly complex but a thick veil was drawn over its workings in order to enhance its mystery. The system was so complicated that it was barely understood by its rulers let alone its subjects; indeed, the many legal disputes which erupted often took decades to solve.[1] Its centralised administration consisted of a rigid hierarchy with the Emperor at the top and power spreading down to the Electors (princes entitled to take part in the election of a new emperor), 'free' cities, secular princes, bishops, higher clergy and large landowners. Structurally it was rather like a ramshackle palace presided over by a strict master who, despite regular inspections and a careful system of spies and informers, did not always know what the servants were up to. Maintaining the empire involved performing a delicate balancing act, one increasingly upset by religious discord.

The peace of Augsburg, signed by Ferdinand I in Bavaria in 1555, had temporarily ended the struggle between Lutherans and Catholics in the Holy Roman Empire and established the principle that each local ruler should determine the religion of his lands: *Cujus regio ejus religio* ('Who owns the region owns the religion'). This was the first time, since the pagan era, that a plurality of belief was recognised – a serious blow to Rome which insisted that religious truth was one and indivisible. What followed was the longest period of peace in German history, though in reality this was little more than an uneasy truce. Being so closely identified with the Catholic cause, the Habsburgs inevitably provided fuel for the Counter Reformation. The spluttering fuse between Catholics and Protestants finally exploded in the Thirty Years' War shortly after Rudolf's death.

Rudolf's paternal grandfather, Ferdinand I, was born in Alcalá de Hernares in Spain in 1503 to an Austrian father and a Spanish mother. Although he was brought up in the Netherlands and died in Vienna he was more Spanish than

Austrian. Reputed to be a kind and approachable man, he only withdrew from life after the death of his beloved wife, Anne Jagellon of Hungary. As a boy, Ferdinand was very inquisitive and became interested in botany, zoology and music but history and architecture became his adult passions. A Venetian ambassador once called him 'a most curious investigator of nature, of foreign countries, plants and animals'.[2] He was a pre-Reformation humanist, a pioneer patron of Renaissance art and architecture. Rudolf no doubt inherited his collecting mania from his grandfather who had established three important collections at the Viennese court: coins and fragments of ancient statues; an impressive library of rare books and manuscripts; and a *Kunstkammer*, a 'Chamber of Art', which contained paintings, jewels and other *objets d'art*.

After the Polish King of Bohemia, Louis, died fighting the Turks in 1526, the twenty-four-year-old Ferdinand had been elected unanimously as the next King of Bohemia. Ferdinand had a particular fondness for Hradčany Castle in Prague and came to reside there for twenty years. The people of Prague appreciated the fact that he understood Czech, although he usually replied in Latin or German. The young King had built for his wife a grandly conceived formal garden and a splendid summer house, later called the Belvedere, inspired by the Italian Renaissance. In the grounds of the brooding medieval castle it felt decidedly new and foreign. Prague nobles were allowed access to the gardens and to the greenhouses on the south-facing terraces where exotic figs, oranges, and lemons were grown.

But Ferdinand also had a ruthless side; he had iron fists within his fashionable velvet gloves. When imperial troops invaded Saxony in a drive against Protestant German princes in 1547, the people of Prague revolted, resentful of the King's drive for centralised, autocratic power. Royal mercenaries occupied Hradčany Castle and the revolt soon fizzled out. In the trials which followed, Ferdinand acted personally as chief prosecutor and high judge, condemning ten rebels to death. In the end, only four lost their lives but many citizens were publicly whipped and exiled. Property was seized and a new permanent beer tax imposed. The result was that the towns of Prague lost a great deal of their autonomy and the Protestant Estates their power.

Having defeated the uprising, Ferdinand handed over Bohemian affairs to his second son, also Ferdinand. Rudolf's uncle lived in Prague Castle for seventeen years as royal governor before moving with his famous art collection to Ambras Castle, near Innsbruck in the Tyrol. Preferring art to politics, the younger Ferdinand deliberately avoided antagonising the Estates, except on the matter of Jewish business which he encouraged. In 1562 when Rudolf came with his parents to Prague, he found a refurbished castle fit for an emperor, with its deep Stag Moat and formal pleasure gardens beyond.

Rudolf's father, Maximilian II (1527–1576), became Holy Roman Emperor on the death of his father Ferdinand I in 1564. He was crowned at Frankfurt, according to an English observer, 'with such triumphal pomp that one could only think that it has not been seen since Charlemagne'.[3]

Maximilian had been educated in Vienna in the Spanish manner but resisted the rigidity and intolerance of the black-clad Spanish court. As a boy, Maximilian was intelligent, cheerful and naturally amiable. Following in his father's footsteps, he became a humanist and, as a typical son of the Renaissance, wanted to learn as much as possible about the world. Throughout his life he remained something of an enigmatic figure with a sharp intellect, a refined artistic taste and an openness to cultural changes. Believing that conflicts and tensions, whether personal, political or religious, could be reconciled through mutual tolerance and sensible discussion, Maximilian made this part of his imperial mission to attain universal knowledge.

Practising his belief in religious tolerance and free enquiry, he accommodated at his court an array of Renaissance humanists who varied from mystical enthusiasts, Neoplatonists and Cabalists to near-atheist sceptics. Indeed, his own personal physician Johannes Crato (Kraft von Crafftheim) had known the Protestant reformer Philip Melanchthon and had lived for at least six years in Martin Luther's house. Although Maximilian went through the externals of Catholic practice, he was inwardly a Christian without any fixed confession and was considered by Rome as no better than a Protestant.

Continuing the cosmopolitan pattern of his own great-grandfather Maximilian I (1459–1519) and his father Ferdinand I, Maximilian was a patron of the arts and a man of learning. He was a fine linguist and spoke German, Latin, French, Italian, Spanish and Czech. Particularly drawn to the natural sciences, his keen interest in botany reflected the changing attitude to nature at the time: it was seen not only as a world waiting to be measured, classified and exploited but also as a place for humans to improve and embellish. As a result, there developed a new fashion for formal gardens.

Although Maximilian preferred to live in Vienna towards the end of his life surrounded by his scholars and painters, he continued to develop Prague Castle, completing a large Ball-Games Hall in the Royal Gardens. He also built a zoological garden which he filled with exotic animals brought by ambassadors and visitors, including lions, tigers, bears and 'Indian crows' (parrots).

Above all, Maximilian delighted in great allegorical pageants. Typical of these state entertainments was the lavish spectacle in 1570 which turned the centre of Prague into a theatre of the world. According to the local publisher, Daniel Adam of Veleslavín:

> The Emperor Maximilian gave the order to stage some strange and unparalleled games, circuses and knightly spectacles lasting several days that were very extravagant and magnificent and took place on the square of the Old Town in the presence of Ferdinand, the Austrian Archduke, his brother and other prominent princes and dignitaries who came in great numbers. Here was Mount Etna, from which sparks and smoke emanated, ravens and other birds flew, fiery tubes shot out. As well as Perseus, holding the head of the Gorgon and sitting astride the winged horse Pegasus, it was possible to behold a lion in a wooden cage. Apart from that and other spectacles a live elephant, a huge creature the like of which has never before been seen in these lands, was led into the square, and Porus, King of India, was seated thereupon . . .[4]

In religious matters, Maximilian was a staunch defender of Christian Europe and checked the advance of the Ottoman Empire on his south-eastern borders in Hungary and Translyvania. At the same time, he was renowned for his religious restraint and tolerance. His religious affiliation was ambiguous: he decided to support the Catholic religion in keeping with his position as Holy Roman Emperor, but he resented the meddling of the Vatican Jesuits in imperial affairs and was impatient with the Catholic fervour of his Spanish cousins. Widely considered to be a closet Lutheran, his father even felt it necessary to remind him that Protestants were excluded from access to the throne. As Emperor, he would sometimes say that he was neither a Papist nor a Lutheran but a Christian.

Maximilian has wrongly been dismissed as a failure with few achieve-ments.[5] True he never overhauled his government, expelled the Turks completely from Hungary or reunited Christendom, but through his religious tolerance and encouragement of the arts and sciences he maintained a precarious peace.

In many ways, Rudolf was the true son of his father. He shared his love of learning, passion for the arts, interest in the natural sciences, and delight in collecting. He also inherited his tolerance and uncertainty but pursued his own religion in a more mystical direction. Drawn to the magical elements in religion, he went out of his way to study the Jewish mystical tradition of the Cabala and the ancient Greek Hermetic texts which had come to light after the fall of Constantinople. And, like his father, by trying to break free of the Protestant and Catholic camps, he offended both. Later in life, he particularly valued an old, long, double-edged sword inscribed with the words: *Ubi regnat odium ibi cecum est iuditium* ('Where hatred reigns, justice is blind').

Rudolf's inheritance from his mother's side was more ambiguous. Maria was the sister of Philip II, the daughter of Charles V of Spain and Isabella of Portugal, and the granddaughter of the Catholic monarchs Ferdinand of Aragon and Isabella of Castile who first united Spain after the defeat of the Moors. This meant that through his mother the Spanish lands and dominions were within Rudolf's reach. But there was another more sinister legacy – that of madness, said to have touched Charles V, Philip II, and Philip II's sons Don Carlos and Philip III. Rudolf's great-grandmother on his mother's and father's side – the Queen of Aragon – was known as 'Juana la Loca', Joanna the Mad, and was incarcerated for much of her life because of her inconsolable love for her unfaithful husband, Philip the Fair. Rudolf was therefore the great-grandson of Joanna the Mad by double lineage.

This tendency to insanity may have been partly explained by the tendency of the Habsburgs to marry their cousins; Rudolf's mother, for example, was the first cousin of his father, with whom she shared the same grandfather, Philip I. The closeness of consanguinity down the generations almost amounted to incest. And there were certain family traits: the Habsburgs were notorious for their lack of humour, their unstable temperaments, their pride and touchiness about rank. They could equally be touched by the fires of genius or the fumes of madness.

In all these respects, Rudolf was a true Habsburg, but his melancholic disposition cannot simply be explained in terms of his genetic make-up. The lack of maternal warmth and an upbringing in vast, draughty palaces full of books, paintings and servants, were probably much more influential in forming his troubled adult personality. And as far as the astrologers were concerned, being born under the star sign of Cancer, the Crab, meant that he would tend to be stubborn and ambitious as well as withdrawn and inward-looking.

Physically, Rudolf was a typical scion of the House of Habsburg: a big nose, jutting chin, a falling lower lip, bad teeth and blond hair. His reserved manner hid his thoughts and feelings from early childhood onwards, but his blue eyes, some observed, hinted at mysterious yearnings and inexpressible suffering.

Rudolf never seems to have been close to his Spanish mother who lacked the grace and beauty of the Portuguese line and also inherited the heavy Habsburgian jaw. Where his father was light-hearted, curious, playful and open to new ideas, his mother was austere and morose, entrenched in Spanish etiquette and fanatical in her Catholicism. When Maria gave birth to Rudolf, she was in a state of deep mourning; three weeks earlier her first son Ferdinand had died and she was inconsolable. As a devout Christian, she refused to take anything for the pain of childbirth – neither myrrh, nor valerian root, nor Turkish poppy nor even a glass of water. When Rudolf came into this world, he was small and sickly and not expected to live. Rather than finding comfort at his mother's breast, he was plunged into the carcass of a freshly killed lamb – then, when it had cooled, into the carcass of another, and yet another, rushed from an adjoining butcher's slab. Only on the second day was he handed over to a wet nurse.

Eventually mother of fifteen children (the bodies of Rudolf's parents met in bed even if their minds remained at the opposite ends of Europe), Maria was cold, stern, remote and devoutly, crabbedly religious at the best of times. She gave Rudolf no caresses, no loving care, no maternal warmth. After her husband's death in 1576, she lived with Rudolf in the Hofburg palace in Vienna, but their relationship was always strained.

Although he made a half-hearted attempt to dissuade her from returning to Spain in 1581 to the court of her brother Philip II, Rudolf was privately pleased to see her go. She spent the last years of her life in the shadow of the convent of barefoot Carmelite nuns in Madrid. When she died in 1603, Rudolf made elaborate mourning arrangements in Prague Castle as imperial protocol demanded, but he also made sure that his presence at the service should remain incognito; in the end, after many delays, he did not even bother to attend.

From the beginning, Rudolf was affected by the split between his two parents. He seems to have been an extremely sensitive child which made the schism all the more painful. More delicate than most aristocratic boys of his age, Rudolf was particularly affected by harsh light, noise and any conflict around him. It did not help matters when he realised that his parents were opposed to each other both emotionally and intellectually: where his mother was an ardent and dogmatic Catholic, his father was a free-thinking and tolerant man with broad humanist sympathies. The young Rudolf, hemmed in by etiquette and court ceremony, responded to the family rows and the long periods of hostile resentment between his parents by retreating into himself, a trait which stayed with him for the rest of his life. From an early age, he developed into a serious, introspective boy, given to fantasy and inclined to melancholy.

Throughout his early years, Rudolf remained close to his father and shared his passion for plants and animals, delighting in his gardens and menagerie. Although he was taught little mathematics, Rudolf's early interest in botany and zoology undoubtedly excited his later passion for science, especially alchemy and astrology. His first teacher was Ogier (also known as Angerius) Ghislain de Busbecq, a man of considerable learning who had been his grandfather's and father's ambassador to Constantinople. De Busbecq not only helped make the temporary peace with the Turks in 1562 but brought back with him to Europe the first tulips and lilac trees which were planted in the palace gardens of Vienna and Prague. He also procured a magnificently illuminated copy of the *De materia medica* by the Greek physician Pedanius Dioscorides dating to the sixth century AD which had been produced for the daughter of the Byzantine emperor.

At his father's court in Vienna, Rudolf came in daily contact with some of the greatest minds of the age. Among these cosmopolitan intellectuals was Maximilian's official historian, the Hungarian Johannes Sambucus (János Zsámboky), who had studied under the German reformer Philip Melanchthon, author of *Loci Communes* (1521), the first great Protestant work on theology. After spending much time in the Netherlands and Italy, Sambucus finally graduated in medicine in Padua. He possessed one of the greatest libraries in Europe and was known principally for a work on symbolism called *Emblemata* (1564), the contents of which were lauded by Shakespeare. Aware of the importance of Egyptian hieroglyphs and mysteries, Sambucus believed that an emblem could correspond to the underlying reality of nature. Another influential figure at Maximilian's court was Jacopo Strada who served as court antiquary, keeper of imperial treasures and senior adviser on all subjects artistic.

So Rudolf's earliest years were spent among such men of learning. When he later came to power, he took on both Sambucus and Strada in their roles of court historian and antiquary and rewarded them greatly for their services. He even managed to buy Sambucus' famous collection of classical manuscripts which he had coveted as a boy.

Despite the unbridgeable rift and periodic rows between his parents, Rudolf was reasonably happy in Vienna. There were new apartments in the Hofburg palace in Vienna, and they occasionally visited the courts at Graz and Innsbruck. He was close to his brother Ernst, a year younger and next in line for succession, but had little to do with his other brothers Matthias, five years younger, Maximilian six years younger and Albrecht, seven years younger. As for his older sister Anna, the first born, and his younger sister Elizabeth, he hardly saw them at all. As soon as they became eligible, the elders of the House of Habsburg ensured that they married well, preferably within the family: Anna eventually became the wife of her uncle, Philip II of Spain, and Elizabeth married Charles IX of France.

In his eleventh year Rudolf's childhood world was torn apart when his uncle Philip invited him and his brother Ernst to complete their education in his country. Since Rudolf would soon be the future Holy Roman Emperor, Philip had wanted to make sure that he remained faithful to the Catholic cause, especially as his own son Don Carlos was already showing unmistakable signs of madness. Though Rudolf's father was reluctant at first – he had himself grown to maturity at the Spanish court and detested its cold formalities and rigid ceremonies – he finally agreed to let his eldest sons go on the condition that Philip renounced all claims to Austria and the rest of the Holy Roman Empire. With good reason he was always wary of his Spanish cousin's ambitions to reunite the House of Habsburg in his own favour.

A BOY OF FEW WORDS

May no one deter you from your faith which is the only true one! Only read books given by your confessor or by men known for their piety. Receive the sacraments very often. In this world, it is as necessary for your salvation as it is for your glory and honour.

Counsel of Philip II, King of Spain, to his nephew Rudolf (1571)

The die was cast. Eleven-year-old Rudolf left with his younger brother Ernst for Spain towards the end of 1563, accompanied by his father's advisers Wolf Rumpf von Wullross and Count Adam von Dietrichstein who served as their tutors. They passed through the Tyrolean Alps and travelled by boat from Genoa across the Mediterranean. Rudolf and Ernst were met in Barcelona on 17 March 1564 by their grave, black-clad uncle, Philip II, inheritor of twenty-one kingdoms and the Americas. Placed at his right side, the young Austrian archdukes received homage from the highest dignitaries of the Spanish court and from the assembled foreign ambassadors. Unlike the more familiar atmosphere of the Viennese court, Rudolf was suddenly being treated as a semi-divine being. Spain was at the zenith of its power and prestige, admired and feared throughout Europe.

Under the rule of Ferdinand and Isabella, Spain had become the centre of European politics. They had defeated the Moors, reconquered the Iberian Peninsula and gained new possessions in the Netherlands. In order to expand Spanish influence, alliances were formed by arranging strategic marriages: their eldest daughter Isabella became queen of Portugal; the second, Juana, married Felipe of Burgundy, the son of the Habsburg emperor Maximilian I;

and their youngest, Catherine of Aragon, became the first wife of Henry VIII of England.

As a result of Spain's expansionist policies, Charles V inherited Flanders, the Low Countries, Artois and Franche-Comté as well as new colonies in America. But just before his own death Charles V's division of the Habsburg dominions between his brother Ferdinand and his son Philip was to sow the seeds of enduring friction between the two branches of the House of Habsburg. Ferdinand was elected Holy Roman Emperor in 1558, the same year that the Protestant Elizabeth I was crowned Queen of England. Philip realised only too well the advantages of educating the future Holy Roman Emperor in his most impressionable years and of making sure that Rudolf remained in the Catholic camp. And there was always the enticing possibility of reuniting the two branches of the troubled House of Habsburg.

When his father Charles V abdicated in 1556, Philip inherited the sovereignty of Spain, the Netherlands and all of the Spanish dominions in Italy and the New World. He remained in Flanders until after his father's death two years later. Hailed as the 'New Apollo' or the 'New Augustus', he returned in 1559, but it was to a Spain that was suffering from a serious financial crisis and increasing religious conflict. He was.[1] Eager to extend his own power and defend what he saw as the true Catholic faith, he involved Spain in a war against France during 1557–9 and against the Turks in the Mediterranean in 1560.

Philip increasingly used the Inquisition as a shield against heresy and subversion. Set up by Pope Gregory IX in the thirteenth century, the Inquisition had increasingly been used after the reconquest of Spain from the Moors as a form of social control. It consisted of tribunals conducted by Catholic clergy who announced – at gatherings called *autos-da-fé* – penalties which ranged from a public reprimand and humiliation to being handed over to the secular authorities for burning at the stake. The procedures of the Inquisition were secret and the suspects did not even know the identity of their accusers. It dominated the life and mind of everyone; a simple denunciation was enough to be arrested, interrogated and tortured. By destroying the seat of evil in the body, its grim reapers claimed to be releasing the soul. Conceived as both an instrument of purification as well as oppression, the Inquisition tracked down Jews, Moors, Protestants, homosexuals, polygamists, humanists, witches; in short, anyone tainted with nonconformist and non-Catholic ideas.

Philip had married Mary Tudor in 1554 opening the prospect of a union between England and the Spanish Netherlands. When Mary died four years later and Philip failed to win the hand of the new queen Elizabeth I, he married Elizabeth of France in the following year, thereby securing the Valois-Habsburg peace.

When Rudolf was introduced to his uncle, he would have recognised the Habsburg features: a slight body, round face and prominent lips, particularly the lower one. While famous for his stiff composure in public, Philip occasionally showed a wry sense of humour in private. His amusements were all tranquil ones. Seeing his young nephews for the first time, fresh from Vienna, no doubt brought a sparkle briefly to his very pale blue eyes.

There was, however, the serious matter of introducing them to the Spanish way. Philip immediately took his young charges to the gloomy and isolated Benedictine monastery of Monserrat, situated high up in the mountains, where St Ignacio de Loyola, the founder of the Jesuits, had meditated forty years earlier. The monastery could only be reached by a steep path which zigzagged up to an isolated ridge at an altitude of 1,238 metres and which was distorted by a series of barren pinnacles, gorges, and hanging boulders. Philip had paid for the monastery to be rebuilt and his nephews would have been at once exhilarated by the giddy ascent and spectacular view and sobered by the oppressive atmosphere of Catholic piety.

After a short stay, Rudolf and Ernst travelled with Philip to the royal palace and park at Aranjuez, 47 kilometres from Madrid, where they spent the summer. It was a leafy oasis in the tawny Castilian plain, famous for its nightingales and wild boar. A summer residence had been built there at the end of the fourteenth century and Charles V had used it as a hunting lodge. Philip had his architect Juan de Herrera expand it into a palace and it proved a pleasant retreat from the summer heat of Madrid. During Rudolf's first stay, Philip was ill with fever, but his younger sister (Rudolf's twenty-eight-year-old aunt) and his twenty-year-old wife Elizabeth of France rode out hunting with Rudolf and Ernst in the cool of the evenings. The sedentary Catholic king also invited the boys to dance before him and demonstrate their skill at fencing.

Only Philip's epileptic son Don Carlos remained in Madrid. The possible future King of Spain was lame and hunchbacked, probably due to the excessive Habsburg inbreeding. According to the Venetian ambassador Hieronymo Soranzo, he was 'ugly and repulsive'. He was both physically and morally twisted: he liked to roast live animals and tried to force a shoemaker to eat the unsatisfactory shoes he had made. Another Italian ambassador, Paolo Tiepolo, wrote of Don Carlos: 'He wished neither to study nor to take physical exercise, but only to harm others.'[2]

Sad news interrupted their summer games at Aranjuez: the death of Emperor Ferdinand on 25 July; Rudolf's father Maximilian II would soon take his place. The court returned to Madrid which Philip had decided a few years earlier to make his centre of government. He not only extended the limits of the town but developed the old palace which had been first built around 1466 by Henry IV to replace a Moorish fort. It was situated on a bare and exposed upland plateau and not an ideal place to live – at 646 metres above sea level, it was the highest capital of Europe. The winters were dry and cold and the summers hot and oppressive. It was not unknown for sentinels on the ramparts to perish of cold at night. An old proverb had it that the air of Madrid 'which will not extinguish a candle, will put out a man's life'. But for Philip it had the inestimable advantage of being at the geographical centre of the recently reunited and newly Catholic Iberian Peninsula.

In Madrid, Rudolf was at the heart of the greatest empire in Europe and Philip made sure that he understood his method of government. Philip insisted on reading all the necessary papers and making the key decisions. Rudolf would have seen how his uncle gave royal audiences, received ambassadors and petitioners and directed his entourage at the court. Charles V's advice to his son Philip had been 'Trust no one, listen to everyone, decide alone' and Philip no doubt passed it on to his nephew. Philip came to believe that travel was useless for a monarch and isolated himself from the rest of his subjects at court, a habit in which Rudolf followed him when he came to power. However, he did not share his uncle's diligent concern for the bureaucracy and paper of empire.

The autocratic and restrained Philip allowed Rumpf and Dietrichstein, the two highly qualified teachers who had come with his young nephews from Vienna, to be responsible for their education but he made sure that they were brought up as strict Catholics. He also provided some diversion with hunting, tourneys and dancing. The two boys were prepared for their future duties of state, shown how to behave in public and taught the secrets of diplomacy. Philip's carefully stage-managed appearances and the reverence he elicited from his entourage made a deep impression on Rudolf and Ernst. Above all, they adopted the restrained manner and elaborate courtly manners of their haughty Spanish uncle. Both boys were taught what has been called the 'Spanish ceremonial', the unbending rituals which involved wearing an elaborate black cloak and court hat and walking in measured paces backwards and forwards, according to the rules of precedence.[3]

Rudolf was a better rider and fencer than his younger brother Ernst but not as quick at learning. His tutor Dietrichstein complained of his slowness and lack of concentration. Nevertheless, under his guidance, the two boys were obliged to read Terence, Cicero, Sallust, Horace and Caesar, study the philosophy of Aristotle and learn about ancient history. They were soon corresponding with their father in Latin. On his own initiative, Rudolf studied mathematics. But when it came to learning Cicero's *De Officiis*, which laid out the maxims of a good head of state, he despaired. Even so Dietrichstein wrote glowing letters about their progress to their father. He argued that Rudolf should be kept in Madrid since he would be next in line to succeed to the Spanish dominions as Philip's son Don Carlos was already showing signs of instability.

When not in Madrid, Rudolf and his brother stayed mainly at the new royal palace which his uncle had ordered to be built at El Escorial, about 40 kilometres north-west of Madrid. Still one of the most remarkable works of European architecture, it was built to fulfil the wishes of Philip's father Charles V to have a royal burial-place. But it was also intended to symbolise the triumphant power of the Habsburgs. Its full name was San Lorenzo el Real de El Escorial to commemorate Philip's victory over the French in 1557 on St Lawrence's Day.

While El Escorial was the greatest monument of its age, it was also a striking symbol of Philip's beliefs and rule. Tuscan in style and alone on a hill covered in trees, the structure was austere and formal, consisting of a parallelogram, more than 200 metres in length. These were towers at each corner and higher towers and the dome of its church in the middle, embodying the principles outlined by Philip to his architect Juan de Herrera: 'simplicity in the construction, severity in the whole; nobility without arrogance, majesty without ostentation'.[4] Built on principles of mathematical harmony it had a deep esoteric symbolism. Astrologers were asked to establish its orientation towards the setting of the sun on St Lawrence's Day (10 August) and priests were consulted to allude in the grand plan to events in the life of the saint: St Lawrence was martyred on a red-hot iron grid which gave the edifice its plan as a building within a building with sixteen courtyards.

The first stone was laid at El Escorial in the year of Rudolf's arrival in Spain in 1563 and it was still not complete when he left eight years later (it was finally consecrated in 1584). Nevertheless, the project obsessed their uncle and they spent most of this time outside Madrid in the palace. In 1568, the boys would have attended the elaborate rituals involved in the reburial of the remains of their grandfather Charles V. The royal palace was originally intended to be a simple appendage to a monastery of Hieronymite monks but vast sums were spent on its lavish decoration, with famous Italian artists covering the walls with frescos and paintings. The books and manuscripts assembled in the library under Philip's surveillance made it one of the most valuable in the world. The palace not only had a seminary and school, but royal laboratories with alchemical equipment and an astronomical observatory. Philip took a keen interest in their findings, an interest passed down to his nephew.

El Escorial contained more than 6,000 holy relics, including an alleged nail from the True Cross, a hair from Christ's beard, a thorn from his crown and part of a handkerchief used by the Virgin Mary and still stained with her tears. Not only were the remains of Charles V transported to El Escorial but the whole bodies and 103 heads of martyrs. Philip would take his children – and presumably his nephews – to kiss the smaller relics. The whole building was intended as a spear against heresy and as a bastion of Catholic faith. Philip insisted that his nephews attend mass every day and participate in the vast processions and ceremonies to celebrate the principal feasts in the Church calendar.

Wandering the dark corridors of this great mausoleum cum monastery on the hot, dusty Spanish plateau, there would have been little for Rudolf to do except pass his days exploring the library with its celestial globe and many rare books and Arabic manuscripts. He would have had ample time to explore his uncle's masterpieces of art, including Hieronymus Bosch's *The Mocking of Christ* and *Garden of Delights* and Titian's *Burial of Christ, St Jerome* and *Ecce Homo*. Titian's *The Last Summer* was painted in 1564 for the refectory at El Escorial when Rudolf was there and both Bosch and Titian would remain two of his favourite painters.

Characteristic of the Catholic fervour embodied in El Escorial was a shrine which preserved a host which was said to have bled at Gorcum in Holland when trampled on by soldiers fighting for Zwingli, the Swiss leader of the Reformation. A bas-relief on the altar depicts the presentation of the miraculous wafer to Philip II by none other than his nephew Rudolf. Philip not only had his bedroom built next to the high altar but arranged to be buried in the magnificent monument where the monks would be able to pray daily for his salvation. On either side of the altar, the centre of the whole complex, were sculptures of the Habsburgs: on one side Charles V, his wife and daughters, and, on the other, Philip II and three of his wives and his eldest son Don Carlos.

Such religious fervour led Philip increasingly to support the Spanish Inquisition which he deemed a useful tool to combat heresy and to increase his control over his own lands. Rudolf's instinctive repugnance for violence and intolerance was strengthened when his uncle arranged for the two brothers to attend with the Infanta Juana an *auto-da-fé* in Toledo in which Protestants were burnt for their beliefs. On one occasion when a condemned noble asked how he could let such a thing happen to a loyal servant, Philip reputedly replied that he would carry the wood to the pyre himself if that was what it took to root out heresy.

Philip spent half an hour each day with his nephews in his private chamber with the intention of shaping their characters and beliefs. He had a strong influence on the sensitive Rudolf, though not always in the way he intended. True Rudolf adopted his haughty manner and stiff comportment and followed him in making decisions slowly and only at the last minute. The Venetian ambassador Tommaso Contarini later wrote that they shared a 'thoughtful hesitation'.[5] But while Rudolf believed no less in absolute monarchy, he reacted against his uncle's theocratic principles and religious intolerance.

Although a lover of books and a patron of the arts, Philip, like Rudolf's mother, was a dogmatic advocate of the Catholic cause. His grandfather Ferdinand of Aragon had not only finally ejected the Moors from Spain but his father Charles V had set up the Inquisition in order to 'purify' any Moorish, Jewish and heretical elements in the newly united Catholic Spain. The purity of Spanish blood became an obsession during Philip's reign: laws of *impieza de sangre* ('purity of blood') covered all Spanish dominions and no one with 'tainted blood' could hold any office, position or title.

Philip was particularly cruel in suppressing the six hundred thousand *Moriscos* (converted Muslims) in Granada who rebelled in 1568–1570 during Rudolf's stay in Spain. As part of their studies, the young archdukes were invited to present a discourse in Latin weighing the pros and cons of the matter and giving their opinion. Rudolf concluded by pleading for mercy for the rebels, while his brother called for a severe punishment. The *Moriscos* were eventually deported to North Africa under Philip III, thereby depriving Spain of some its most industrious subjects and precipitating its economic decline.

Philip was no less ruthless with the Protestant rebels in the Netherlands. Rudolf, like his father Maximilian, was dismayed when two of their leaders, Counts Egmont and Horn, were executed in 1568 by the notorious Duke of Alva, even though they were fellow knights of the Order of the Golden Fleece. Rudolf intervened on their behalf but to no avail. 'Nothing', wrote Rudolf at the time, 'is more harmful, more inhuman and more shameful than to let oneself be overcome by anger.'[6]

Philip also contributed greatly to the Catholic Holy League which he formed with Venice and the Italian princes; it was designed as a union against the powerful Ottoman Empire which had seized Cyprus and was a constant threat to Christian Europe. Under Philip's half-brother, Don Juan of Austria, the League achieved a decisive victory over the Turkish fleet at Lepanto in 1571 in the Gulf of Corinth in Greece. In both domestic and foreign affairs, Catholic supremacy was always at the forefront of Philip's ambitions.

The period in which Rudolf grew up in Spain was, therefore, one of neo-scholasticism and mysticism, of persecuted illuminists and burnt heretics, of extreme religious bigotry and political absolutism. He could not escape being touched by this. While being drawn to the mystical elements of the period and endorsing its political absolutism, like his father he rejected its intransigent bigotry, organised persecution and merciless intolerance.

At the same time, Rudolf appreciated Philip's refined aesthetic sense and his discerning appreciation of art. In the libraries of his uncle, he was able to indulge his growing interest in esoteric art and the occult sciences. Alchemy, astrology and magic were all considered mainstream; indeed, 'natural magic' was the Renaissance name for the scientific investigation of nature. He no doubt read avidly the works attributed to the Spanish alchemists Ramón Lull and Arnald de Villanova who had benefited much from Islamic learning. For the rest of his life, Rudolf remained fascinated by the possibility of unveiling the mysterious body of external nature and penetrating its essence. To understand the riddle of existence became his greatest passion, of far greater importance than the intimate affairs of the heart or the power politics of empire.

*

While in Spain Rudolf and his younger brother Ernst were inseparable; they not only enjoyed each other's company but clearly needed each other in the cheerless and austere palaces and among the arcane and exaggerated customs of the Spanish court. They delighted in the company of the young French queen Elizabeth who gave birth on 17 October 1567 to the Infanta Isabella Clara Eugenia. She in turn was to become the light of her father's eyes and betrothed to her cousin Rudolf at the age of five.

The two brothers observed with curious disbelief, however, the mad antics of their first cousin Don Carlos, Philip's son by his first wife, seven years their senior. He was mentally unstable as well as physically handicapped and after he had thrown a page out of a window and attacked the Duke of Alva with a knife, Philip eventually had him locked up, like Juana la Loca before him, in a tower with walled-up windows. Thereafter, it was forbidden to mention his name in conversation or even in prayers. On 28 July 1568, the prince died from self-starvation. Elizabeth was greatly upset, made all the more by her implacable husband who forbade her to shed

Archduke Rudolf of Austria, aged sixteen, at the court of his uncle, Philip II of Spain. Alonzo Sanchez Coello (1567)

tears. Inconsolable, she had a miscarriage and died on 3 October, aged twenty-three, pining until the end for the lost paradise of the Court of Valois where she had grown up.

Rudolf missed Don Carlos and was reported by courtiers to have cried at his young aunt's funeral; he probably felt closer to her than any other woman in his life. The two unexpected events traumatised him. He would have realised that for all their power and glory, kings are just as susceptible to the arrows of outrageous fortune as anyone else; perhaps more so.

The Spanish court, immersed in official mourning, was gloomier than ever. Rudolf and Ernst continued to study, write letters in Latin to their father, and assist in the ritual of mass on Sundays. A portrait painted at this time by the court artist Alonzo Sanchez Coello depicts a slim 'Rudolf, Prince of Hungary' looking directly at the spectator. He has a high ruff under his jutting chin which touches his ear lobes. His hair is chestnut and his long nails are painted red. Showing no visible signs of emotion, he has one hand on his dagger in the belt of his ballooning breeches and the other hanging down by the ornate handle of his sword. The design of his codpiece makes it look as if he has an erect penis. It is the pose of an emperor-to-be as well as that of a repressed and wistful teenager. His large nose and forehead recall his German ancestors while his melancholic and dreamy look evoke the Portuguese side of his family.

Early in 1570, Rudolf and Ernst travelled with their uncle through southern Spain and spent Easter in a monastery in Córdoba which had been the centre of the Muslim empire in Iberia. During Holy Week, they were expected to fast and pray and experience the Passion of Christ. In a chapel lit by hundreds of candles, they saw their uncle prostrate himself on the ground in a frenzy of religious fervour. He then presented to God an offering of tortured heretics. Rudolf was disgusted by a dogmatic religion which preached love and forgiveness but which tortured and burnt those who did not share its doctrinal purity.

The brothers also visited the massive palace in Granada which their grandfather Charles V had deliberately built into the side of the delicately proportioned Moorish palace of Alhambra, thereby destroying its subtle symmetry. It was a crude symbol of the Christian reconquest of Spain and of Habsburg rule. It took the form of a perfect square surrounding a circular courtyard with a double portico of Doric columns. To reinforce Philip's claim that he was the ruler of the world, its walls were decorated with scenes of his triumphs, including his victory over the Protestant princes at Mühlberg in 1547.

Later in 1570, the young archdukes were joined by their elder sister Anna, then aged twenty-one, and their younger brothers whom they hardly knew, Albrecht and Wenzel-Ladislas, aged eleven and nine respectively. It was not a joyous reunion. The boys had come to undergo a similar education to their older brothers. Anna had been destined to marry her cousin Don Carlos but it had been subsequently decided that she would be the fourth wife of her forty-four-year-old uncle. Anna was warm and playful and had hoped to become the Queen of France. She would now have to submit to the dogmatism and rigidity of an ailing and morose middle-aged man and live in an austere court which one French ambassador likened to a convent of nuns.

Rudolf must have been horrified to see his sister take the place of the beloved Elizabeth in the bed of her pustular uncle. Such a union was prohibited both in the Bible and by Rome. But the Habsburgs felt that their blood should not be diluted and Philip was determined once again to strengthen the ties between the two branches of the House of Habsburg.

The wedding took place on the 12 November 1570 in Segovia. A few weeks later, Rudolf's sister, the Archduchess Elizabeth, married Charles IX of France.

Having sacrificed his daughter to Philip, Maximilian reclaimed his two eldest sons. But it was only when their sister became pregnant that Philip consented to let them go in the spring of 1571.

After nearly eight years in Spain, the nineteen-year-old Rudolf and his brother Ernst were at last allowed to return to Vienna. At the end of his life, the habitually melancholic and reserved Rudolf recalled how: 'I was seized with such joy that the following night it was impossible for me to sleep.'

On the 28 May 1571, Philip II said farewell to his two nephews with the words:

Since you return to countries dangerous for your soul, I wish to put you on your guard as if you were my own children. May no one deter you from your faith which is the only true one! Only read books given by your confessor or by men known for their piety. Receive the sacraments very often. In this world, it is as necessary for your salvation as it is for your glory and honour.[7]

Fruitless advice for the future Holy Roman Emperor! It may have made an impression on the pious Ernst but, coming from Philip, it made Rudolf want to read all the books on the Vatican's forbidden list.

After their Spanish sojourn, the two brothers remained close to each other for the rest of their lives; indeed, Ernst seems to have been the only member of the family whose trust and support Rudolf could always count on. Ernst was later appointed Governor of the Netherlands by Rudolf as a gesture of appreciation; Rudolf was devastated when he died two years later. As the second son of the family, he would have been the candidate for succession after Rudolf. One aspect, however, distinguished them: whereas Rudolf imbibed his father's religious tolerance, Ernst seems to have taken after his mother and uncle in his devout Catholicism.

Rudolf's experience in Spain marked him deeply and helps to explain his complex personality and the later direction of his life. He retained the haughty air and ceremonial manners of the Spanish court and invariably dressed in black as was the custom there. He preferred to speak Spanish formally and placed great store by his Spanish connections and advisers, especially his former tutors Dietrichstein and Rumpf. His uncle's collections of art and libraries only confirmed his father's interest in these matters. And he never forgot the grand palaces he had lived in, especially El Escorial. Later when Rudolf lived in Prague he asked his Spanish envoy to send him architectural details of El Escorial and there are striking affinities between its western main entrance and the one to the Castle ordered by Rudolf which came to be known as Matthias' Gate.[8]

Despite his long stay in Spain and the close family ties, Rudolf had an ambivalent attitude to the country. His exposure to the bigotry, religious pomp, intrigue, and persecution of the Spanish court made him suspicious of the Vatican. He disliked its rigid dogma and the Inquisition's pursuit of anyone with faintly heretical views. He saw his uncle Philip's desire to expand his part of the Habsburg empire as a serious threat to his own dominions. In the long run, his early exposure to the humanist circle of his father in Austria proved stronger than the Catholic entourage of his Spanish uncle. In assimilating such a mixed heritage, he later developed a highly personal form of spirituality.

At the same time, he learned how to adopt the persona required by the autocratic Habsburg monarchy – so much so that it became increasingly difficult for him to know the boundary between his private and public self and to have a strong sense of his identity as an individual. He did not feel comfortable in himself and, without exactly knowing why, would swing suddenly from boredom to sadness to fear.

Rudolf did not question, however, the vainglory and boundless majesty and absolute rule which were expected of him. From his earliest childhood, he had lived in a world of intrigue and suspicion, of words exchanged behind curtains, of gossip circulating in antechambers, of dissembling courtiers. As a sensitive soul, it is hardly surprising that he became oppressed by a morbid sense of paranoia and a deep-seated persecution complex. No wonder, among the constant whispers and shadowy plots, that he craved solitude and peace.

On his return to Vienna, the main features of Rudolf's personality had already been shaped. He was shy, melancholic and somewhat austere. Observers there noted disapprovingly his stiffness and pride. Rudolf certainly preferred to listen to others than to express his own views; the Venetian diplomat Giovanni Michele called him '*Rodolpho di poche parole*' ('Rudolf of few words').[9] Few could read his thoughts and feelings.

Indeed, the Venetian ambassador Corato detected a certain pride in Rudolf's and his brother Ernst's

> way of walking and in each of their gestures which makes them – I do not want to say hated so as not to use a disagreeable word – but less loved than they might be. This is entirely against the custom of this country which wishes to find in a Prince a rather familiar manner of speech and seems absolutely unbearable when it is a question of behaviour learned in Spain which is detested. . . . Those who know the Archdukes say that they are intelligent and polite. But those who do not know them are offended by their appearance and judge them to be too proud, all the more since by nature they are not talkative.[10]

Their father brought this widespread perception to their notice and reproached them on several occasions but was unable to change their habits. In Rudolf's case, it was more than just a question of manners. The experience at the Spanish court fashioned for him a royal mask to hide his true feelings.

There can be no doubt that Rudolf found study and contemplation more interesting than politics and diplomacy. At the same time, when he did become engaged in the affairs of empire, he did not want his personal rule challenged or curtailed by advisers and councils. He was extremely prickly about his rank and even the suggestion of insubordination infuriated him. For most of the time, he was lethargic and procrastinating, but the slow burning fuse within him would suddenly explode and he could be consumed by a paroxysm of anger from which it took a long time to recover.

Yet while haughty and dignified in public, Rudolf could also be engaging and friendly in private with people of high or low status, depending entirely on whether they had something interesting or original to say to him about nature or art. Although he wrote virtually nothing – only a few official letters have survived and his juvenilia are entirely unremarkable – all observers noted his intelligence, sensibility and discerning aesthetic sense. The future Emperor had an enquiring mind and was interested in anything new or unusual. Like his father, he was also a considerable linguist, speaking German, Spanish, Italian, Latin, French and some Czech. He became a brilliant patron of artists and scientists, but was incapable of producing anything notable himself.

Born in the late Renaissance, brought up in Austria and educated in Spain, Rudolf lived in a period of transition when the medieval world view was giving way to a recognisably modern outlook. By his ancestry and rank, he was steeped in the Middle Ages, but by his aesthetic and intellectual interests he was drawn to and excited by the latest developments in art and science. The conflict made him a great patron but it made his own life full of doubt and uncertainty. Although it may have proved a personal disaster, his life and patronage marked an intellectual turning point in the history of Western culture.

DOMINUS MUNDI

Holy by inclination given to the warres, few of wordes, sullein of disposition, very secrete and resolute, nothinge the manner his father had in winninge men in his behaviour, but yet constan[t] in keeping them . . . extreemely Spaniolated.

Sir Philip Sidney on Rudolf II (1577)

The two brothers set sail from Barcelona in grand manner as part of a flotilla commanded by Don Juan of Austria who was about to defeat the Turkish navy at Lepanto. After disembarking in Genoa, they passed with their large entourage through the Tyrolean Alps and called at the magnificent castle of Ambras in Innsbruck. It was the residence of their father's brother Ferdinand, Archduke of Tyrol, who ruled the Bohemian lands and had returned from Prague in 1567.

Rudolf studied carefully his uncle's famous art collection, gathered painstakingly during his stay at Prague Castle and at Ambras. His *Kunstkammer* contained all manner of rare and wonderful things: paintings, portraits, furniture, precious stones, cameos, suits of armour, weapons, coins, inscriptions, and classical relics among other exotic items. Its organisation was encyclopaedic and intended to represent the beauty and diversity of the world.

Ferdinand was interested in Neoplatonism, inspired by the rediscovery of the late Greek Platonists, and Hermeticism, based on the writings of the legendary Hermes Trismegistus ('Thrice Great') who claimed to pass on the wisdom of the Egyptians. Ferdinand was also a practising alchemist and believer in astrology. His extensive library contained several works dedicated to him by alchemists, including the *Ettlich Tractatus* (1570) by Michael

Toxites and the *Archidoxa* (1569) by Leonhard Thurneysser zum Thurn. Ferdinand took a keen interest in mining and used the services of Thurneysser who was not only an alchemist, physician and publisher but a mining and furnace construction expert. Ferdinand created his own architectural masterpiece, the Hvězda (Star) Summer House built in the royal game park outside Prague. It took the shape of a six-pointed star after the seal of Solomon and had five storeys and a magnificent vaulted ceiling rising from the central rotunda. The French Surrealist André Breton was so taken by its sacred geometry that he later described it as '*construit en pierre philosophale*' ('made wih the Philosopher's Stone').[1]

On their arrival in Vienna, the brothers were met by their father and mother, now Emperor and Empress: a year after their arrival in Spain, Maximilian II had ascended to the throne. His mother was delighted with Rudolf's Spanish manners and dress; his father despaired of his stiffness and reserve. He repeatedly told him to be more relaxed in Vienna but the influence of the Spanish court prevailed.

Nevertheless, soon after their return to Vienna, Rudolf happily participated with his father in a courtly pageant during the festivities for the wedding of Charles of Styria and Maria of Bavaria. Intended to glorify the House of Habsburg, such festivities were highly ritualised attempts to depict a symbolic world in which the nobility lived out high chivalric ideals. They had both magical and sacred aspects and were a way of confirming the social order of feudal society.

The festivities were organised and designed by the Milanese artist Giuseppe Arcimboldo and his assistants.[2] At first, an artificial hill and two pyramids were raised in a field outside the city walls to mark the tilting-ground. The pageant began with Juno, the patron goddess of weddings, who entered the scene first standing in a carriage pulled by peacocks. She was accompanied by three kings of the continents, Africa, Asia and America. All four characters were played by the members of the imperial family.

Other goddesses then appeared: Europa riding a horse disguised as a bull, followed by the Sirens and the Seven Liberal Arts. The latter, presented as the children of Mercury, were played by the Emperor's chamberlains. Next in the procession came Diana, Neptune, Pallas Athene, Venus and Bacchus. The cardinal virtues (justice, prudence, temperance and fortitude) were also represented. Finally came groups representing Spain, France and Germany. In the first, Rudolf was the personification of the Sun carrying the Spanish element gold. In the last, his father Maximilian was dressed as Winter wearing a ceremonial tournament helmet decorated with mythological and astrological motifs centred on Venus and Mars, with Aeneas depicted fleeing from ruined Troy and founding Rome.

The first day of tournaments ended with a dinner and ball, to which the guests came in extravagant, allegorical costumes. On the second day, there was a further procession watched by thousands. The whole was intended to impress the subjects of the House of Habsburg with its majesty and power, as inheritors of the ancient past and conquerors of the present world.

Soon after his return to Austria, Rudolf, already Prince of Hungary, was crowned King of that country at Stuhlweissenburg on the 26 October 1572 at the age of twenty. It was first rung on the imperial ladder to becoming Holy Roman Emperor upon his father's death. His father's respected artist Giuseppe Arcimboldo once again organised the celebrations which included a triumphal procession, feasts and tournaments.

The new king at the centre of the court festivities was a delicately built and pale-faced young man with a receding forehead and deep-seated eyes. He was small and lean at this time, only 5 foot 3 inches tall, and looked more like an overworked student than the future *Dominus Mundi* (Ruler of the World). Yet Martino Rota's engraving of him at the time shows him wearing parade armour and carrying a baton in a pose recalling Titian's portrait of Julius Caesar. It shows his thick blond eyebrows, strong nose, full lower lip and protruding Habsburgian chin.[3]

Now that he had some real power of his own, his repressed sensuality was allowed to erupt in private at least and a series of 'imperial women' were brought to his private chambers at the Hofburg palace in Vienna. But while they temporally assuaged his lusts, his Catholic upbringing afterwards ensured that he felt only shame and remorse. He was no ascetic but a man who enjoyed hunting, meat, wine and sex; as he grew older, however, only sex retained its hold, and that was more often sublimated into contemplating works of erotic art rather than being acted out in the boudoir.

Rudolf could not escape the fact that it was a time of deepening religious conflict. After the defeat of the Turkish fleet at the Battle of Lepanto in 1571 the route was open to Constantinople at the centre of the Ottoman Empire but the victors did not press forward. There was also increasing unrest between the Protestant North and the Catholic South in Christian Europe. In the year Rudolf received the Hungarian crown, about 2,000 Protestant Huguenots were massacred on St Bartholomew's night in Paris. Rudolf's family was at the centre of the maelstrom; his younger sister Elizabeth had married Charles IX of France two years earlier. Rudolf's father Maximilian wrote to the Lutheran Elector of Saxony:

> Believe me, such tyrannical acts do not please me in any way; I am profoundly afflicted by them . . . It is neither just nor justifiable. It is atrocious and against all Christian faith . . . Religious questions cannot be resolved by the sword, but by the divine word and by a just *entente* between Christians.[4]

It was a troubling time for the Habsburgs as well as for Europe. Maximilian tried in vain to get his son Ernst elected king of Poland; the Duc d'Anjou, brother of Charles IX, was chosen instead. On his brother's death the twenty-three-year-old duke returned to Paris to become Henri III. On his way, he passed through Vienna where great celebrations were held in his honour on 23 June 1574. Rudolf was at the centre of them but, unfortunately, there is no record of his meeting with the future king of France. Maximilian was doubly upset by the turn of events: not only had his son Ernst failed to gain the crown of Poland but the future king of France refused to marry his brother's widow, Rudolf's sister Elizabeth.

An ominous celestial event confirmed for many the growing disharmony in Europe. Comets had long been considered omens of war, plague and famine. But then a new tailless star – a supernova – appeared in the Cassiopeia constellation in 1572, the very year that Rudolf had been crowned king of Hungary. It suddenly shone brightly and then gradually changed colour and eventually disappeared from the sky during 1574. It was observed by the court astronomer Tadeáš Hájek in Prague and by the aristocratic Danish astronomer Tycho Brahe in his observatory on his island called Uraniburg (City of Heavens). Since the appearance of the star implied that the heavens were not perfect after all, as the traditional Aristotelians claimed, Brahe interpreted the celestial drama as a sign that the world would perish by fire. Some in the Holy Roman Empire, possibly including Rudolf himself, concluded that the new king would shine brightly only to have his power gradually wane.

*

However much he tried, Rudolf simply could not ignore the growing religious tensions within and outside the Holy Roman Empire. It was almost a miracle that the tolerant policies of his father had prevented a civil war between Catholics and Protestants in Austria. Bohemia had been all but lost to Rome since the time of the Hussite Rebellion in the first half of the preceding century. Although Rudolf's uncle, Ferdinand, had tried to weaken the powers of the Bohemian Estates and tried to bring about an absolute monarchy the Protestant majority constantly checked his plans.

The Jesuits were on the counter-attack in Bohemia and making some inroads in the populace but the Utraquists, who advocated the freedom to practise both Protestant and Catholic forms of communion, stood firm. The towns of Prague were generally run by a conservative alliance of Catholics and Utraquists, but gaining ground were German and Czech Lutherans and the Czech Brethren (also known as the *Unitas Fratrum*). The Czech Brethren had formed the first Reformation church in Europe.[5] They were descendants of the radicals led by Jan Huss, who in the previous century had repudiated violence, claimed that all people were equal, and practised the simple life of early Christianity in closely knit communities. His burning at the stake by the Inquisition in 1415 triggered the Hussite Wars (1415–22) which eventually brought about the independence of Bohemia.

To stem the demands of the Protestants and to ensure that his son would be crowned king of Bohemia, Maximilian verbally agreed in 1575, just before his death, to the so-called 'Czech Confession' at a Diet, or parliament, summoned in Prague. It was a protocol, drawn up by the Protestant Utraquist and Czech Brethren nobility in Bohemia, which declared that subjects were not obliged to espouse the same religion as their gentry and nobility, following the principle of the Confession of Augsburg. Maximilian had always opposed the policy of force employed by his brother Philip II in the Netherlands and by Charles IX in France which he believed only encouraged extremism on both sides. But under the influence of the papal nuncio and the Jesuits, he refused to put his concession in writing. 'Truly', he declared to the Diet, 'you must have confidence in my words since I have pronounced them in good German and good Czech.'[6]

Continuing his climb up the imperial ladder, the twenty-three-year-old Rudolf was proclaimed King of Bohemia on 7 September 1575. The Diet of

Bohemia elected Rudolf unanimously on 27 October 1575 in Regensburg and on 1 November he was crowned king of the Romans. Since the crown was not hereditary, the Emperor had to be elected by seven Electors. His official title was now 'Son of Maximilian II, Roman, Hungarian and Bohemian King'. He was thereby placed along with the Pope at the apex of European society, embodying the temporal power of Christendom. It was his sacred duty to assure the integrity of the empire, to protect the faith and to defend it against all its enemies.

Like his father and grandfather before him, Rudolf was crowned in the majestic Gothic cathedral of St Vitus within the walls of Hradčany Castle in Prague. It was a grand, imperial affair, attended by most of the Bohemian aristocracy.

The imperial insignia and the Bohemian and Hungarian jewels were brought up from the Coronation Chamber in St Vitus cathedral – which required seven keys to open it – and carried in the grand procession. They included the ancient Crown of Charlemagne and the sword and crown (dating from 1345) of St Wenceslas, the prince who encouraged German Christian missionaries to come to pagan Bohemia in the tenth century, and hence became the patron saint of Bohemia. As the twenty-four-year-old emperor sat on the antique throne, with a sceptre in one hand and a globe in the other, the princes of the realm came to swear allegiance and to kiss his feet.

Arcimboldo made a simple sketch in profile which shows the fact that the imperial Wenceslas crown was two fingers too large for him on all sides, underlying the physical frailty of the young king and the heavy burden being placed upon him.

A year after Rudolf's coronation as king of the Romans, the forty-nine-year-old Maximilian II died suddenly on 12 October 1576 while trying to raise funds to stem yet another invasion threatened by the Turks across the Hungarian plain. On his deathbed, the papal legate, the Spanish ambassador and his wife all implored him to take the final Catholic rites, but true to character he refused, claiming that his priest was in heaven and he had already made peace with him.

The Catholic world was scandalised. The Holy Roman Emperor refused the last sacraments! The Spanish ambassador wrote to Philip II: 'The unfortunate man has died as he has lived.'[7] Rudolf drew a different lesson from seeing his beloved father harassed by religious fanatics right until the end. He would, like him, follow the path of tolerance and compromise.

Rudolf, King of Bohemia and the Romans, wearing the St Wenceslas crown. Sketch by Giuseppe Arcimboldo (1575)

Rudolf inherited a vast, ramshackle empire. It had been founded when Pope Leo III crowned Charlemagne emperor in 800. Consisting mainly of a loose federation of German states, it stretched from the borders of Denmark in the north, France in the west, Venice in the south to Poland and Hungary in the east.

Rudolf adopted the Habsburg ideal of absolute authority and tried to encourage its mystique yet in reality he had no choice but to deal with the democratic concessions which earlier struggles had won in the administration of his dominions. As King of Bohemia, he was only one Elector among others to approve the choice of the Holy Roman Emperor and his rule over Bohemia was further tempered by the fact that the Hussite Wars of the previous century had reduced the property and power of Crown and Church. Bohemia was in fact a free union of provincial communities in which the Imperial Diet, the royal dignitaries and the landed gentry all had an important say. This internal federalism made the kingdom difficult to control from the centre while affiliated provinces such as Moravia, Silesia and Lusatia were virtually independent nations.

Immediately after being crowned Holy Roman Emperor, Rudolf visited the countries he ruled and familiarised himself with the empire's arcane administration. The Emperor's political power was in theory absolute and based on the imperial authority of ancient Rome and despite the democratic demands of his subjects, Rudolf considered his imperial majesty to be universal, not only above mere kingship, but with a divine dimension. He believed in burnishing its mystique through elaborate rituals, ceremonies and pageantry.

Not surprisingly, one of his most valued works of art was the *Gemma Augustea*, a marble representing the apotheosis of Augustus. Rudolf identified with him as an emperor of peace and saw himself as his legitimate successor as King of the Romans. Despite being born under the sign of Cancer, he even adopted Augustus's zodiacal sign of Capricorn, depicted by a creature with the tail of a fish. This symbol was placed on many works depicting Rudolf as the new Augustus as were the words *Astrum fulget caesareum* ('The imperial star shines').

For all Rudolf's grand aspirations, the crown of Charlemagne was undoubtedly a heavy burden. He may have felt rather exalted at the prospect of absolute power, but his whole character was directed towards the cultivation of art and the discovery of knowledge. His heart detested the Church's fanatical schisms and yearned for a mystical union with God through the peace which passed all understanding. He abhorred the messy intrigues of the court but he still had to rely on the leading aristocrats to get anything done.[8] The approach of a wily ambassador filled him with dread while the company of artists and scientists made him feel at ease.

Rudolf's first public act as Holy Roman Emperor was to arrange the funeral of his admired father at huge expense and in the presence of all the imperial nobility. The ceremonies began in Vienna on 5 August 1577. In keeping with court etiquette, careful instructions were issued about the guests, their dress, their station and their duties. The body of Maximilian II was then brought to Prague and laid to rest in the imperial vault in the middle of St Vitus cathedral in a grand ritual, the like of which Prague had never witnessed before. The symbolic pageantry, entirely endorsed by the young Rudolf, was once again intended to impress his subjects, as well as foreign dignitaries, of the power and wealth of the Habsburg dynasty.

No doubt with El Escorial in mind, Rudolf then had a marble mausoleum completed over the vault. Portrait reliefs of his ancestors adorn its sides, including those of Emperor Charles IV and Wenceslas IV. Rudolf arranged for three monumental figures to be carved on the upper panel: his grandparents Ferdinand I and Anne Jagellon of Hungary and his father Maximilian II.

Below the mausoleum in the foundations of the cathedral was the royal crypt containing the sarcophagi of the kings of Bohemia. Pride of place was reserved for Charles IV; behind, Rudolf arranged for his own lead coffin to be set. It is still there today.

Maximilian left one final shock. In his will, he broke with the tradition of distributing his lands among his sons and left them all to his eldest, Rudolf. The other sons – Ernst, Matthias, Maximilian and Albrecht – only received from their father some works of art and financial compensation. The Archdukes were understandably angry and disappointed. Moreover, Rudolf himself had few funds he could call upon for his own use. The young poet and diplomat Sir Philip Sidney who had been sent to represent the English Queen Elizabeth at Maximilian's funeral reported to Sir Francis Walsingham: 'I understand by men of good judgement, that he is left poore, the division with his brethren not yet made, warres with the Turke feared, and yet his peace little better, considering the great tributes he paies, and the continuall spoiles his subjects suffer upon the Frontiers.'

In the following month, he observed to Walsingham that the new emperor was 'holy by inclination given to the warres, few of wordes, sullein of disposition, very secrete and resolute, nothinge the manner his father had in winninge men in his behaviour, but yet constan[t] in keeping them'. While his brother Ernst was 'more franke and forward', he found both of them 'extreemely Spaniolated'.[9] Rudolf seems to have listened politely to his pleas on behalf of Protestants. But there was little warmth between the two young men even though Sidney was a polished example of the Renaissance gentleman and a fellow star-lover (the name 'Astrophel' from the title of his sonnet sequence Astrophel and Stella is a Greek pun on his name).

Determined to treat his brothers 'graciously, fraternally and paternally', Rudolf named Ernst Governor of Lower Austria and Maximilian Governor of Higher Austria. But he made the serious mistake of doing nothing for his younger siblings Matthias and Albrecht and he would pay for this oversight later.

The twenty-year-old Matthias was already meddling in the troubled affairs of the war-torn Low Countries. In the autumn of 1577 and without authorisation from his brother or his uncle Ferdinand, he acceded to the request of local nobles to act as an intermediary between Philip II and William of Orange in the hope that he would one day become the governor. When Rudolf heard the news, he was furious; the last thing he wanted was to get embroiled in his Spanish uncle's religious maelstrom in Northern Europe. Rudolf also saw it as a direct threat to his rule. In a flurry of letters, Rudolf chastised his brother for endangering the House of Habsburg and the Catholic religion, while Matthias asserted, somewhat feebly, his good intentions.

Rudolf never forgave his brother for his impetuosity. He further built up trouble for himself by preventing Matthias from marrying and by refusing to deny the rumour that he was impotent. Matthias began to nurture a dislike bordering on hatred against his older brother which would eventually become all-consuming.

Rudolf would not be gainsaid. In 1578 he engineered a succession treaty to ensure that his brothers rendered him due homage as the senior member of the family. Any move against him by his brothers would thereafter be considered a case of *lèse-majesté*. They agreed to 'remain mutually friendly, peacefully united, without mistrust'.[10] In return they received substantial incomes. Matthias was absent and got nothing.

As for the Habsburg treasures and works of art, Rudolf was determined to try to reacquire them from the members of his family to whom they had been bequeathed. He particularly coveted two talismans which had been given to his uncle Ferdinand of Tyrol: an *Ainkhuern*, allegedly the horn of a unicorn which had magical powers, and an ornate agate cup which had been pillaged from Byzantium during the 1204 crusade and which was said to be nothing less than the Holy Grail.

In the same year of his father's obsequies a comet appeared in the sky which inspired many pamphlets and astrological predictions throughout Europe. In general, it was interpreted as a portent of evil and an augury of troubled times ahead. Tycho Brahe stressed its Saturnine aspect and the dark red hue of Mars at the time – both associated with misfortune and disaster. Rudolf, who was a great believer in astrology, must have shuddered; he was born under the sign of Cancer which is ruled by the melancholy Moon.

The effort of burying his father, inheriting the Holy Roman Empire and forcing a settlement on his brothers was all too much for Rudolf. Within a year of becoming emperor, he fell seriously ill. All observed that he disliked the everyday intercourse of the court and the affairs of state. At the same time, he had a strong sense of duty and was tortured by the thought that he would be unable to live up to the grand ideals of his illustrious ancestors. Moreover, he had no confidant whom he could trust; his estranged mother

Maria, the daughter of Charles V, was out of the question. Her confessor, the Jesuit Maggio, had become his own and he avoided him as much as possible, correctly suspecting that he was spying for his mother, Philip II and the Vatican.

Rudolf's emotional turmoil eventually led him to withdraw to his private rooms. His entourage feared only too much that he would succumb to the ancestral 'melancholy' of the House of Habsburg. In 1578, he fell both physically and mentally ill. At first his doctors put it down to fish poisoning but he soon suffered from general exhaustion and had to be carried upstairs. He also developed severe stomach pains. His gradual recovery was helped by the elderly Johannes Crato, the Protestant humanist who had been a physician and adviser to his grandfather Ferdinand as well as to his father.

It was Rudolf's first major crisis and it took him a couple of years to begin to emerge from his slough of despond. Even as late as 1581, his minister Wolf Rumpf wrote to his mother, Empress Maria, that his melancholy would not fade away despite 'the number of medical men and surgeons of which there are ten attending the Emperor all day long'. He would never feel the same again. His chronic stomach pains, doubtlessly aggravated by his nerves and medicines, only made him more morose.

It is difficult to know exactly what Rudolf was feeling during this period. Indeed, it is virtually impossible to be certain of his thoughts, let alone his inner feelings, for he never wrote them down.[11] What we do know is that Rudolf's mother Maria took advantage of his weakened state. Since her husband's death she had failed to find a satisfactory role for herself at the court in Vienna. Unable to emulate Catherine de Médicis in France and become the guide and confidante of her son, now, as the daughter, wife and mother of emperors, she felt increasingly superfluous. Brought up as a staunch Catholic in Spain, she had never felt at home surrounded by Protestants in Austria and wanted nothing more than to return to her native land. In addition, she had money concerns: a letter exists from a wealthy Jew, Mordechai Maisel of Prague, who had bankrolled her husband on occasion, requesting the interest on a loan of two thousand thalers lent for kitchen expenses.

She had despaired at the news that her daughter Anna, her brother Philip's third wife, had died during her sixth pregnancy at the age of thirty. She immediately proposed to her brother that her last daughter Marguerite should fill the gap and intimated that she would like to return to her native land. Rudolf reluctantly let her return to Spain, fearing that she too would plot with her brother against him. As it turned out, the fifteen-year-old Marguerite was relieved that her white-haired and crabbed uncle did not like her; she suddenly found a religious vocation and retired to a convent.

Rudolf's mother was not, however, prepared to leave it at that. She sought once again to tighten the knot between the two branches of the Habsburgs by trying to persuade Rudolf to become betrothed to Philip's daughter, the thirteen-year-old Infanta Isabella Clara Eugenia. In a series of grandiloquent letters, the ageing Empress exhorted her son to consider his sacred duty as well as his self-interest:

> Man makes his destiny by his own courage . . . You also have received some gifts from God, and that is why you must fight like your ancestors. You fear losing your States and your peoples? Who could better help you to conserve them than the Catholic King, who would never leave his daughter in misfortune? Your mother and your ambassador have asked on your behalf the hand of the Infanta. What figure will you make before God and before the world if you repay his goodness with an insult and put your mother in an intolerable situation? Fear that the King gives his daughter to another and that your heritage escapes from the House of Austria.[12]

After much evasion and hesitation, Rudolf eventually agreed to the engagement. The thought of uniting the two branches of the House of Austria was too important a prize to throw away. But the negotiations on a dowry soon became bogged down: Rudolf asked for the Low Countries and Spanish possessions in Italy; Philip refused and insisted on himself becoming Imperial Vicar in Italy; now it was Rudolf's turn to refuse. They soon dropped the negotiations: the Infanta was still young and both men turned to more pressing affairs.

External events eventually obliged Rudolf to stir himself. All he desired was to be left alone in peace and quiet but all around him religious struggles were deepening and the clouds of war were rolling ominously across Europe. The forces of the Counter Reformation, spearheaded by the Jesuits and supported by his brother Ernst, were making ground. Catholicism had triumphed in Austria while the Protestant northern part of the Low Countries had proclaimed independence from Spain under the name of the United Provinces. Philip II invaded Portugal and crowned himself in Lisbon. Yet more threateningly, Islamic troops of the Turkish Ottoman Empire were pressing on Rudolf's southern and eastern borders.

Rudolf was well enough to open his first imperial parliament in June 1582 in Augsburg. Huge crowds invaded the city, along with the ambassadors of the Pope, the Protestant Electors, and most of the Catholic kings. Even the recently crowned Czar of Russia, Ivan IV, who was soon to earn the soubriquet of 'the Terrible', attended. The meeting proved to be the first step of Russia towards the West.

The principal decision of the parliament at Augsburg was to adopt the new Gregorian calendar which replaced the old Julian calendar, which was twelve days out of kilter with the cycle of the Sun. Pope Gregory XIII accepted the new calendar and chose the first day of January rather than Easter as the beginning of the New Year. At the parliament, the Catholics accepted the proposal; the Protestants, suspicious of a papal plot, rejected it. One Lutheran prince saw it as a sign of the impending Apocalypse.

Rudolf, who was fascinated by astrology and astronomy, found the subject far more interesting than affairs of empire. This was his natural intellectual territory. 'It's a question of mathematics which has nothing in common with religion', he said quietly in one of his rare interventions. 'The essential is that the calendar is good. Its origin does not matter.'[13]

THE WORLD'S STAGE

All the world's a stage,
And all the men and women merely players:
They have their exits and their entrances;
And one man in his time has many parts . . .

Shakespeare, *As You Like It* (1599)

W hen Rudolf was proclaimed Holy Roman Emperor, the city of Vienna was as densely populated and lively as Elizabethan London. Reconstructed behind strong walls after 1529, its buildings reached for the heavens. Thanks to Ferdinand I, a beautiful Renaissance garden cheered up the forbidding fortress of the Hofburg where the imperial family lived. Visitors remarked on the flowers which decorated the doors of the town and the birds singing in cages hanging from the windows. The people of Vienna loved music, carnivals and luxury. According to the German writer Wolfgang Schmeltzl, the city was a 'garden of roses, a place of delights, a veritable paradise'.[1]

Although his father had built the *Rudolfsburg* for him in Vienna, Rudolf was increasingly drawn to Prague Castle on the hill known as the Hradčany. Vienna was simply too gay, too noisy and too intimate for the frail and melancholy introvert. He preferred the comparative peace and austerity of Prague to the frivolity and extravagance of the Austrian capital. In 1576 and 1577, he was often in Prague and began to supervise new projects: the building of a summer house and a study, a residential wing, and the west end of the south façade of the castle. Two years later the construction of a new palace within the castle had reached a stage where it was possible to decorate the interiors.

From 1580, Rudolf remained in Prague on a regular basis and in 1583, by a royal decree, established Prague Castle as the imperial seat. Besides his personal convenience, this enabled him to distance himself from his brothers' ambitions and from his meddling mother, who preferred the life at the Hofburg palace in Vienna. Temperamentally, Rudolf appreciated the strong elements of water and earth of Prague to balance the air and fire of his upbringing in Spain; its brooding black spires and scudding grey clouds suited his melancholic disposition. He not only liked the weather in Prague – cold in winter and hot in summer – but the mountains on its borders made it comparatively safe from attack by the Ottoman Turks who were constantly threatening to cross the Hungarian plain to Vienna. Situated in the middle of the Bohemian basin created a billion years previously by a gigantic meteorite, surrounded by green forests and sturdy hills, it rose on a great outcrop which made it a natural fortress. Prague moreover was at the geographical centre of Europe; a remarkable allegorical map of Europe as an Empress from the period, created by Johannes Putsch and engraved and published by Daniel Adam of Veleslavín, depicts Hispania as her head and Bohemia as her heart.

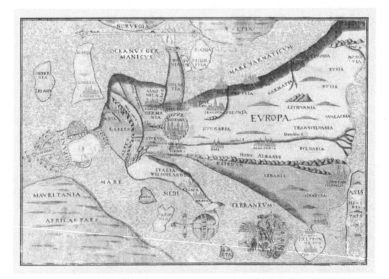

Europe as an Empress, with Hispania as her head and Bohemia as her heart. Printed by Daniel Adam of Veleslávin (1591)

Prague also had other attractions. The special atmosphere – the *genius loci* – of the ancient city further appealed to Rudolf. One legend popular at the time has it that Libussa, queen of Bohemia, sought out a husband. With the help of the gods, she mounted a magic white horse which took her to a place where she met a handsome young peasant called Přemysl. Then, one summer's evening, while she stood with her new husband and the elders of her people on a cliff overlooking the great Vltava River, she pointed across the water to the wooded hills beyond and was moved to prophesy: 'I see a great city whose fame will touch the stars!'

She led her people to the spot on the hill where there was a man raising the threshold (*prah* in Czech) of a house and asked them to build a castle. Together they founded a dynasty and the city of *Praha*, Prague.[2]

According to Roman records, Bohemia was inhabited by Celts as early as 500 BC. They were driven from the territory by a German tribe around 100 BC and were followed by Slavs after the disintegration of the Roman Empire. The first Christian ruler of Prague was Duke Bořivoj in the ninth century who founded the Přemyslid dynasty. From the tenth century onwards, Jews came from all over Europe, attracted by the tolerant atmosphere and a thriving economy.

Prague was not only a crossroads of cultures and peoples but truly a threshold where the visible and the invisible met, where objective reality slid off into subjective fantasy. As the title of an early sixteenth-century essay, *Praga Mystica* by Jan Bechyňka, puts it, Prague has always been a mystical and radical place. The heretical ideas of Jan Huss had not been forgotten, especially among the Czech Brethren. During this period the city attracted dissidents, visionaries and seekers after truth from all over Europe. The same was to happen at the turn of the seventeenth century during Rudolf's reign.

Prague, with its countless spires and underground network of dungeons and cellars, has always been a city of the imagination and of the unconscious. No wonder legend says that the Golem, an artificial man made from mud by a Jewish rabbi, haunted the narrow alleys by night. No wonder it was thought that alchemists in the Stygian darkness of their laboratories were manufacturing the Philosopher's Stone. No wonder the Holy Grail was said to reside in the innermost chambers of the great Castle dominating the city on the hill.

From the Middle Ages, the layout of Prague had four elements: the Old Town, the New Town, the Lesser Town and the Jewish Town. To the south, on the lowland plain, was the Old Town of cobbled streets and large open squares.

The architectural details of the medieval buildings suggested to the visitor not only an ancient city but evoked a fabulous world, depicting basilisks, rams, lions, skeletons, stars and other esoteric symbols. Along the main Celetná Street leading to the Old Town Square and adjoining alleys, dark taverns called the Unicorn, the Stone Table, the Blue Star, the Vulture and the Spider enticed the passer-by to risk his purse and his reason.

The great meandering river Vltava divided the Old Town, the New Town and the Jewish Town from the Lesser Town and the Castle which rose up on a steep hill to the north and dominated the city. The buildings, with their towers and spires, shot up to heaven out of the great bowel of Bohemia. Rudolf's revered ancestor Charles IV had modernised and embellished the city with a fine array of public works, such as St Vitus cathedral (where he was buried), churches, monasteries, and the university. In 1348, he founded the New Town with three major squares (including Wenceslas Square and Charles Square) and surrounded it with massive walls. It was laid out on the same plan as Jerusalem and was intended to represent the coming of the New Jerusalem on earth as described in the Bible.

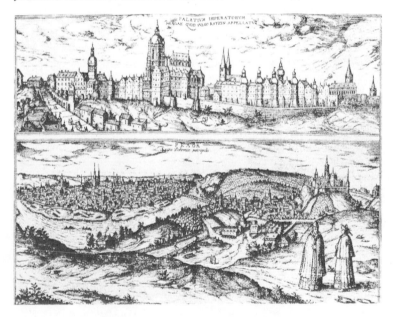

View of Prague, c.1590, by Joris Hoefnagel

During Charles's reign the Church of Our Lady Before Týn was built, with the tapering spires of its Adam and Eve towers reaching for the sky and the alchemical carving of a green dragon lying in its well. By the time the Emperor died, Prague was larger than London or Paris and, on account of its rich heritage and magnificent architecture, it had become known throughout Europe as the 'Golden City'.

Rudolf looked out from his castle to the Charles Bridge, founded by his ancestor Charles IV on 9 July 1357 at 5.31 a.m., a time chosen carefully for its propitious astrological and numerological associations. At that very moment a conjunction of the Sun with Saturn occurred, with the great luminary of the sky overpowering the gloomy influence of the malefic planet. As a student of the Cabala as well as astrology, Rudolf was fascinated by its sacred numerology: the date and time of its foundation consisted of favourable odd primary numbers which ascended and descended palindromically: 1 / 3 / 5 / 7 / 9 / 7 / 5 / 3 / 1. In addition, the setting sun on the summer solstice lined up Charles Bridge with an architrave of the Castle's cathedral.[3]

Rudolf, who loved moving mechanical objects, would also have appreciated the large astronomical clock, made in 1410, on the front of the Town Hall in the main square. It indicated the time of day in Babylonian time and Old Bohemian time. The clock, which still exists, also depicted Ptolemy's model of the universe with the Earth at its centre and charted the movements of the sun and moon through the signs of the zodiac. Moving figures were added in 1490. On the hour, the twelve Apostles appeared in windows before disappearing back inside the clock. Perched on pinnacles at four corners were figures representing what was considered to be the chief threats to Bohemia at the time: the lender with his money bags; Death, depicted as a skeleton carrying an hourglass and tolling a bell; a Turk shaking his turbaned head; and Vanity admiring his reflection in a mirror. Four other immovable figures symbolised Philosophy, Religion, Astronomy and History.

Rudolf shared his ancestor's vision of Prague as the centre of the empire but went one step further: he saw it as the hub of the universe. As a result, Prague became the most cosmopolitan city in Europe.

During Rudolf's reign, Prague not only attracted some of the greatest minds of the day in art and science, but also hordes of alchemists, astrologers and magicians on the make as well as soothsayers, fortune-tellers, charlatans, mountebanks and puffers who delighted in telling a tall yarn and fleecing the gullible. The gloomy streets of the Old Town swarmed at night with hired thugs, *banditi,* swordsmen and cut-throats from all over Europe. Legend has it that even Faust came to stay. Catholics worked and lived side by side with Protestants and Jews in tolerant acceptance. The large Jewish Town itself was experiencing a Golden Age of comparative calm and prosperity. Ancient beliefs from pagan times lived on. The arrival of so many foreigners made the city a melting pot of languages. It also made it a vibrant and creative place in which to live.

The writer David Gans who lived at the time in the Jewish Town was ecstatic about the charms of Prague and Bohemia and described them in terms of a Holy Land:

> Prague, that great, splendid and populous city is the capital of this Land of Bohemia. It is situated exactly in the centre . . . And as for Bohemia, what an abundance of population, of unfortified towns, of villages, of great and splendid cities, of palaces, of castles which out-rival one another in their beauty! This land is full of the blessings of God: wheat, wine and must exist there in such quantities that the neighbouring countries draw their subsistence from it. It is also a land of rivers, great and small – many majestic waterways: an abundance of fish, pastures, forests. It is a land where the stones are iron and the mountains are brass . . .[4]

As in most European cities at the time, however, great splendour went side by side with squalor. Apart from the grand stone houses in the Lesser Town and around the Old Town Square, most of the houses were made from timber and clay with little beauty or art. The English traveller Fynes Morison who visited at the end of 1591 was unable to avoid the terrible stench in the streets of Prague, strong enough to 'driue backe the Turks'.[5] But not everything was squalor: in May or June women wore garlands of flowers on their left shoulders and the men sported little wreaths of roses in their hats, to celebrate the spring.

There was always something to keep the tongues of the burghers wagging. Foreign delegations of diplomats, courtiers and merchants came and went, often having to wait for months before seeing Rudolf or leaving without an audience at all. Even up at the Castle, there was a regular fair of luxury goods from all over the known world in Vladislav Hall in the Old Royal Palace. The well-to-do of Prague would come to exchange court gossip and political intrigue and to see what latest wonders had come to the city.

*

The beauty of Hradčany Castle for Rudolf was that it was protected on all sides by hills and forests. Being situated on a steep hill, it had uninterrupted views of the palaces and villas of the Lesser Town below and the churches and grand buildings of the Old Town on the other side of the river. Soon after moving in, Rudolf undertook some major changes and new building projects. In the process, he transformed the old draughty castle, which had been partly destroyed in a fire in 1541, into a grandiose late Renaissance residence.

The Old Royal Palace, formerly used by Charles IV, became the administrative centre of the empire. The Palace contained the magnificent Vladislav Hall, a masterpiece of late Gothic architecture, which was so large that knights on their horses once rode through it to get to their tournaments. Two rooms on the same level as the hall, with a fine panoramic view over Prague city, were used by the Bohemian Chancellor and Governor, who presided over the country's affairs when the king was away. Above the Bohemian Chancellery was the Imperial Court Council, decorated with portraits of the Habsburg rulers. It was from here that the whole of the Habsburg empire was governed. Yet amidst this grandeur an almost inconspicuous detail on a side door to the Old Royal Palace reflected Rudolf's interest in the curious and erotic: it consisted of a Renaissance knocker which when used brought together two stylised figures of a naked woman and man in an act of fellatio.

Within the castle walls rose the spires of St Vitus cathedral, first constructed during the reign of Charles IV. On the Great South Tower Rudolf added his mark. At the top of the gilded lattice window a plaque was erected bearing a crowned 'R' – the signature of the Emperor – surrounded by the emblem of the Order of the Golden Fleece, represented by a ram's fleece with dangling head and legs. The Golden Fleece was associated with the Lamb of Christ but Rudolf would have been fully aware of its Hermetic symbolism as the Philosopher's Stone which the alchemists throughout Europe were searching for as the universal panacea.

The symbol of the Golden Fleece became one of the most potent symbols of the Habsburgs. Charles V mentioned holding the meetings of the Order in the same terms as he did the greatest matters of state and Rudolf was inordinately proud of joining the Order in Innsbruck in 1585. A print shows his investiture in which the Archduke Ferdinand presents Rudolf with the chain of the Order, while his brother Ernst and his cousin Charles of Styria look on. Rudolf invariably wore the emblem around his neck and it was buried with him in his coffin.

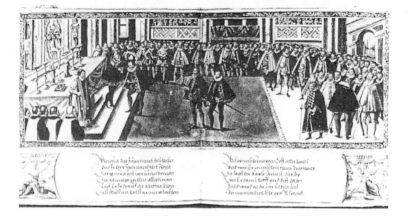

Rudolf's investiture into the Order of the Golden Fleece in Prague, 1585. Rudolf kneels before Archduke Ferdinand; Ernst and Charles of Styria stand forth

Founded in 1429 by Philip the Good, Duke of Burgundy, the Order of the Golden Fleece was a chivalric order of knights dedicated to the defence of the Church. The knights were enjoined to be dignified, sober and always zealous for the honour of God and their order. However august, they had to accept the criticism of their fellow knights. They were expected to wear a heavy golden collar in battle and no knight was allowed to leave the field once the banners had been flourished; it was a fight to the end. They entertained each other with lavish banquets and followed elaborate rituals. The knights were meant to be as steady and intrepid in their defence of Christianity as Jason's Argonauts – the archetypal warrior band – were in their pursuit of the Golden Fleece. The aim of the order was to bring peace and harmony to a troubled world.[6]

The Order of St George was another favourite chivalric fraternity of the Habsburgs. In the courtyard in front of the cathedral, there was a bronze statue of St George mounted on his horse killing the dragon with a lance. While many saw it as a symbol of Christianity overcoming paganism, Rudolf would have known its esoteric meaning of drawing on the serpentine energies of the earth.

Wishing to separate his private life from public affairs, Rudolf decided to leave the Old Royal Palace largely to his officials and built a sumptuous new residence for himself above the southern ramparts. With the help of the Italian architect Ulrico Aostalli, he supervised a grandly conceived second courtyard surrounded by spacious and elegant Renaissance buildings.

From 1586 onwards, Giovanni Gargioli of Florence continued to embellish the palace. In the same year, Rudolf had built splendid stables on the northern medieval foundations of the Castle – known as the Spanish Stables – to house his favourite animals. He had a particular penchant for grey Andalusians. The diplomat Pierre Bergeron remarked enthusiastically in his report on his travels in 1603: 'Within the castle are stables, some of the best looked after in Europe; there are nearly always three hundred horses there, originating from every possible country, and they are the most beautiful in the world.'[7] Rudolf not only took a great interest in the well-being of the horses but regularly went out hunting in the Krivoklát forests. Although he never once went into battle, he was often depicted in portraits intended for his subjects on a fiery steed routing the Turks. One of the best ways to gain one of his rare audiences was to offer some fine equine specimens; if he was particularly pleased by a visiting dignitary, he might give him a team of his finest greys. It was said that he spent as much time with his horses as his state duties would allow – perhaps like Swift's Gulliver he came to prefer their company to that of humans. Towards the end of his life, when he hardly left his rooms, he would have his favourite horses paraded in front of his windows.

Above the Spanish Stables on the north side of the castle grounds in the west of the Castle, Rudolf also had built the New Hall (today confusingly called the Spanish Hall) to house his statues and the Spanish Hall (now known as the Rudolfine Gallery) to house his paintings. The clean light from the north-facing windows was ideal. As was the custom, the paintings themselves were not hung up but placed on ledges, tables and special stands. The two rooms probably offered for the first time among the collections of European nobility a large space entirely devoted to the display of sculpture and painting.

The north wing of the Castle with its stables, hall and gallery was joined in the 1590s by the 'Long Corridor' (*Langer Bau*) stretching 100 metres to connect with Rudolf's private chambers in the new Summer Palace on the south side, facing the city. The corridor housed Rudolf's famous collections of precious objects on three levels: on the ground floor, his collection of rare saddles and harnesses; on the first floor, divided into four separate rooms, his celebrated *Kunstkammer* or 'Chamber of Art'; on the second floor, more paintings and sculptures. Midway between the north wing and his apartments rose The Bishop's Tower (also known as The Mathematical or Astronomical Tower) from the flat roof of which the night sky could be surveyed.

Not all the buildings in Prague Castle, however, were devoted to affairs of state, horses and works of art. At the eastern end of the castle ramparts, the Daliborka Tower and Black Tower had long been used as prisons. The Daliborka Tower was named after its first prisoner, a young Czech noble who had supported a peasants' rebellion at the end of the fifteenth century. He was said to have learned to play the violin in the tower and his sweet music filled the castle until he was executed.

Rudolf used the New White Tower further west on the northern ramparts to hold part of his collection of armour and commissioned Bartolomeus Spranger to paint an allegorical fresco on the second floor of Hermes and Pallas Athene. Rudolf would have appreciated the reference to Hermes, the

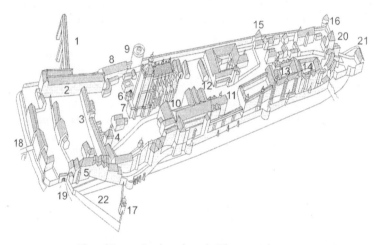

Plan of Prague Castle at the end of the sixteenth century

1 – Powder Bridge
2 – Northern Wing
3 – Bishop's (Astronomical, Mathematical) Tower
4 – Old White Tower
5 – Rudolf's Palace (Summer Building)
6 – Chapel of St Vojtěch
7 – Cathedral of St Vitus
8 – Foundry
9 – Powder Tower
10 – Royal Palace
11 – Church of All Saints
12 – Basilica of St George with the Convent
13 – Rožmberk Palace
14 – Pernštejn Palace
15 – New White Tower
16 – Daliborka Tower
17 – Tower of the Trumpeters
18 – Western Gate
19 – Gate to the Castle Stairs
20 – Black Tower
21 – Eastern Gate
22 – Garden of Eden

legendary father of alchemy, whom the Greeks associated with Thoth, the Egyptian god of wisdom. He would also have celebrated Pallas Athene, the Greek goddess of wisdom and patron of arts and crafts. The allegory of Hermathena, representing the union of Hermes and Athena, was a symbol of eloquent wisdom and hence the academic ideal, and was to become a recurring image in Rudolfine iconography.[8]

In the Powder Tower set in the northern ramparts of the castle, Rudolf established an alchemy workshop and filled it with the latest instruments – vases, tubes and stills – produced by his glass blowers and by the most competent alchemists who managed to catch his eye. He would often visit the laboratory unexpectedly to see how the Great Work was progressing and even engaged in some of the experiments himself.

Beyond the castle walls lay another of Rudolf's great passions, the Royal Gardens which he had connected by a covered passageway to his private apartments. Visitors from all over Europe waxed enthusiastically about the rich profusion of plants and animals in the grounds. Below the northern ramparts was a long and dried-out moat, known as the Deer Moat because of the immense number of game which grazed on its steep slopes. As with his horses, deer were often presented as special gifts to visiting dignitaries and envoys.

On the south-facing slope of the Deer Moat, a heated walled aviary was made which housed many rare birds, among others parrots and birds of paradise and, after 1598, a dodo; it was the finest aviary in all Europe. Rudolf also had replaced on the same slope the wooden menagerie of his grandfather Ferdinand I with a larger, stone-walled one. It was called the Lions' Court but also contained tigers, wild cats, bears, and wolves. The lion, ancient symbol of power and rank, was one of the oldest emblems of the Bohemian kings; as Holy Roman Emperor, Rudolf was often associated with the king of the jungle. A fine bronze bust by Adriaen de Vries depicts him with the head of a lion on his shoulder. A pet lion, which Rudolf played with when it was a cub, was allowed to prowl on occasion around the palace workshops and studios.

Rudolf was particularly fond of a lion given to him by the Sultan of Turkey in a rare lull in the fighting between the Ottoman Empire and the Holy Roman Empire. It was reported that Tycho Brahe, who became Rudolf's court astronomer, declared that since they shared similar horoscopes they would suffer a similar fate. The prophecy proved to be accurate: when the lion eventually died, Rudolf locked himself in his chambers, refusing all medicine and help, and died three days later.

Beyond the Deer Moat, taking full advantage of the southern sun, lay the Royal Gardens planned in the Italian style at the behest of his grandfather. George Braun, in his celebrated six-volume work on the most outstanding places in the world, described Rudolf's gardens as a small *theatrum mundi* in which trees and plants of all types from all over the world flourished: apples, palms, olives, cedars, as well as shrubs and flowers. They were laid out with extraordinary care: some were formed into individual letters, while others took the shape of whole sentences. In a raised parterre brightly coloured flowers against green grass formed the letters of Rudolf's talismanic device *ADSIT*, which probably stood for *a Domino salus in tribulatione* ('In trouble, deliverance comes from the Lord', a paraphrase of Psalm 36:39). *ADSIT* is also the Latin for 'May He be Present'. The allegorical nature of the Royal Gardens was further enhanced by a maze, symbol of life on earth for the pilgrim searching for the celestial city.

The gardens were not only intended to be a living encyclopaedia of trees and plants, but contained specialised areas for growing herbs for medicine and alchemical experiments. Just before Rudolf's enthronement, the gardens were already despatching exotic orange, pomegranate and cherry trees to the courts in Dresden and Vienna. Among the original features of the Royal Gardens opposite the grim Black Tower were a Fig House and an Orangery also built by Rudolf's grandfather, Ferdinand, on the south-facing terrace below the formal gardens. The first Fig House was built in 1571 in a wooden and glass building which had its roof open in the summer and closed in the winter. A more elaborate Orangery was started by Rudolf in 1590 and became the first permanent one of its kind in Europe.

Another first was the planting of tulips in the grounds of the Royal Gardens. Ogier (Angerius) Ghislain de Busbecq, Rudolf's early tutor and his grandfather's envoy to Constantinople, had brought the exotic bulbs back to Prague in 1563 and Ferdinand's botanist and physician, Pietro Andrea Mattioli, personally supervised their cultivation. They were considered sacred plants in the Middle East, particularly as the Turkish word for them, *lalé*, resembles the word for Allah in Arabic script. The flower was often worn in the turban, the *duliband*, which explains how the mistranslation into 'tulip' was made. The Turks preferred them all of one colour with long, narrow, upright petals like flames or daggers.

At the eastern end of the Royal Gardens stood the beautiful Belvedere, commissioned by Rudolf's grandfather for his beloved wife. Resembling an upturned boat, it was the finest example of Renaissance building north of the Alps, offering harmonious proportions and colonnades decorated with reliefs illustrating Greek myths. On many occasions, Rudolf and his court astronomers observed from its wide balconies the movement of the heavenly bodies.

If Rudolf was not happy with his palaces and gardens he could always decamp to several other residences outside Prague. The most intriguing was the Star Summer House, built on the instructions of Rudolf's uncle Archduke Ferdinand of Tyrol, king of Bohemia before him. It was probably used to undertake certain esoteric rituals. Its ground plan formed two overlapping triangles making the six-pointed star which had been used as the Seal of Solomon and was a powerful magical symbol. The time of the laying of its foundation stone on 28 June 1555 was, as with Charles Bridge and El Escorial, determined astrologically. Its sacred geometry was further enhanced by four storeys, including a basement, which may have represented the principal stages and colours of the alchemical process or the four Cabalistic orders of being: black, white, yellow and red. The acoustics of this ingenious building are so extraordinary that the voice of a person standing at the centre of the first floor vibrates throughout the edifice. The Star Villa proved to be one of the most magical buildings in central Europe.

Rudolf also developed the Stromovka, the oldest and largest of Prague's royal parks. Fish ponds were created, artificial lakes with islands and bridges were made and rare species such as elks and aurochs were kept within its fenced boundaries. He turned the existing Gothic hunting lodge into a Royal Summer House in the Renaissance style in 1578 and connected the Royal Park to a refurbished mill by a wide path; he was said to take his baths there, often accompanied by courtesans. He also commissioned in 1583 a kilometre-long tunnel with a very gentle gradient to bring water from the river Vltava to a fish pond used for water games in the park. The court scribe Isaac Pheniller drew up a beautifully illuminated scroll depicting the profile of the construction with an accompanying text in Spanish. It was an outstanding artistic and technical work exemplifying the close links between art and science in Rudolfine Prague.

Rudolf's most favoured country residence, however, was the castle of Brandýs nad Labem, situated by a river about 19 kilometres north-west of Prague. He spent considerable funds on improving its fabric and grounds and particularly admired the huge elephant etched with the sgraffiti technique on to the wall of its inner courtyard. Whenever the plague threatened Prague, he would retreat to Brandýs. In addition, Rudolf established his own Imperial Stud Farm at Kladrubylt and had a castle and stables built there so he could be with his favourite animals.

Prague Castle then, with its satellite palaces and parks, became Rudolf's world's stage, filled with everything in which he delighted. Despite being the most powerful man in the empire, Rudolf preferred the retired life of the scholar and connoisseur to the public life of the emperor and courtier. The Venetian diplomat Hieronymo Soranzo left a sympathetic portrait of him and his way of life in the castle he had spent so much effort and so many riches improving. Rudolf, he recalled,

> was rather a small figure, of quite pleasing stature and relatively quick movements. His pale face, nobly formed forehead, fine wavy hair and beard and large eyes looking around with a certain forbearance, made a deep impression on all who met him. The Habsburg family likeness was evident in the largish lips which curled towards the right. There was something haughty in his comportment: he behaved rather shyly, avoided all noisy society and took no part in the usual amusements; jokes pleased him not, and only rarely was he seen to laugh: these were the characteristics he had in common with his brother Ernst, with Philip II and Philip III. Apart from hunting, he also enjoyed a game with a ball and riding on horseback, but the older he became, the more he made it clear that he did this not for amusement but for the needed physical movement. During audiences he was patient, and otherwise he was kindly disposed towards his surroundings, open to conversation, though he himself spoke rarely, and if so, then with evident ease. He had mastered several languages: German, Latin, French and some Czech; and Spanish, being the language he was brought up in, was entirely normal for him; nonetheless, he had a special affection for German, and used it almost exclusively.[9]

Prague Castle was ideal for Rudolf's purposes. It was a town within a town, separate from the city but providing all the services required for an imperial court. It was the official residence of the King of Bohemia and the Archbishop of Prague. It contained an old palace for the emperor's administration and a new palace for his pleasure. It sheltered St Vitus cathedral where his ancestors were buried and a monastery where monks could pray for his salvation. Its precincts embraced sumptuous *palazzi* provided for the Bohemian nobles. It had houses for the officials of the court and the canons of the cathedral as well as dwellings for the servants and artisans who made the court life possible. In 1597, he gave the castle fusiliers permission to build houses in the aprons of the northern walls, thereby creating the alley known today as Golden Lane and wrongly associated with alchemists. Above all, the vast, inaccessible walls and the steep moat of the castle on the top of Hradčany hill provided the kind of security and seclusion that Rudolf craved.

While living there, Rudolf disliked being observed and valued his privacy so highly that he had made roofed wooden staircases which extended across the whole complex as well as connecting the castle with the gardens. He did not go out and see the world; he let the world come to him. And of those who came, he chose to see only a few. He appeared briefly on this stage of his own creation, acting like the magus Prospero in Shakespeare's *The Tempest*, directing and receiving courtiers and ambassadors, organising artistic and alchemical experiments and neglecting the affairs of empire. Above all, he invited to join him scholars of immense learning from all over Europe, men who appeared like the 'Merchants of Light' in Francis Bacon's scientific utopia *The New Atlantis* (1627). As a result, he helped bring about nothing less than a cultural revolution in later Renaissance Europe.

Prague Castle for Rudolf became a microcosm of the macrocosm. He transformed what had been an old castle into a unique centre of learning and an inspirational milieu for creative and original work. He opened the doors of its chambers and vaults and built galleries, workshops, laboratories and studios for anyone who could help him in his grand project to unveil the mysteries of the world.

It was the perfect place for Rudolf to reside and he came with his great powers of patronage of the arts and the sciences at exactly the right moment. A true son of the Renaissance, he provided just the catalyst needed to fixate the ideas bubbling in the crucible of Central Europe. Under his aegis, he turned Prague into the principal centre of art and science in Europe. Rudolf could not compare with the imperial glory of his other contemporary monarchs, Philip II of Spain, Henri IV of France and Elizabeth I of England, but none of them had such a powerful influence on the cultural history of the West. He may not have changed the political face of the earth, but he transformed the artistic and scientific landscape.

THE GREATEST ART PATRON
IN THE WORLD

Whoever so desires nowadays has only to go to Prague (if he can), to the greatest art patron in the world at the present time, the Roman Emperor Rudolf the Second; there he may see at the Imperial residence, and elsewhere in the collections of other great art-lovers, a remarkable number of outstanding and precious, curious, unusual, and priceless works.

Karel van Mander (1604)

Rudolf, in his own lifetime, would become known as the Maecenas of Bohemia after the trusted counsellor of Augustus who was synonymous with great patronage. Making no hard distinction between the world of art and ideas and everyday life, Rudolf invited into his magic theatre of the world many inspired painters, sculptors and craftsmen from all over the continent. From the mid 1580s into the new century, they flocked to Prague and made it the cultural capital of Europe. Some came from Germany and the Low Countries, bringing with them the latest sculptural style of the Northern Renaissance, while others from Italy brought the more picturesque manner of the South.

He was following in a long family tradition. His grandfather Ferdinand and his father Maximilian had attracted many artists to their court in Vienna from both Italy and Flanders. The basis of Rudolf's collection was therefore inherited from his father who, with the help of Jacopo Strada of Mantua, had amassed a prodigious number of Renaissance works. After studying the ancients at the University of Pavia, Strada became an expert in numismatics, sculpture and architecture and he quickly realised how profitable the market was north of the Alps for Italian art and artefacts. He moved to Vienna and was appointed by Maximilian as Court Antiquary to advise him on architecture but he soon became the curator of his galleries in Vienna. Within a year of ascending to the throne, Rudolf invited Strada to join him in Prague and made him his own Court Antiquary. He valued his discerning judgement and organising abilities to such an extent that he knighted him von Rossberg after the family name of his wife Ottilie Schenk von Rossberg. Strada's portrait by Titian presents a well-dressed courtier offering a little silver Venus to a client but one Venetian rival who resented his power at Rudolf's court once described him as a man of 'unbearable arrogance'.[1]

It was a family affair. Their son Ottavio, who sat for Tintoretto, looked after the library and took over his father's role when he died. Rudolf's appreciation of the Strada family was further strengthened by his passion for Jacopo's beautiful and captivating daughter Katherina who had been well educated in Vienna.[2] Like those of her brother, her features were fine and gracious with a hint of sadness. Although intelligent, disinterested and attentive, she remained Rudolf's invisible mistress for most of his life, never involved in intrigue at court or appearing publicly in his company. She patiently bore six children for him, three boys and three girls. The oldest son, Don Giulio, was born around 1585 and became the light of his father's life until he descended into madness like his Spanish cousin Don Carlos, the son of Philip II.

Rudolf recognised Katherina's children as his own but he did not remain faithful to her. He was well known for the vagaries of his sexual passion. Referring to his 'troops of concubines' and 'virgins who greatly valued their chance to be deprived of that title', the hostile Scottish novelist John Barclay wrote that he preferred 'free love to marriage'.[3] More decorous observers of the Prague court spoke simply of Rudolf's 'imperial women'.

Unfortunately, neither Katherina nor Rudolf's other amours were able to calm the troubled nerves of their lover and dispel his phantoms. His only true solace was the *ars magica* of his collections which grew steadily with the gifts of diplomats, princes and kings of Europe as well as from the bequests of his relatives. He gained little from his sister Elizabeth, widow of King Charles IX of France, but from his brother Ernst, Governor of the Spanish Netherlands, he acquired many great works of Northern European art, including paintings by Hieronymus Bosch, Hubert van Eyck, Roger van der Weyden and Pieter Brueghel. At the end of Rudolf's life, his collection contained, according to the Venetian diplomat Soranzo in 1612, almost three thousand paintings.

Art became a less than subtle form of diplomacy. It was widely known that the gift of a special work of art could secure the good will of the Emperor and speed up an audience. Foreign nobility, local grandees and wealthy citizens all used art to influence and gain access to Rudolf. The Burgomaster of Nuremberg, for example, sent Holbein's *Isaac Blessing Jacob* and Dürer's *Trinity*; the Elector of Palatinate gave a carved ivory altar; the mining magnate Johann Fugger offered a marble sarcophagus found near Athens; and the Spanish count Khevenhiller gave several paintings by Titian, Pietro Rosa and Parmigianino. To be invited to see his private and closely guarded collections was not only a major privilege but a clear sign of imperial recognition and approval.

Rudolf's passion for art was awakened as a boy when he saw on a daily basis the fine collections that his paternal grandfather Ferdinand I and his father Maximilian II had brought together in Vienna. During his stay in Spain with his uncle Philip II, he not only refined his aesthetic judgement but learned as a future patron of the arts how to choose the right artists, architects and craftsmen.

Rudolf developed his family's taste for certain artists who were to become the central figures in his collection. Rudolf's grandfather Ferdinand I had been a great patron of Dürer; Titian had been the favourite artist of his grandfather Charles V; and Leonardo da Vinci, Dürer and Bosch had been treasured by his uncle Philip II. He also inherited or acquired works by Caravaggio, Paolo Veronese, Corregio, Parmigianino, Tintoretto, Leoni, Holbein and Cranach among many others. Brueghel was much admired for his monumental composition and precise detail. Rudolf possessed at least twelve works by Dürer and wanted to amass all his principal works. He had to negotiate for a year with the town of Nuremberg to acquire the *All Saints* and paid seven hundred gold pieces for it. On one occasion, he borrowed from Fugger thirteen thousand écus to buy the *Retreat of the Ten Thousand*. And of course to bring the *Feast of the Rosaries* from Venice was a major achievement as well as a labour of love.

Rudolf's agents, such as Giuseppe Arcimboldo who searched for German masters, and Giulio Licinio who worked in Venice looking for Italian works, over time brought so many works back to Prague that it was found necessary to build new galleries for the growing collection. Agents were sent out in coordinated searches throughout Europe. Not content simply to possess the masterpieces of past artists, Rudolf commissioned from Veronese a cycle based on allegories of love – one of his favourite themes and pastimes – and from Jacopo Tintoretto four paintings with mythological subjects.

Despite his admiration for the works of the early Renaissance, Rudolf was exceptionally open to artistic innovation and his collection was mainly of contemporary art and based on the artists at his court. By patronising artists such as Giuseppe Arcimboldo, Bartolomeus Spranger and Hans von Aachen, Rudolf presided over the development of a new affected style, full of conceits, which became known as Mannerism. Spranger and von Aachen, for instance, produced a series of allegorical paintings presenting curvaceous women with elongated or contorted bodies for their master's delectation.

It did not take long for Rudolf's reputation as a discerning art patron to spread throughout Europe. After a visit to the court of Rudolf in 1597, Jacques Esprinchard remarked:

> The Emperor's chamberlains, Hans von Aachen and Bartolomeus Spranger, both truly outstanding in the art of painting, led me to three Castle rooms, and showed me there the most splendid paintings, old and new, and the rarest that one will ever see these days anywhere in Europe. The Emperor has them brought here from all corners of our part of the world, at great cost and expenditure.[4]

Rudolf valued his practitioners of art so highly that he had built for them well-equipped studios and workshops in the Castle. In April 1595, he issued a 'Letter of Majesty' to the Prague Painters' Guild which not only confirmed their existing privileges but added a new one: 'Because their art and mastery is very different from other handicrafts . . . it shall . . . no longer be regarded or described as a craft by anybody, but rather shall be termed altogether the art of painting'.[5] They were exempted from the rules of the guilds, given annual stipends, and could expect additional payments for commissions.

Nowhere in Europe before 1600 were artists so highly valued as at Rudolf's court. They not only enjoyed royal protection and a right of residence but, most important of all, freedom to express themselves. From their royal studios, buoyed up by handsome salaries and titles, they poured out works of art, the majority of which were either mythological paintings with an erotic quality or complex allegories glorifying the Emperor. As a Prague style developed, the works became increasingly arcane so that their several layers of meaning could only be visible to the initiated. Indeed, it might well be described as a form of poetry in painting.[6]

The allegorical style was not peculiar to Prague: mythological subject matter, with gods and goddesses, heroes and heroines, was in fashion throughout the German-speaking world. But the lubricious elements, with naked women placed in alluring poses, were particularly emphasised for Rudolf's imperial pleasure. For their part, the artists repaid their generous patron by turning out canvases of imperial propaganda, politely referred to as the art of rhetoric. They decorated his galleries and rooms with works which presented him as a new Augustus and as a new Maecenas who commanded the world from his castle. He was even likened to Jupiter, the supreme god of the gods.

Rudolf's highly intellectualised view of art was part of his interest in the occult: whether in art or nature, he wanted to see the essence behind the surface appearance. Rudolf was not simply interested in the faithful reproduction of nature, but the implied metaphysical content behind the subjects. In the artistic terms of the day, the artist would have to combine *natura* (nature) and *ingenium* (talent), but Rudolf also liked them to be directed towards *historia* – full of personifications and symbols illustrating complex mythological and allegorical themes.[7]

Rudolf inherited many of the artists, scholars and craftsmen who had worked for his father in Vienna. The most imaginative and original was Giuseppe Arcimboldo, a high Mannerist painter and designer later admired by Oskar Kokoschka and Salvador Dali. He has been celebrated as anticipating Surrealism and Pop Art but he perhaps best represents the kind of magical realism which prevailed at Rudolf's court.[8] Looking back from the twentieth century, Roland Barthes rightly called him a magician and a rhetorician: while his imagination was poetic, he had a linguistic base to his work. He was also very modern, moving from a 'peinture newtonienne', founded on the fixed objects represented in painting, to an 'art einsteinen', according to which the movement of the observer is part of the status of the work.[9]

Arcimboldo had not only studied the notebooks of Leonardo da Vinci but knew the techniques used by Bosch, Brueghel and Cranach. In addition, he appreciated the new literature influenced by the humanists in which medieval and ancient symbols combined, often in a contradictory and paradoxical way. His work, more than that of any other artist, was a kind of *ars magica*, presenting the magical transformation of matter, and it best reflected the ambience of Rudolf's world in Prague. In his severe self-portrait, however, he is far from humorous or fantastical: he presents himself wearing a black overcoat and conical hat. Moreover, he was the first artist employed by Rudolf to produce illustrations of natural history.[10]

The Milanese painter and designer had been the *Hof-Conterfetter* ('Court Portraitist') to Rudolf's father Maximilian and his grandfather Ferdinand. He excelled as an engineer as well as an inventor, making among other things his own musical instruments. He was a brilliant designer of costumes for balls, banquets, masques and tournaments and the chief organiser of the lavish court celebrations in Prague in 1570 when Rudolf's younger sister Elizabeth married King Charles IX of France in Vienna. Rudolf and Ernst, fresh from their return from Spain, witnessed his work a year later at the marriage of Charles of Styria. He was not only responsible for the festivities when Rudolf was crowned King of Hungary in 1572 but made a striking sketch of him at his coronation as King of Bohemia in 1575. Arcimboldo produced for Rudolf in 1585 a red leather folio containing pen-and-ink drawings of 148 designs for costumes, headgear and decorative wear he had made for processions and balls, dedicated to 'The Invincible Emperor of the Romans, his Everlasting and Most Benevolent Sovereign and Majesty Rudolf II'.

A typical entertainment which he organised in Prague in the mid 1580s involved cortèges and cavalcades parading before Rudolf and his entourage for days on end. One tableau had Europe, Asia and Africa presented in subjection before the Emperor; courtiers would perform in sketches interpreted from Italian farces; and there would always be music. The Imperial Orchestra under the direction of Philippe de Monet played Dutch and Italian music, while Jacques Regnard, composer of motets and villanelles, broke with tradition to write the text for his melodies in German. There were also imperial singers, among them two castrati, to perform in the cathedral and at state dances and banquets. As a lover of modern art and as a sensualist, Rudolf always preferred the elaborate polyphony of Renaissance music to the austere plainsong demanded by his uncle Philip at the Spanish court.

Arcimboldo's most memorable works were, however, his strangely surreal portraits made from compositions of *objets trouvés*. His composed heads are ambiguous and enigmatic, combining satire and wit, yet at the same time embodying a system of correspondences between humans and the natural world. His peculiar method was to disguise subtly the external appearance of nature in order to reveal its inner essence.

No one had seen anything quite like Arcimboldo's pictures. He drew inspiration from the natural world but juxtaposed objects such as fruits, vegetables, game, books, kitchen utensils and farm implements to a grotesque and surrealist effect. *The Librarian*, a portrait of the imperial historian and bibliophile Wolfgang Lazio, is entirely made from books, with an open book as his hair and the spine of his book as his nose. *The Cook* is a grotesque visual pun: it depicts a rough-looking head under a helmet; turned upside down, the helmet turns into a dish containing a fried suckling pig and chicken.

Rudolf especially prized two series of paintings depicting *The Four Seasons* and *The Four Elements* which Arcimboldo had presented to Rudolf's father on New Year's Day in 1569. In the former, *Winter* is painted as a gnarled tree trunk and *Spring* as a young man composed of flowers. In the latter series, the element *Water* consists of a head entirely made from an agglomeration of sea creatures, with red coral as hair. In *Earth* the head is composed entirely of animals, forming a veritable bestiary. Different creatures represent particular human features and attributes: the fox, the craftiest of animals, is the brow while its tail forms the eyebrows; the cheek is portrayed by an elephant, which in turn symbolises modesty. But the paintings are more than charming expressions of wit. They were intended to glorify symbolically the House of Habsburg: the would-be harmony in the empire is reflected in the harmony between the elements and the seasons.[11] Arcimboldo went on to paint the *Four Seasons* twice for Rudolf in 1577. He liked the paintings so much that he hung them in his bedroom.

Rudolf used Arcimboldo as his agent and sent him to Germany in 1582 in search of valuable works of art and rare animals and birds for his collections. In 1587, he reluctantly allowed his long-serving artist and scout to return to his native Milan in order to enjoy his old age. For his long, faithful and conscientious service to the Habsburgs he was awarded the handsome sum of 1,550 Rhenish guilders and in 1592 given the title of Count Palatinate.

From Italy, Arcimboldo continued to send works to the Emperor, including the most famous portrait of Rudolf entitled *Vertumnus*. It depicts him as the Roman god of the seasons, with a face composed of painted fruits, flowers and vegetables from the four seasons harmoniously brought together. The grave and melancholic Holy Roman Emperor was delighted to see himself represented with his nose as a pear, his hair as millet, grapes and sheaves of wheat; his forehead as a melon; and his beard as nuts and chestnuts.

Rudolf painted as Vertumnus, Roman god of the seasons, by Giuseppe Arcimboldo (1590–1). Rudolf much appreciated the work

The work was inspired by the Latin poet Propertius who celebrated Vertumnus as a god of permanence through change. But Vertumnus is much more: he is brother of Hermes, the father of alchemy. The painting appealed to Rudolf's appreciation of the interplay between the natural and the artificial, the sensuous form and the pure idea. Far from simply making a joke, Arcimboldo intended to glorify his patron as a protector of the arts and sciences. He implies that the Emperor not only rules over his subjects, but even the elements and the seasons; indeed, the eternal cycle of the seasons evokes the everlasting rule of the Habsburgs. Arcimboldo's paintings, just like the festivities and celebrations he organised, were intended as allegories of the power of the Emperor and the harmony of the world under his rule.[12]

Arcimboldo's friend Don Gregorio Comanini wrote a poem about the painting which brings out well its deliberate depiction of the ideas of diversity in unity, of ugliness subsumed in beauty, and of reality behind appearance:

> Unless you clearly see that ugliness
> Which makes me beautiful,
> You cannot know that there's a certain
> Ugliness more beautiful than any beauty.
> There's diversity within me,
> Though despite my diverse aspect, I am one.
> That diversity of mine
> Renders faithfully and truly
> Diverse things as they are . . .
> Though my aspect may be monstrous,
> I bear noble traits within,
> Hiding thus my kingly image.
> Tell me now if you are willing
> To discern what I conceal:
> Then my soul I will reveal.[13]

While Arcimboldo was Rudolf's most original artist, his most valued master was undoubtedly Bartolomeus Spranger who first trained in his native Antwerp as a painter of landscapes but later became court painter to Pope Pius V. Rudolf's father had invited him in 1576 at the age of thirty to the court of Vienna where he worked on the triumphal arch for the return of Rudolf from Spain in the following year. Typically Mannerist, it had fantastically decorated towers with irregular beds of flowers and various water features. It became so well known throughout Europe that the English diplomat Henry Wotton tried to find a copy of the design as late as 1591.

When Rudolf moved the court to Prague he took Spranger with him where he was appointed Master Painter (*Hofmaller*). He lived in a grand house in the Lesser Town, just below the castle walls, where he soon acquired other properties. By the early 1580s Spranger had made himself indispensable to Rudolf and the Emperor would often spend days conversing with him and watching him at work in his studio. He provided for Rudolf a steady stream of paintings consisting of mythologies, allegories, religious scenes and occasional portraits. Spranger became the chief arbiter of cosmopolitan taste in painting during the last two decades of the sixteenth century.[14] The Emperor rewarded his loyal services by conferring on him in 1588 a coat of arms as liegeman and by elevating him in 1595 to the ranks of hereditary nobility. When Spranger died in 1611, he left five handsome town houses to his heirs.

A year after Rudolf's move to Prague, the merchant Hans Ulrich Krafft noted during a visit, accompanied by Spranger, that the rooms were decorated not only with his guide's works but with 'magnificent works made in Spain, most of them nudes, painted from life, and, apart from that, mainly Roman and other splendid Italian pieces'.[15]

Beyond the decorative works he produced, as Rudolf's appointed Imperial Court Painter Spranger unashamedly promoted the mystique of the Emperor in works which mixed military prowess with cavorting, contorted, half-naked or completely naked bodies. In his highly stylised *Allegory of the Virtues of Rudolf II* (1592), Bellona (the Roman goddess of war) sits on a globe surrounded by Athene, Bacchus, Venus and Amor with emblems symbolising Hungary and the Croatian river Sava, the moving border in the Turkish wars. The message is clear: in Rudolf's hands, all will be well in the empire. But while it was part of the anti-Turkish propaganda and ostensibly intended to show that the virtuous will be victorious in battle, it clearly aims at erotic stimulation.

In *The Triumph of Wisdom*, Spranger presents the sexually provocative figure of Athene (Greek goddess of war, handicrafts and wisdom), with helmet on head and naked breasts, stomach and thighs. She treads down Ignorance who has the ears of an ass. Bellona and the nine Muses gather around her, with the figures representing astronomy (Urania with a celestial globe) and mathematics (Geomatria with compasses) standing out. Another

The Triumph of Wisdom *by Bartolomeus Spranger (c.1605). Athene,*
Greek goddess wisdom, steps on the neck of Ignorance who has the ears of an ass.
Supporting her are Bellona, Roman goddess of war, and the nine Muses

typical work but with a more personal theme is the *Allegory of the Triumph of*
Fidelity over Fate – Allegory of the Life of the Sculptor Hans Mont. Mont was a
friend of Spranger who lost an eye playing tennis and was unable to continue
his work. Painted in 1607, it remains in Prague Castle, one of the few works
of art left over from Rudolf's reign to be found in the city.

As an exceptional patron, Rudolf took a keen and direct interest in the activities of his artists, regularly observing them at work in their studios. Spranger told Krafft that the Emperor usually visited in the early morning to see what the artists had done the day before. No doubt his overweening interest was not always welcome but then he was a generous patron and respected them as inspired artists rather than as employed artisans. He even took a direct hand in the choice and treatment of their subjects and his artists were expected to work according to his 'impressions'. The iconography of the Prague Mannerists undoubtedly reflected his desires and fantasies, especially in its glorification of the power and splendour of the Habsburgs (of which he saw himself as the supreme expression), in its playful symbolism (which drew wantonly on classical mythology), and in its love of the erotic (which some sterner critics called indecent and even decadent). Many of the allegories were drawn from Homer and Ovid. While the women were invariably depicted as curvaceous and serpentine, the men were muscular and hairy. It was a highly distinctive blend of intellectual interest and sensual desire.

The salacious aspect was particularly prominent in one of Rudolf's favourite artists, the Swiss Josef Heintz. He depicted voluptuous and contorted bodies in somewhat predictable canvases, using such mythological themes as Leda and the Swan, the Rape of Proserpine and Venus and Adonis as a veiled excuse to present the erotic. In his *Declining Venus*, Heintz transformed one of Rudolf's imperial mistresses by giving her more beautiful features than she possessed in life. Rudolf's eyes were thus able to take over when his body tired of love. The castle corridors soon became decorated with dozens of canvases by court artists of Venuses, Circes, Dianas, Nymphs and Muses as well as Mars, Mercury and Adonis. It was no doubt for this reason that the novelist John Barclay presented Rudolf as a prurient old man wandering his corridors, the walls of which were adorned with 'Prostitute Paintings'.[16]

Another one of Rudolf's most trusted artists was Hans von Aachen. He was a Flemish painter but he developed his distinctive style during a long stay in Italy and was particularly influenced by Paolo Veronese. Rudolf invited von Aachen to Prague early in 1592 and like Spranger named him Imperial Court Painter. He was not obliged to live in the castle and in 1595 Rudolf elevated him to the hereditary nobility like Spranger and Arcimboldo.

Rudolf admired von Aachen's heroic paintings as well as his genre works. He completed a series of portraits of Rudolf in the first decade of the seventeenth century depicting him as an Imperator in armour conquering the Turks. In reality, however, Rudolf had a horror of battle and never visited the front during his lifetime but a portrait of a king in armour at the time was considered the supreme expression of his claim to power and was deliberately intended to send out a hostile message to any potential enemy. Hans von Aachen fully understood that in the art of rhetoric it was crucial that the form and expression of a painting should match the occasion, the subject and the intended audience. The vainglorious and belligerent message of his imperial portraits is all too obvious. Indeed, von Aachen's rhetoric is so extreme that it often bordered on caricature.

Hans von Aachen could, however, be an outstanding and realistic portrait-painter, as exemplified by his beautiful and simple painting of his daughter, Marie Maxmiliana. It is now known as *Head of a Young Girl* (1611) and remains in Prague Castle. The engaging directness of this portrait shows how he could capture a likeness in its most disarming light.

Like Arcimboldo, von Aachen played an important role in acquiring works from Italian collections for Rudolf. In 1603, he left for Italy to examine the works in Turin, Mantua and Modena and wrote up a detailed report on each. He also painted the daughters of the dukes he visited to help the declining and jaded Rudolf choose a bride to fill the still empty throne of the empress. Rudolf often instructed his artists to engage in personal and artistic business during their diplomatic missions on his behalf.

Several of von Aachen's and Spranger's allegorical works were engraved by Aegidius Sadeler, an artist from Antwerp who came to Prague in 1597 after working in Munich, Venice and probably Rome. He was appointed the Imperial Engraver (*Kaiserlicher Kuperferstecher*) and lived in the Lesser Town in one of the houses owned by Spranger.

Sadeler produced a fine engraving of Vladislav Hall in the Old Royal Palace of Prague Castle in 1607. He called it a *sciographia* or architectural perspective; it shows the crowd of courtiers visiting booths selling art objects dwarfed by the great Gothic vaults of the Old Royal Palace. He is best known, however, for his superb panoramic view of Prague and etched map of Bohemia.

Sadeler also engraved, after Adriaen de Vries, a conquering Rudolf on a rearing stallion with the imperial troops routing the Turks in the background. In a complex relief called *Rudolf II as Patron of the Arts*, de Vries further has the Emperor with rippling muscles in armour on horseback but instead of holding a lance tilted metaphorically at the Turk, he reaches down to grasp the out-reached hand of a naked female – much more to his taste. He is thus depicted as a peacemaker, turning from warfare to embrace the liberal and plastic arts. The disciplines which Rudolf most appreciated – architecture, sculpture and painting – are shown nearest to him.

Not all artists though continued the Rudolfine tradition of mannered erotic scenes and allegorical images of imperial might. As the new century dawned there was a move towards greater realism. Prague became renowned for the landscapes and townscapes produced by Rudolf's artists. While striving for the realistic portrayal of natural details they also tended to heighten the decorative and picturesque aspects of their compositions. The first landcape painter to come was Pieter Stevens from Mechelen who was appointed as a court painter in 1594. He was inspired by the Bohemian landscape, woods and peasants for his rural themes. As his *Landscape with a Mill* and *Mountain Landscape with Waterfall* show, he delighted in tightly packed natural forms

The great Vladislav Hall in Prague Castle, engraved by Aegidius Sadeler (1607)

and tangles of foliage and plants. But he was not a realist and gave his rural subjects a sense of picturesque fantasy. By looking at his paintings, Rudolf, who did not like travelling, could contemplate his own lands, transformed by the artist's imagination in accord with his own taste.

The most outstanding landscape painter and naturalist at Rudolf's court was undoubtedly the Flemish Roelandt Savery. He is thought to have arrived in 1603. He not only walked with his sketchbook throughout Bohemia and Prague but drew many corners of the capital – decrepit homes as well as the grand approaches to Charles Bridge. He was a penetrating observer of city life and its disparate peoples, even attending services at the New Synagogue in the Jewish Town. He was also a great stickler for detail: in a sketch of a group of old men, he noted in Dutch in the margins the colour and type of clothes they wore.

A conquering Rudolf II on horseback. He never went into battle.
Engraved by Aegidius Sadeler, after Adriaen de Vries (c.1603)

Between 1606 and 1608, Savery undertook a long walking tour in the Tyrolese Alps to make drawings for Rudolf. The majority of the works were both dynamic and picturesque, depicting waterfalls tumbling down rocky cliffs and deep ravines, the ordered chaos of broken trees and fragmented rocks, the spontaneous flow of rich vegetative life and turbulent waters, all set against a backdrop of magnificent mountains. His work was greatly ahead of its time in that it offered one of the first glimpses of the sublime in rugged landscapes later beloved by the Romantics.[17] Through his painting Rudolf was able to recall the scenes of his return from Spain as a young man. Savery was unique among Rudolf's artists in producing no imperial hagiography but he made good use of Rudolf's botanical and zoological collections, menageries, aviaries and gardens in order to paint wonderful compositions of different animals and birds placed in luxuriant vegetation. Every branch, every stem, every stone and every hair in his paintings are carefully detailed. Savery's landscapes betray a close observation of nature, but the studied juxtaposition of animals, birds and plant life are fantastical and the themes allegorical. They create a reassuring paradise of natural harmony at a time when the social fabric of Central Europe was beginning to be torn apart.

Rudolf's collection of artistic treasures became the greatest in Europe, unrivalled in a lavish age. He not only enjoyed the possession of his paintings but he also delighted in their aesthetic contemplation. In July 1605, Carlos Francesco Manfredi, the ambassador for the Duke of Savoy, reported that Rudolf had spent 'two and half hours sitting motionless, looking at the paintings of fruit and fish markets sent by your Highness'.[18]

The artists at Rudolf's court undoubtedly developed a self-conscious virtuosity, panache and allusiveness. Their style has many Mannerist features, especially in their elongated proportions, graceful gestures and complicated poses. Yet the subject matter of the majority of the works depart from mainstream Mannerism in that they are not anti-classical, as Spranger and von Aachen demonstrate, nor are they anti-natural, as the landscapes of Stevens and Savery show. But while the Mannerist painters of the Prague school observed 'nature', their work was not simply 'realistic', that is, a direct reproduction of what they saw. As the microcosm of the macrocosm, nature for them was always infused with symbolism. It was seen as a repository of marvels, secrets and mysteries.

THE *KUNSTKAMMER*

He loved only what is extraordinary and miraculous.
What he knows, he feels obliged to have.

Archduchess Maria of Styria

Rudolf's passion for collecting was by no means limited to the realm of painting. Throughout his adult life he collected rare and exotic items which he appreciated for their aesthetic value as much as their scientific interest, ranging from precious metals and stones to works of art and instruments of science. He entertained no firm distinction between their artistic and useful aspects: Rudolf appreciated, for instance, the art involved in glyptics (the cutting and engraving of gems) but he also employed gems as talismans with astral powers. He was particularly drawn to natural oddities and rarities, to those objects which lay on the borderline between the human and the natural worlds.

In all this, he was driven to lift the veil of external nature in order to understand its essence. As the historian R.J.W. Evans observed: 'The art of Rudolfine Prague was essentially a revelation of mystery, whether through the medium of canvas, or the manipulations of stones, or the alchemical and Cabalist "arts".'[1] Rudolf's artists and scientists, partly because it was the spirit of the time and partly because they were encouraged by their patron, all strove to transcend the everyday world with its constant change and infinite variety to perceive a universal and eternal Oneness.

They made no rigid separation between art and science, the natural and the artificial. The allegorical canvases of Rudolf's favourite painters – Spranger, Arcimboldo and Savery – were based on the careful observation of nature. His collections were full of unusual stones and minerals which were often fashioned into works of art in his ateliers. He encouraged the composition of beautifully illustrated herbals and bestiaries. Just as God had created the universe, so Rudolf's artists and scientists were refashioning and transmuting the Creation. Interest in 'particulars' was fired by an appreciation that they stood as emblems, symbols and signatures of the 'general'. In his view, the world of created things and beings therefore made up the symbolic language of God which was waiting to be deciphered.

Collecting was, of course, a widespread phenomenon in Central Europe during the Renaissance. Rudolf's grandfather Ferdinand I, his father Maximilian and his uncle Ferdinand had established impressive collections in Vienna and Ambras, but Rudolf's in Prague was by far the greatest in its value and diversity.[2] Although the more bizarre aspects of his collections caught any privileged visitor's attention, Rudolf amassed many important works of art and nature, both old and new, from all over the known world. As a learned and cultured monarch, he saw the whole world as a precious cabinet of curiosities to collect and classify. The collection also provided a peaceful retreat from a troublesome and uncontrollable world. 'When our arduous tasks of government permit', he confessed to the Neopolitan Giovanni Battista della Porta, author of *Magia naturalis* (1558), 'we enjoy the subtle knowledge of natural and artificial things in which you excel.'[3]

In addition to paintings, drawings and sculptures, Rudolf sought out allegorical costumes and other curios. He had a reputation for acquiring whatever he fancied, regardless of cost or the need for restoration. Whenever he heard word of some rare manuscript, celebrated work, precious gem or oddity, he despatched agents on official and clandestine missions to track them down.

Rudolf's collecting mania, partly inherited from his family and partly fired by his acute possessiveness, reached its supreme expression in his *Kunstkammer* ('Chamber of Art'). It was contained on the first floor of the Long Corridor which connected his private living rooms in the palace's south wing to the Spanish Hall and New Hall which he had built on the northern rampart. Below were his collection of saddles and harnesses and possibly an alchemical laboratory.

Rudolf's *Kunstkammer* was divided into four large rooms and housed his collections of small paintings, folios of drawings and curiosities. It had its own inventory (drawn up in 1607 to 1611) of cherished objects placed in specially designed cabinets and chests.[4] The antiquarian Daniel Fröschl arranged it into three sections, starting with *naturalia*, turning to *artificialia* and ending with *scientifica*. Visitors usually entered the *Kunstkammer* through an ante-chamber decorated with images of the four elements and the twelve months, a microcosm of the universe presided over by Jupiter.

It was an extraordinary and magical place. Although classified into different realms the boundaries constantly broke down. Rudolf's love of the marvellous and monstrous mixed the animal and the vegetable, the animal and the human. It was, as Roland Barthes wrote, a revelation of '*excess*, in so far as it changes the quality of things to which God has assigned a name; it is *metamorphosis*, which tips from one order to another; in short, in another word, it is *transmigration* . . .'[5] As such, the *Kunstkammer* was the artistic equivalent of the laboratories of the alchemists who sought to understand the riddle of existence and the inner essence of reality through the transformation of matter.

Contemporary engravings show cabinets reaching halfway up the walls covered in antique bronzes, shells, medals and amulets. Paintings are piled up as high as the ceiling. Skeletons hang from strings like strange marionettes. Keeping guard are pieces of armour from famous knights. But the real gems are hidden away within the drawers of the large cabinets.

Rudolf's *Kunstkammer* was a veritable cornucopia of arcane phenomena, remarked on by all who visited the castle. But it was not just simply a cabinet of curiosities, collected with no organising principle. It was intended to be a *theatrum mundi*, a 'theatre of the world', a systematic encyclopaedia of nature which could be used to unlock its secrets. Rudolf shared the Neoplatonic view that the everyday world is not entirely real, but believed that reality could be glimpsed through the extreme and strange, through natural oddities and contrived rarities.

The range was astonishing. His collection included drawings, prints, busts, statuettes, carved and bejewelled bowls in hardstone (such as jade, jasper and heliotrope), amulets, cameos, weapons, coins and medals. He sought out musical, astronomical and scientific instruments, clocks and automata as well as ethnographical, zoological and botanical items. Among his antiquities, he had the famous *Ilioneus*, a Hellenistic sculpture of the Niobids, and the *Gemma Augustea*, an onyx cameo representing the Divine Emperor Augustus.

Although Rudolf rarely left Hradčany Castle, his collections also reflected the sudden explosion of voyages of exploration to distant lands

Watercolour of Albrecht Dürer's Hare, one of Rudolf's
most prized possessions in his Kunstkammer.

and the new researches into natural history in the sixteenth century. Artefacts came from all around the world, such as Egyptian antiquities and mummies, objects made by American Indians and stuffed birds and eggs from the Indian Ocean.

The vast array of items varied from intricately mounted Seychelles coconuts washed up on the shores of the Maldives, a wonderful watercolour of a hare by Dürer, to a table-top made in Florence from Bohemian stones. Rudolf particularly valued his large collection of bezoars, gall stones taken from the stomachs of animals thought to be an antidote to poisons, and even used them to keep the plague at bay. He was delighted when his mother sent him a huge bezoar, a gift from the viceroy of the Portuguese Indies.

Rudolf valued precious stones and crystals for their secret virtues and he always carried one next to his heart to calm his palpitations, an inherited Habsburg weakness. His magical arsenal, which he increasingly drew on when normal methods to influence the course of history failed, included dried roots of mandrake, bizarre foetuses, a basilisk, parrots' feathers, corals, fossils, ancient stones with indecipherable markings, whales' teeth, rhinoceroses' horns, the jawbone of a Greek siren, a fur fallen from the sky and a crystal lion.

He also had such wonders as unicorns' horns and dragons. One of the court physicians, Anselm Boethius de Boodt, kept a sketch with the caption: 'This is the figure of a Dragon which the Emperor Rudolf II has; dried it is this exact size, where it is preserved.'[6] Clearly it was greatly reduced by desiccation. Rudolf was not alone in believing in the existence of dragons: many Renaissance naturalists such as Conrad Gesner wrote extensively about the anatomical, etymological and moral meaning of the fabled creatures. Anselm Boethius de Boodt, on the other hand, was convinced that the unicorns' horns in Rudolf's collection were either from rhinoceroses or narwhals.

Religious relics were highly prized throughout Europe in the Middle Ages and the Renaissance and Rudolf's collection reflected this, boasting a grain of earth from which God created Adam, two iron nails from Noah's Ark, Moses' rod with which he struck water from rock. There were even parts of fabulous creatures which his agents persuaded the Emperor were real: the feathers of a phoenix, the claws of a salamander and demons imprisoned in blocks of glass.

Absurd as this might appear now, Rudolf was one of the first to collect the bizarre and wondrous as part of his attempt to create a universal encyclopaedia of nature. They all found their place in Rudolf's collection since he believed that they participated in the sacred mystery of the Creation. His collection reflected both his fascination for natural history as well as human contrivances. As a Venetian ambassador asserted, Rudolf's interest lay in the secrets of natural and artificial things', observing that he who has a chance to treat of these matters will always find 'the ear of the Emperor ready'.[7]

Rudolf delighted in collecting books as well as *objets d'art*. He took on his father's Imperial Librarian Hugo Blotius, a native of Delft, who greatly augmented the collection, and soon set about acquiring books and manuscripts, partly by purchase and partly by the gifts of authors. The library he acquired from the heirs of his father's court historiographer Johannes Sambucus ran to 2,600 volumes alone. His many astrological and astronomical works not only included those of the Arab Albumazar but a copy of Copernicus's *De Revolutionibus*. Rudolf was particularly interested in many of the key texts of the alchemists, both ancient and modern, in his library. These included a Greek manuscript of Stephanus of Alexandria, the Hermetic texts of *Pymander* and *Asclepius* (translated by Marsilio Ficino), the *Summa Perfectionis* of Geber (known as the 'prince of the Arabian philosophers'), the *De mirabilis potestate artis et naturae* of Roger Bacon (sometimes called the first scientist), Ramón Lull's *De Secretis naturae* (bound with a tract by Albertus Magnus), and the works of Paracelsus (the founding father of modern medicine and chemistry).

Rudolf went out of his way to collect manuscripts which reflected his interest in Christian mysticism, such as the *Liber de laudibus sanctae crucis* by Hrabanus Maurus. He acquired the *Codex giganteus*, a vast medieval work full of number mysticism and symbolism, from the Bohemian monastery of Broumov. The greatest treasure in his collection, however, was the *Codex argenteus* which contained the Gothic translation of the Gospels by Bishop Ulfilas and came from the Abbey of Werden in the Rhineland. In keeping with his astronomical interests, Rudolf possessed a copy of Ptolemy's *Geography* and a hand-coloured edition of Abraham Ortelius's *Theatrum orbis terrarum*.

Rudolf also commissioned illustrated books, many of which are superb. One of his most valued works was by Sadeler, who produced the beautifully illustrated emblem book *Symbola divina et humana* (1601–3). The engravings depicted a long series of emperors, popes and monarchs with devices and mottoes, culminating in Rudolf himself who receives sixteen separate emblems. Not surprisingly, he is depicted as an eagle and a lion fighting against the Ottoman Turks and embodying the Christian virtues.

A massive work commissioned by the Holy Roman Emperor was called the *Museum of Rudolf II* and consisted of two volumes of studies of natural wonders, mainly in oil on vellum, by different artists. It included illustrations of the rhinoceros which arrived in Lisbon in 1577 which Rudolf tried unsuccessfully to acquire; a cassowary (a flightless bird which inhabited the forests of New Guinea and north-east Australia), the first to be seen in Europe which Rudolf received as a gift in 1601; and a dodo that seems to have been taken alive from Mauritius to Prague at the turn of the century.[8] One page has two pieces of narwhal horn lying on a green desk; another page a goblet with a lid made from a rhinoceros horn; another shows two pieces of bezoar.

The illustrator who benefited most from Rudolf's animal and plant collections was Joris Hoefnagel, self-styled '*Inventor Hieroglyphicus et Allegoricus*'. Despite his grand title, what he became celebrated for were his

From Mira calligraphiae monumenta, *a masterpiece of manuscript illumination commissioned by Rudolf, showing Georg Bocskay's calligraphy and Joris Hoefnagel's art work*

drawings of towns, national dresses and customs. When he came to Prague and entered the service of the Emperor around 1590, he illustrated several books with animals from Rudolf's menagerie, especially the more exotic ones. He drew on his collections of flora and fauna in his beautifully illustrated book on natural history called *The Four Elements*. Again, this reflected Rudolf's interest in the wondrous, the exotic and the odd. The opening image of *Ignis: Animalia rationalia et insecta* presents Petrus Gonzales, a mythical wild man inflicted with hirsutism and dressed in splendid court clothes. The work also included other oddities of nature: birds with two heads or three legs and a snake whose tail sprouted a branch of leaves.[9]

Hoefnagel's greatest work for Rudolf was undoubtedly the fabulous illustrations he made for a calligraphy primer known as the *Mira calligraphiae monumenta* ('Wonderful Monuments of Calligaphy'). It had been written by the Hungarian Georg Bocskay for Rudolf's grandfather Ferdinand I whom he served as imperial secretary. Hoefnagel illustrated the extravagant examples of calligraphy with exquisite emblems which explored the world of flowers, insects, fruit, small animals and other forms of natural minutiae. They were all drawn from life but gave a sense of pictorial illusion. The book was one of the last important documents of the medieval tradition of manuscript illumination.[10]

Hoefnagel's work was only part of the general programme to amass, classify and present the new knowledge acquired at Rudolf's court, especially knowledge about the natural world. The lively imagery of his illustrations of natural history parallels the striving of the court painters like Spranger and Aachen to attain artistic virtuosity. Yet it also implies that even the wonders of nature were under the Emperor's sway.

Rudolf's ateliers produced not only a steady stream of paintings and illustrations but superb works of artifice. In the late 1580s, he invited to Prague some of the best goldsmiths from Augsburg and Nuremberg in the north and from Milan and Florence in the south. The art of cutting stones, known as glyptics, had traditionally been cultivated in Milan, but Rudolf made Prague another European centre. He attracted Ottavio Miseroni and his brothers from Milan and Cosimo Castrucci from Florence who produced pictures from finely worked jasper, agate and carnelian, including a fine mosaic of Hradčany Castle. One of the finest goldsmiths of Europe, Paulus van Vianen, came to create elaborate works of Mannerist art.

Goldsmiths, engravers and painters often worked together, one drawing a design, the other executing it. Sadeler was soon joined by his friend Caspar Lehmann, a stone cutter from Westphalia, who was appointed *Kammeredelsteinschneider* ('Stonecutter of the Royal Chamber') in 1601. He had the revolutionary idea of applying to high-quality glass the methods he had been perfecting to cut precious stones and mountain crystals. The result was sparkling crystal glass, an invention for which Bohemia became famous in the decades that followed.

In addition to his love of works of art, Rudolf shared the passion of his revered grandfather Charles V for clocks. He collected many different timepieces, large and small, and employed many clockmakers. He was often found in their workshops while escaping some irksome envoy from his far-flung empire; perhaps the steady work of the craftsmen and the regular beating of the clocks calmed his nerves.

Throughout the 1590s Rudolf tried to entice to his court the instrument maker Jost Bürgi, who had for many years worked at the court of Landgrave Wilhelm IV of Hesse-Cassel. Bürgi finally consented to take up a post at the court of Prague in 1604. He produced for Rudolf all manner of highly decorated clocks, some of which were the first to allow the measurement of seconds. Bürgi's finest work, however, was a planet-clock which represented both the old Ptolemaic and new Copernican systems. It was appropriately decorated with gold-worked scenes with mythical as well as astrological symbolism. He also created a 'perspective instrument' which had crystal and glass mirrors as well as a square crystal and ebony table with Cabalistic symbols inscribed on parchment underneath. This observation timepiece also boasted a cross-movement, which until the introduction of the pendulum was the most precise method to mark the passage of time and was used to measure the position of the stars with accuracy.

Not surprisingly, Rudolf took a particular interest in astronomical instruments and his *Kunstkammer* housed a vast array of them, from old and new celestial and terrestrial globes, astrolabes and quadrants, to geometric compasses. He had many Venetian lenses used for telescopes. Erasmus Habermel designed some 300 instruments for Rudolf, including fountains, astrolabes and a huge sextant which, because of its size and intricate decorations, was probably intended to be kept inside the *Kunstkamme*r. But the instruments produced at Rudolf's court were invariably beautiful as well as useful; they were made by advanced mathematicians and skilled designers.

One of Rudolf's most prized instruments was a celestial globe made in 1603 by Willem Janszoon Blaeu, a Dutch student of Tycho Brahe. The globe was fixed to wood and a tripod by means of a terrestrial axis and meridian. Brahe's observations were used to illustrate the northern sky while the southern sky was plotted in accordance with the findings of the astronomer Fredericus Housman. On the southern hemisphere, there was a portrait of Brahe.

Rudolf also went out of his way to acquire mechanical objects with hidden properties. One of his most precious possessions was a bell decorated with magic symbols which he reportedly used to call up the spirits of the dead. Rudolf was not only dazzled by bright and uncommon objects but the more extravagant the claims made for them, the more he held them dear.

He preferred to spend his time in the company of his artists and artisans rather than that of ministers, ambassadors and courtiers. As his desire for seclusion increased, the latest wonders of his *Kunstkammer*, studios, workshops and laboratories eventually became more important than the affairs of state. Although little more than an amateur, he loved to try his hand at watch-making and inlaying as well as at painting and drawing.

The *Kunstkammer* certainly offered Rudolf a tranquil place to observe the works of nature and art as his hopes of universal peace for Christendom collapsed. But it was much more than simply a solitary retreat from the world. As a repository of gifts, it played a role in his political activities: giving gifts was a central part of diplomacy at the time.[11] It also served as an emblem of his vision of the world and of himself as the earthly equivalent of Jupiter and the reincarnation of Augustus, responsible for creation in its entirety.

According to the Venetian ambassador Tommaso Contarini, Rudolf seemed less melancholic than usual after the death of his uncle Archduke Ferdinand of Tyrol in 1595. There was good reason for this. He was delighted to inherit his collection which he had amassed in his chateau of Ambras near Innsbruck. The inventory alone stretched to 736 pages. The collection contained many portraits, musical instruments, furniture, manuscripts, books, armour; one of the highlights was an ornate salt cellar, topped by a man and woman facing each other, made by the Florentine Benvenuto Cellini and given at the marriage of Rudolf's sister Elizabeth of Austria to Charles IX. Since Ferdinand had married a commoner and had two morganatic sons, they were unable to inherit their father's possessions. They all went to Rudolf, including the region of the Tyrol.

From his uncle, he at last managed to acquire two of his father's treasures which he most coveted. One was the large bowl of precious agate, found in 1204 by the Crusaders during the conquest of Constantinople which had the name of Christ in the vein of the stone. Rudolf believed that it was none other than the Holy Grail and was convinced that, by drinking from it, he would be filled with holiness and good health. This he did in private and found its effect was always positive.

His other favoured object was the *Ainkhuern*, a six-foot-long unicorn's horn (probably a narwhal horn) which allegedly bestowed special powers on its owner. During his increasing bouts of melancholy, Rudolf would often take both objects and draw a magic circle around himself with a special

Spanish sword in order to protect himself against the baneful influences of his enemies.

The best way a diplomat could gain an audience with Rudolf was to offer him curious gifts to add to his collections. Knowing what was expected of him, Manfredi, the ambassador of Duke Heinrich Julius of Brunswick, brought with him on 9 March 1605 an Indian dagger, a ruby-encrusted rhinoceros horn, three bezoar stones, a crown and 'a large silver ship that contained inside it half of an Indian nut, larger than a man's head'. It was such gifts that enabled Manfredi to see the Emperor at last after waiting nine months at his court. Rudolf only then extended him the privilege of visiting the *Kunstkammer* where he claims to have seen the unicorn's horn and the great agate basin in which he discovered to his astonishment the word Christ was 'written by nature's hand in big letters'.[12]

What fired Rudolf's mania for collecting? In the first place, it provided an escape from the life of the court. He found his real solace not in the arms of his mistress Katherina or the other 'imperial women' but in the heavy silence of his *Kunstkammer* where the *ars magica* of his collection occasionally worked its effect. He went to it like an opium addict to his pipe in order to escape the entanglements of this world and to imagine a more beautiful and harmonious realm where he really was Augustus and Maecenas rolled into one.

Secondly, there can be no doubt that Rudolf suffered from an acute sense of possessiveness. Archduchess Maria of Styria observed acutely: 'What he knows, he feels obliged to have.'[13] Although to covet the goods of his neighbouring monarchs was technically a sin, it did have its positive side: Rudolf's love of art and science made him amass the greatest collection in Europe at the time.

Thirdly, his inflamed desire to possess rare works of art and nature may well have come from an uncontrollable drive to avoid the inescapable existential fact of his own mortality. The modern historian Angelo Maria Ripellino observed shrewdly: 'Rudolf's obsession with objects derived from a longing to fill the void around him, to suppress the fear of solitude, but also from thanatophobia: by assembling a forest of rare gadgets, he hoped to stave off death.'[14]

While this may have been part of his unconscious motivation, his collecting obsession was both intellectual and sensuous. His passion for art was intimately connected with his passion for science. He wanted to penetrate beyond appearances and attain a vision of the ultimate nature of the universe; hence his interest in the arcane sciences of alchemy and astrology, the occult, magic and the other speculative arts. He wished nothing less than to solve the riddle of existence, to foretell the future and to find the key to immortality.

Rudolf's *Kunstkammer* was not, therefore, just a random collection of curious items nor was it merely for his private contemplation. It provided him and his court with a magic 'theatre of the world', a distorting mirror of the universe. It was also more than one man's folly for it offered a special source of learning for his growing band of seekers after truth by gathering together all aspects of available knowledge, arranged systematically according to their artistic, scientific, technical and natural character.

Just like the mazes in Rudolf's gardens and the Mannerist art at his court, it showed a fine example of the principle of *concordia discors*, of how harmony could emerge out of apparent discord. It was not only an encyclopaedia of the visible world but revealed the common unity underlying the apparent diversity of the world. And just as in an alchemical laboratory the experimenter was not a passive observer but an active participant, so Rudolf affected his collection and was affected by it in turn. Far from being a dusty museum of dead objects, his *Kunstkammer* was a living, evolving organism bringing together the best of contemporary art and science.

AS ABOVE, SO BELOW

> True it is, without falsehood, certain and most true. That which is
> above is like to that which is below, and that which is below is like to
> that which is above, to accomplish the miracles of the one thing.
>
> *Emerald Tablet*

N o work, no language, no culture was considered out of bounds by
Rudolf if he thought it might help him in his ceaseless search for
enlightenment. However heretical the books placed on the Index
drawn up by cardinals in the Vatican and forbidden to faithful Catholics, he
felt he was above such prohibition and would read whatever he wished.
Indeed, if a book had been placed on the Index, such as many Hermetic and
alchemical works which favoured the ancient wisdom of the Egyptians, it
made it all the more enticing.

Despite his strict Catholic upbringing and the constant reproofs of the
Vatican, as he grew older and his sphere of enquiry grew broader, Rudolf
refused to distinguish between Catholic, Protestant, Jew or Muslim in the
pursuit of truth and beauty. A staunch advocate of free enquiry and religious
tolerance, he allowed his subjects to follow their intellectual and spiritual
investigations to wherever they might lead them. The Catholic Vilém
Slavata of Chlum was forced to admit that 'While he was monarch the
inhabitants of this kingdom were for many years not hindered at all in their
various religious deviations; each man thought and believed whatever suited
him best.'[1]

During his reign, the court at Prague was both tolerant and learned. Rudolf
transcended the sectarian differences between Catholic and Protestant camps
and sought a more universal cosmology. He welcomed anyone who could help

push forward the frontiers of knowledge. Despite being the Holy Roman Emperor, he even welcomed to his court heretics like Francesco Pucci and Giordano Bruno who were later burnt by the Inquisition.

In this liberal approach Rudolf reflected the secular Renaissance humanism of his father and grandfather which, inspired by the rediscovery of classical learning, sought to realise the full potential of humans. He was further advised by a small circle of highly gifted councillors with a humanist background, such as Johann Matthias Wacker von Wackenfals and Johannes Barwitz and, towards the end of his reign, Duke Heinrich Julius of Brunswick.[2]

But he also drew on Neoplatonism which was based on the rediscovery of the ancient Greek philosophy of Pythagoras, Plato and their followers; the Hermetic tradition of arcane knowledge which stretched back to Egypt; and the Cabala of mystical Judaism which first emerged in the thirteenth century in Spain. They combined, with magic, alchemy and astrology, to form the *ars magica* of the Renaissance. They all advocated inner spiritual growth through the acquisition of greater insight: every human being has a divine spark, ran the argument, and can find his or her way back to God through *gnosis*, the illumination of knowledge.

Within a few years of becoming Holy Roman Emperor, Rudolf had turned Prague, an ancient city of flying buttresses and dreaming spires, into a centre of occult and magical knowledge which eventually spawned the new science of the seventeenth century. While he was reluctant to give audiences to diplomats, the Venetian envoy Tommaso Contarini observed: 'He delights in hearing secrets about things both natural and artificial, and whoever is able to deal in such matters will always find the ear of the Emperor ready.'[3] And being one of the most powerful and wealthiest men of his day, there was no practical obstacle which prevented him following his interest wherever it might lead him.

As the *Dominus Mundi*, God's representative on earth, Rudolf could enjoy all earthly experiences and play a major political role on the world's stage if he so wanted, but he chose rather to spend his time in his castle trying to understand the hidden forces operating in nature. As for all the thinking members of his generation, he lived in a period of doubt and uncertainty: he could no longer count on the old verities of Catholic dogma and the new science was questioning the traditional place of the Earth at the centre of the universe. As an enlightened monarch, he and his fellow 'Merchants of Light' – to use Francis Bacon's phrase – were looking for a universal knowledge which consciously involved recovering the wisdom of ancient Egypt and Greece and attempted to create a new harmony on earth.

The first element in the Renaissance world view which Rudolf and his fellow seekers after truth espoused was Neoplatonism. In the sixth century BC Pythagoras, famous for his theorem of right-angled triangles, had declared that numbers are the ultimate essence of reality and can render visible the structure of the universe, usually hidden from the experience of the senses. The correspondences he discovered between arithmetic ratios and the chief musical intervals supported the idea and gave rise to a belief in the 'harmony of the spheres', a celestial music created by the planets turning in their orbits.

Plato was strongly influenced by Pythagoras and stressed the inextricable connection between mathematics and cosmology. In his dialogue *Timaeus*, Plato argued that while organising the universe god 'placed water and air between fire and earth, and made them so far as possible proportional to one another'. The result was a close relation between beauty, perfection and divinity. At the same time, Plato believed that the cosmos was a living being – 'a blessed god' – and the components of the universe were its living limbs.[4]

Neoplatonism had been an undercurrent in Western Christian thought ever since it had been attacked by Augustine in the fourth century. For the Renaissance Neoplatonists if God is immanent in the world, then mathematical truths, the movements of the stars and planets, the attributes of natural phenomena are all expressions of the mind of God in the world. There is, therefore, no gap between things, thoughts and signs. Moreover, by examining the parts, one can comprehend the whole.

The corollary is that art is as real as science. Both the artists and scientists at Rudolf's court shared the Renaissance drive to go beyond the world of appearances and sense experience. They studied the forces operating in the world around them not as discrete and mechanical patterns of cause and effect but as a dynamic system of divine correspondences. Since both art and science reveal the signatures of God, examining a painting, an emblem, an animal, a bird, a flower or a stone involved decoding divine hidden meanings in nature.

The second key element in the Renaissance world view which found favour at Rudolf's court was Hermeticism. The Hermetic texts, of which the *Corpus*

Hermeticum and *Asclepius* are the best known, were written down probably in the second century AD in Alexandria, a vibrant cultural melting pot of Egyptian, Jewish and Greek cultures.

Hermetic ideas, as well as Neoplatonic ones, were given a fresh impetus during the Renaissance when Bessarion, the patriarch of Constantinople and a cardinal of Rome, brought back to Italy his unique library of ancient texts just before the fall of Constantinople to the Turks in 1453. They included the *Corpus Hermeticum*, which was first translated into Latin from Greek in 1463 by Marsilio Ficino and was soon widely read by Renaissance intellectuals. Unlike the earth-centred cosmology of the Roman Catholic Church, Hermeticism espoused a heliocentric view of the universe: the sun stands at the centre of the cosmos created by God. Rudolf's library contained not only Ficino's translations but a copy of the 1585 Cracow edition of the Hermetic work *Pymander*, which was thought to have originated in Egypt.

Hermetic philosophy saw God, the cosmos and humanity forming an organic whole. God as One can never be known completely but is manifested in the universe, particularly in humanity. As the *Corpus Hermeticum* put it: 'A human being is a great wonder, a living thing to be worshipped and honoured: for he changes his nature into a god's as if he were a god.'[5] By studying man, one can understand the universe, and by studying the universe, one can understand man. Since invisible God is revealed in visible nature, through the exploration of matter, one can see the divine light. The heavens moreover mirror the earth: as above, so below. It follows that phenomena are all interconnected and correspond to each other.

The alchemist and physician Oswald Croll, who lived in Prague, wrote in 1609 of the 'divine Analogy of this visible World and Man' in his influential *Basilica chymica*:

> Heaven and Earth are Mans parents, out of which Man last of all was created; he that knowes his parents, and can Anotomise them, hath attained the true knowledge of their child man, the most perfect creature in all his properties; because all things of the whole Universe meet in him as in the Centre, and the Anotomy of him in his Nature is the Anotomy of the whole world . . .[6]

As a man of his time, Rudolf would not have questioned the notion that heaven and earth are linked by a subtle web of correspondences. Cosmology of the late sixteenth century not only assumed that there was a dynamic system of correspondences but an unbroken and hierarchical Chain of Being throughout the created world. And as an absolute monarch, Rudolf would also have approved of Sir Walter Raleigh's defence of universal hierarchy and the natural right of kings to rule:

> For that infinite wisdom of GOD, which hath distinguished his Angells by degrees, which hath given greater and lesse light and beautie to Heavenly bodies, which hath made differences betweene beasts and birds, created the Eagle and the flie, the Cedar and the shrub, and among stones given the fairest tincture to the Rubie, and the quickest light to the Diamond, hath also ordained Kings, Dukes or Leaders of the People, Magistrates, Judges and other degrees among men.[7]

The third element in the world view prevailing at Rudolf's court was the Jewish mystical tradition of the Cabala. Rudolf was deeply engaged in this subject which had become popular among Christian thinkers during the Italian Renaissance. Its most famous texts are the *Zohar* ('Splendour' or 'Enlightenment') by Moses Leon which dates back to thirteenth-century Spain, and the *Sefer Yetzirah* ('Book of Creation') which dates back to perhaps five hundred years earlier.

The Cabala teaches that God created the world by means of ten *Sephiroth*, male and female emanations of God. Between God's Light and our world there are four levels which divide into ten spheres; the Cosmic Tree connects them all. The paths connecting the *Sephiroth* were expressed by the letters of the Hebrew alphabet, the first language spoken by Adam, and it was believed that a contemplation of the letters could lead to the divine. It was thought that by becoming a creator oneself on earth, one could experience the mystical rapture of union with the Creator. The purpose of the Cabala is to bring God down to Man and to raise Man up to God.

The Cabala further embraced the art of *gematria*, a form of magic which assigned numerical values to Hebrew letters. Through complex calculations and combinations they could not only depict the organisation of the world but manipulate the natural forces of fire, earth, air and water. The social message of the Cabala was apocalyptic, prophesying a new harmonious age based on moral and spiritual regeneration. It coincided with a widespread *fin de siècle* belief in the imminent transformation of Europe, which would sweep away the old, corrupt regimes. Its influence was widespread and long-lasting: the occult thinkers Agrippa, Paracelsus and John Dee were all strongly influenced by the tradition.

Rudolf's confessor and one of his closest confidants, Johann Pistorius, produced in 1587 in Basle the first volume of a widely influential compendium of Cabalistic texts called *Artis Cabalisticae* with commentaries by leading Christian scholars. It not only included the *Sefer Yetzirah* but became a standard text of the so-called Christian Cabala which flourished alongside the older Jewish tradition during the Renaissance. A record dating from 1600 notes that Rudolf wanted to obtain a copy of the *Sefer Yetzirah* for himself.[8] Rudolf, moreover, had close relations with the Jewish community in Prague.

The Habsburgs had been accommodating towards the Jews for some time, drawing on their economic energy and intellectual knowledge. Jews had been coming to Prague since the tenth century and were generally tolerated in the Middle Ages. The Jewish Town and its extensive cemetery in Prague were situated on the right bank of the Vltava next to the Old Town. It was sometimes referred to as the Prague Ghetto because it was set apart from the city.

But there had been troubles as well. After a Jew confessed under torture to starting the fire in 1541 which had destroyed much of the Lesser Town and the Castle, including the state archives which contained ancient documents recording privileges held by the Bohemian Estates over the king, there were angry calls for their expulsion. Ferdinand I, who had been educated at the Spanish court just before the expulsion in 1492 of the Jews from Spain, acquiesced and many Jews moved to Poland or Moravia.

Rudolf's father, Maximilian II, however, revoked all the expulsion orders on 4 April 1567 and confirmed the ancient privileges of the Jews in Bohemia. On a cloudless day in the summer of 1571, he walked with great pomp and ceremony with his Spanish wife Maria and the nobles of Bohemia through the cheering streets of the Jewish Town to demonstrate his imperial approval. On gaining the throne, Rudolf confirmed the Jewish privileges to trade in 1577 and protected the self-rule of the Jewish Town by legal measures. During his reign some eight or ten thousand Jews came to live in Prague, the largest community anywhere in the diaspora. Not only was the city called the 'mother-in-Israel', but the period of Rudolf's reign also witnessed a great flowering of Ashkenazi culture which came to be known as a 'Golden Age' in

Jewish history.[9] There was a long-established and lively printing press – the first book in Hebrew had been printed in Prague in 1512. The rabbis of Prague were also famously learned and well travelled, studying in the Jewish schools in Germany, Poland, Italy or Egypt.

The large Jewish community in Prague, compared to those in other European capitals, enjoyed considerable privileges and were some of the wealthiest citizens. They were expected to contribute handsomely to the coffers of the empire. The richest man in Prague and mayor of the Jewish Town, Mordechai Maisel, maintained a close contact with the court and nobility. Although the medieval church had decreed that Jews could not take part in trade and finance, Rudolf granted him a special trading privilege in 1592. Among his many projects to help his community, Maisel paid for two Renaissance synagogues, a hospital, ritual baths and schools. Rudolf made him his privileged *Hofjude* ('Court Jew') and leaned on him heavily to finance his war with the Turks.

Another prominent member of the Jewish Town was David Gans, historian, geographer, mathematician and astronomer. Born in Westphalia, he had studied in Bonn, Frankfurt, Cracow and Prague. In the 1580s he had even worked in England as a metallurgist. He boldly tried to reconcile the new sciences with Jewish tradition, and praised the Cracow Rabbi Moses Isserles for suggesting a compromise between them presented as appealingly as 'oranges in a silver basket'.[10] He particularly appreciated Euclid and believed his teachings created 'a ladder thrown between earth and heaven'.

Gans was also the first Jew to compile a chronicle called *Zemah David* ('Branch of David') which included Gentile history. Printed in Prague in 1592, it was the first secular literary work to be produced in Ashkenazi culture and gave a summary of his Renaissance view of the human sciences.[11] A staunch local patriot, he praised Prague as a 'great, splendid, and populous city'. He further claimed that it was founded before Troy and that a Prague Jewish community existed at the time of the Second Temple of Solomon.

To help him in his occult and Cabalistic studies, Rudolf called in the Supreme Chief Rabbi of Bohemia, Rabbi Judah Loew, who was a friend of his physician and alchemist Michael Maier. He was the most original mind in the Prague Jewish community, a renowned Renaissance scholar as well as a Cabalist.

Loew was probably born in 1520 in Worms in Germany.[12] He became the rabbi of Mikulov (Nikolsburg) and then from 1553 the Chief Rabbi of

Moravian Jews for twenty years, a post specially created by Maximilian II. In 1573, he moved to Prague.

The principal aim of Loew's many writings was to justify the irrational and the supernatural in traditional Jewish teaching, calling for a return to the traditional sources – the Torah, the whole body of the Jewish sacred writings, and the Haggadah, the rabbinical interpretations of the Hebrew scriptures outside the law. He had grave reservations about the ability of the new Renaissance science, especially the disciplines of mathematics and astronomy, to offer a reliable account of the ultimate nature of reality compared to the sacred essence of the Torah.

Yet Loew was strongly influenced by Neoplatonism and steeped in the Cabala.[13] He used the mystical texts of the *Zohar* to demonstrate that the Torah is above all history and the evolving knowledge of peoples and nations: 'Only those who really know the Torah', he wrote, 'are able to reveal the secret of wisdom and truth.'[14] But while the Torah offers the true plan of the order of the world, it has an esoteric meaning: 'The whole supramundane content of the Torah is enclosed in material shapes, and when man touches the material part he is drawn towards the hidden one.'[15]

Loew was trying to reconcile two contradictory philosophical principles: the 'horizontal' relative power of humans which took the form of science and creativity and the 'vertical' and absolute power of God. He also had original views on the *Sephiroth* which are central to Jewish mysticism. According to the Cabalists, God the invisible is manifested in the visible world through the ten *Sephiroth*, sometimes translated as 'powers', 'energies' or 'essences', which reveal the divine Unity. While accepting the invisibility of God, Loew argued however that the *Sephiroth* are merely categories of human perception – they are useful to our understanding but cannot be taken as divine attributes. The only way to come close to God was not therefore through adherence to the *Sephiroth*, which he called a form of 'clinging' or 'cleaving', but through the close study of the Torah and the practice of the Ten Commandments.[16] By insisting on the primacy of the Torah as a source of divine knowledge, he confined the sciences to a secondary realm concerned with a fragmentary view of nature. In this, he was at odds with David Gans who actively advocated the new astronomy and mathematics.

Loew earned the reputation as a Zaddick, a man of special powers and wisdom, and many legends grew around him in the Prague Ghetto over the centuries. One story claims that he stopped the Emperor's carriage on Charles

Bridge at a distance by some kind of kinetic energy. Another presents him magically conjuring up the patriarchs of Jewish history for Rudolf. His most celebrated act was said to be the creation of a 'Golem' (Hebrew for 'unformed or imperfect matter') from the mud of the river Vltava. Loew gave life to its clay body, it was claimed, by placing under its tongue a *shemhamforash* – a parchment on which was written one of the names of God. Another version has it that the Golem was brought to life by the letters 'EMETH' ('Truth') traced on its forehead. It became a much appreciated servant and protector of the wider Jewish community but of course it was not allowed to work on a Sabbath. One Friday, however, the Rabbi forgot to erase the first letter of the magic formula from its forehead, leaving the word 'METH' (Death). The result was that the Golem began to run amuck. It was only when all the letters had been erased that it collapsed and slowly reverted to clay. The moral, of course, is that even the most perfect creation can be transformed into a destructive force.

In fact, the first mention of the creation of a Golem – the Jewish prototype of Frankenstein's monster – antedates its appearance in Prague by many centuries. Nevertheless, it was typical of the magical atmosphere at Rudolf's court that such stories should gain credence.

Rudolf would have heard of the alleged powers of Chief Rabbi Loew and of his interest in the Cabala. He had further been deeply impressed by a sermon on brotherly love on the Day of Atonement in which Loew called for all religions to work together for universal peace, and he invited him to the Castle so that he might benefit from his occult knowledge and esoteric skills. They may have had several interviews, but unfortunately there is firm evidence of only one meeting taking place. David Gans mentions in his chronicle *Zemah David* the audience which he says took place on Sunday, 13 February 1592, the centenary of the great expulsion of the Jews from Spain by the grandfather of Charles V, Ferdindand of Aragon. Gans describes Rudolf as 'a just ruler, the source of great and brilliant light' and says that he received Rabbi Loew in his residence 'most graciously, speaking face to face as a man speaks to his equal. As for the substance and purpose of this dialogue, it remains a secret which the two men decided not to disclose.'[17] Whatever the exact nature of their lengthy and closeted conversation, to have had an audience with the most powerful man in Christendom was undoubtedly a dramatic event in the Rabbi's life.

The Rabbi's son-in-law, Isaac Katz, on the other hand claims that they met a week later on 20 February and that the Rabbi was only allowed to talk to a courtier while the Emperor listened behind a closed curtain. Katz promised to reveal later the *nistarot* ('secrets') which they shared 'in due time' but never did.[18] This account would seem less reliable than Gans's; it was written much later and it was not Rudolf's custom to talk to scholars and adepts in such a roundabout way. It seems certain that they debated aspects of the Cabala.

Some nine months after their meeting, Loew left Prague to become the Chief Rabbi of Poland in Posnan. He returned to Prague around 1599 and for the last ten years of his life became the Chief Rabbi of Bohemia and head of the Jewish community. He remained a close friend of his benefactor Mordechai Maisel and was shocked when Rudolf, who had earlier guaranteed the execution of his will by imperial decree, had his fortune confiscated when the financier died in 1604. It was a mean act which reverberated throughout the Jewish communities of Europe. Loew was buried in the Old Jewish Cemetery in 1609; it is still a place of pilgrimage, for Jews from all over the world light candles on his tombstone and leave wishes and prayers on pieces of paper in order to draw on his alleged healing powers. His reputation as a Cabalist and as a Zaddick, which first drew Rudolf's attention, still lives on.

ARS MAGICA

These metaphysics of magicians,
And necromantic books are heavenly;
Lines, circles, scenes, letters, and characters;
Ay, these are those that Faustus most desires.
O, what a world of profit and delight,
Of power, of honour, of omnipotence,
Is promis'd to the studious artisan!..
A sound magician is a mighty god:
Here, Faustus, tire thy brains to gain a deity.

Christopher Marlowe, *Doctor Faustus* (c.1588)

After Neoplatonism, Hermeticism and the Cabala, the fourth element to make up the world view which held sway at Rudolf's court was magic. Magic attempted to reconcile the apparent opposition between the perception of the diversity of things in the external world and an underlying cosmic unity. It was understood to be a skill (*ars* in Latin) which could attain particular effects on objects or individuals by hidden – occult – means which are beyond the senses. Magic drew on a mystical rather than a rational understanding of the universe and its practitioners tended to be hostile to both brands of established religion – Protestant and Catholic – as being too dogmatic and rigid. Organised religion, on the other hand, rightly considered magic a threat since it assumed that adepts had a direct relationship with and could manipulate the divine forces of nature.

What in the Middle Ages and the Renaissance was called 'natural magic' was their closest approximation to science.[1] Giovanni Pico della Mirandola saw in magic 'the sum of natural wisdom'. He wrote in *The Dignity of Man* (1486):

> Magic does not create miracles, but, as a kind of adoring servant, it calls up the living forces of nature. It studies the connection in the Universe which the Greeks called Sympathy, it deepens the understanding of the very essence of things and brings out from the bosom of the earth and from its mysterious reserves miracles and carries them into the open . . . The magician marries heaven and earth and puts in contact the inferior world with the superior world.[2]

Pico defended natural magic as 'the practical part of the science of nature, which only teaches us to achieve admirable works by means of natural forces'.[3] It concerned itself, in his view, with the hidden properties of natural bodies in the animal, vegetable and mineral realms.

But there was also magic which worked by calling up daemons: good, divine, 'white' magic (sometimes called 'theurgy') which Shakespeare's magus Prospero drew on; and evil, diabolical, 'black magic' (sometimes called 'goety') which Faust evoked. Theurgy called upon good spirits and angels and prepared the soul to communicate with them, while goety developed techniques to call up demons for evil purposes which in Faust's case involved selling one's soul to the Devil. Both involved miracles in the sense of suspending the common laws of nature which govern the world.

In his work *De magia* (1590) Giordano Bruno, who visited and worked in Prague during Rudolf's reign, identified at least ten different kinds of magic, varying from *sapientia* – the art of the wise magus – at one end to *maleficium* – demonic magic involving a pact with the Devil – at the other. Among the former, he counted the natural magic of *medicina* and *chymia* or alchemy and occult philosophy which relied on words, numbers, images and characters. The widespread persecution of witchcraft in the second half of the sixteenth century reflected the commonplace belief that malevolent devils could be raised as well as benefic spirits. In both cases, the attempt to evoke hidden forces was motivated by a desire to control and manipulate them: one to good ends, the other to evil.

One important strand of Renaissance magic in particular and occult philosophy in general was Lullism. Ramón Lull, a thirteenth-century Christian mystic living in Spain influenced by the Muslim Sufis and the

Cabalists, developed a model based on geometrical figures and letter-notations which allegedly mirrored the structure of the universe. He designated the 'Divine Dignities' by letters of the Latin alphabet and placed them on a series of revolving concentric discs. Any combination of letters could thus represent a possible form in the universe. These relationships and categories could be extended by analogy to other fields, such as principles, virtues, mental faculties and even medical ideas. Lull also drew up symbolic names, numbers, diagrams and alphabets which were widely used by alchemists in their pursuit of the Philosopher's Stone.[4]

An aspect of natural magic which greatly excited Rudolf was the belief that man-made instruments could extend the limits of the human senses and artificially manipulate nature. Galileo's telescope was an obvious contemporary example while the English adept John Dee made use of magical mirrors. Renaissance magi also looked back to the 'artificial' magic of Roger Bacon and Albertus Magnus, both adepts of alchemy. In *De Mirabili potestate artis et naturae* ('On the Wonderful Power of Art and Nature', 1542) Bacon imagined great advances in technology, such as flying and travelling underwater, as well as the discovery of the Philosopher's Stone which would enable one to live for ever. According to alchemical tradition, Albertus owned a talking head of brass, recalling the Egyptian belief in living statues, but his best pupil, the future St Thomas Aquinas, was said to have smashed it because it interrupted his studies. Hydraulic, pneumatic and clockwork machinery were examples of artificial motion that Rudolf collected avidly for his *Kunstkammer*. He even tried his hand at making them himself in his workshops, as he did mixing substances in his alchemical laboratories.

With this late Renaissance fascination with magic, it is no coincidence that Johann Spiess's *Faustbuch*, the first printed version of the famous legend, was published early in Rudolf's reign in 1587. It inspired many works, including Christopher Marlowe's play *Doctor Faustus* (1604) in which the hero eventually sells his soul to the Devil in pursuit of power through knowledge. While he comes to a sticky end, Marlowe shows sympathy for his desire for complete experience and boundless longing for the infinite.

Faust allegedly lived in a house in Melantrichova Street in Prague. After it was demolished, Mladota's Palace at the south end of Charles Square became known as Faust's House because of its association with magic and alchemy, especially when it was occupied by Rudolf's astrologer Jakub Krocínek. Little

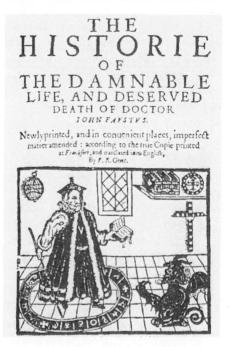

A seventeenth-century woodcut showing Faust, within a magic circle, conjuring up the Devil. The Vatican accused Rudolf of dabbling in magic

is known about him but his two sons came to a bitter end: the youngest killed his brother, apparently for alchemical treasure hidden in the walls of the house, and ended up on the gallows. The notorious English alchemist Edward Kelley, who engaged in 'angelic communications' with John Dee, is also said to have bought the house in 1591. Certainly, alchemical symbols have recently been revealed beneath the plaster.

Johann Trithemius of Sponheim was often associated with Faust. Trithemius was a Benedictine monk steeped in natural magic, the Cabala, Neoplatonism, alchemy and astrology. He taught at Basle University where the great alchemist Paracelsus later came under his influence. His most famous work was called the *Steganographia* which was written in 1499 and first offered to Maximilian I; it was distributed in manuscript form at Rudolf's court but not printed until 1606. It was based on a combination of angel magic, secret writing and ciphers and, rather like the modern internet, his angelic network was intended to transmit messages and gather knowledge 'of everything that is happening in the entire world'.[5]

Rudolf's fascination with such secret writing is demonstrated by one of the most intriguing documents that came into his hands. He apparently bought it and then passed it on to his physician Jakub Sinapius (Hořčický) of Tepenec. It is handwritten with curious drawings in ciphers which have never been decoded. It was probably a magical tract disguised so that it would not get into the wrong hands. Writing in ciphers was a common practice among magicians and alchemists. Later attributed to Roger Bacon, the work could well have arrived with John Dee, who had a strong interest in Bacon and who came to live in Prague and met the Emperor.

Throughout Europe at this time there was a close network of seekers after occult knowledge which formed a kind of invisible college. Henry Cornelius Agrippa of Nettesheim was one of them. Trithemius checked the proof pages of his *De occulta philosophia* (1533), a remarkable survey and analysis of Renaissance magic, copies of which were held in the imperial libraries of Vienna and Prague. As a Hermetic philosopher, Agrippa worshipped the One behind the many forms taken by the gods and angels. As a Neoplatonist, he believed that the hidden virtues of things are infused 'by the Ideas through the World Soul and the rays of the stars'. And as an alchemist, he declared that the Philosopher's Stone was not to be talked about lightly and condemned all practitioners who did not practise the spiritual Art. Agrippa moreover distinguished between three types of white magic which he called natural, celestial and ceremonial:

> Natural Magicke then is that, which having intentively behelde the forces of all natural thinges, and celestiall, and with curious searche sought out their order, doth in such sorte publish abroade the hidden and secret powers of nature: coupling the inferiour things with the qualities of the superior as it were certain enticements by naturall joyninge of them together, that thereof oftentimes doe arise marvellous miracles: not so much by Arte as nature whereunto this Arte doth proffer herself a servaunte, when shee worketh these things.[6]

Agrippa insists that magic was the active part of natural philosophy. The magician can often produce effects before the normal passage of time which the vulgar take for miracles but which are in fact only natural operations. However, he readily admitted that evil spirits, pretending to be divine, can be invoked by men, while angelic spirits may reveal themselves only to upright and holy men since they are sent on the command of God.

One of the most influential and notorious works on magic which Rudolf possessed was the treatise known as the *Picatrix* which first emerged in Toledo in the thirteenth century. It was a translation of the Arabic work *Gayat al-hakim* ('The Final Aim of the Wise') attributed to the tenth-century alchemist Al-Majriti. As its subtitle implies, the *Libro de la magia de los signos* ('Book on the Magic of Signs') was primarily a work of talismanic magic drawing on ancient Egyptian, Hebrew, Chaldean and Greek sources. The works opens with the usual Hermetic and Cabalistic doctrines: there is One Truth and One Unity behind the diversity of things; the earth mirrors the heavens ('as above, so below'); and man is a little world reflecting the macrocosm of the universe ('as within, so without'). Through his divine intellect (*mens*), man can raise himself above the seven heavens to reach God.

The work makes clear that the 'virtues' of superior bodies (*spiritus*) are the form and power of inferior bodies (*materia*). The art of *magia* is thus to channel the spiritual into the material. The magician using talismans seeks help from the spirits of the planets, the secrets of numbers, and the position of the celestial spheres. Through careful rituals, he can transmit power from the heavens into objects on earth – talismans – in order to achieve his ends. Although the book was banned by the Inquisition, Rudolf carefully followed its instructions on how to draw down the energies of the planets through the use of talismans and spells in order to protect himself from his enemies and to cure his bouts of melancholy.

Natural magic did not seek to call up supernatural beings as demonic magic did but focused on the manipulation of hidden, natural causes for desired and predictable effects. Such occult forces included gravity, magnetism and musical resonance. Its exponents claimed that they were following an ancient sacred tradition of the *prisca theologia*, the original theology. It was believed that God had revealed to Adam supernatural knowledge about the structure and processes of the Creation. This *scientia* had been passed down through the centuries from initiate to initiate, including Abraham, Moses, Hermes, Pythagoras, Plato and others. It was no accident that on the threshold of Sienna Cathedral a large floor carving of Hermes Trismegistus was made during the Renaissance.

Magic for Rudolf's contemporaries was not, therefore, something created, but a power summoned; it was not neutral, but bore responsibility and had a purpose. To prevent the sacred science getting into the wrong hands and to hide it from the vulgar, it was disguised in secret symbols, myths and allegories which only the initiated could comprehend. Its potency, however, was assured by the energy which suffuses and flows throughout the whole of creation and made up the *spriritus mundi* or World Soul. This subtle, invisible fluid medium ensured the efficacy of magic as well as alchemy and astrology.

The wielder of black magic was the necromancer or witch; the practitioner of white magic was the magus. The magus was considered during the Renaissance a powerful figure, a prophet and a reformer who could invoke powers from a higher world. Francis Bacon, founder of the modern scientific method of experiment and observation, may have rejected the magus as a prophet and seer but he still saw the new scientist as a 'Merchant of Light', as a powerful figure capable of transforming the physical world. He not only asserted the old adage 'knowledge is power' but in his book *New Atlantis* called for a dedicated elite to reform society.

Although the Catholic Church defended miracles as the suspension of otherwise immutable natural laws, it was in general opposed to magic if it meant the attempted harnessing of supernatural powers. It was worried that the Renaissance magi would offer a different path to knowledge other than their own carefully laid-out route and feared that they might invoke the powers of the Devil rather than those of God. The example of Rudolf, the most powerful temporal representative of Christianity, listening to such men and collecting their works rather than following the counsels of the Church's appointed priests was considered a grave threat indeed. Not only was his religious orthodoxy at stake, but the entire edifice of the Catholic Church was being undermined.

While Neoplatonism, Hermeticism, the Cabala and magic were essential elements in the world view of Rudolf's court, alchemy and astrology were the main sciences that shared the same perspective. Alchemy attempted to transform nature by drawing on invisible energies as well as physical means, while astrology assumed that the subtle web of correspondences between heaven and earth ensured that celestial events would influence those on earth. Although they were considered – with magic – part of the 'occult' sciences, their higher purpose was to banish the darkness of ignorance and to attain enlightenment through knowledge.

The word alchemy comes from the Coptic word for Egypt *Al Kemia*, meaning the 'Black Land', and alchemy had first emerged in Alexandria in the second century BC. The Arabs had brought it to Europe during their occupation of Spain and Sicily and the greatest thinkers of the Middle Ages – Thomas Aquinas, Roger Bacon, Ramón Lull and Arnald de Villanova – had all been involved in the pursuit of the Philosopher's Stone.

The Philosopher's Stone was the Holy Grail of the art and science of alchemy. The Philosopher's Stone, the alchemists believed, could not only transmute base metal into gold and offer untold riches but prolong life indefinitely and provide the key to the riddle of the universe. Alchemy was a sacred science, blending mystical religion and philosophy with medicine and chemistry. The alchemists believed in the alchemy of matter as well as the alchemy of spirit: if an alchemist was not spiritually pure, he would never achieve success in his experiments. To discover the Philosopher's Stone was therefore an outward sign of inner enlightenment: the two aspects were inextricable. The alchemists' aim was to attain personal harmony which mirrored the ultimate harmony of the universe. Moreover, they sought not only the transmutation of metals but the moral and spiritual transformation of mankind. Underlying their obsessive pursuit of the Philosopher's Stone was undoubtedly a drive for harmony and perfection and for the truths of revealed religion. The alchemical dream of the Renaissance was nothing less than a search for the Creator through his created works.[7]

Rudolf would have known about the fiery dreams of the alchemists ever since he was a boy. The libraries of his father in Vienna and of his uncle in Madrid were full of the works of the German, Italian and Spanish alchemists and physicians who wrote and communicated with each other in Latin. Rudolf's quest for miraculous knowledge would have been excited by the imperial court physician and astronomer-astrologer Dr Tadeáš Hájek of Hájek (Thaddaeus Hagecius). A native of Prague and a master of *ars magica* and occult philosophy, Hájek had been first engaged by his father. He conducted alchemical experiments in his house on the corner of Bethlehem Square in the Old Town and it became the meeting place for many alchemists, physicians, scientists and scholars. Hájek completed Rudolf's Spanish education by introducing him to the writings of the medieval philosophers Albertus Magnus and Roger Bacon (whose works were on the Index forbidden by the Vatican), the infidel physician Avicenna (the 'Aristotle of the Arabs'), the alchemist Geber (the 'Prince of the Arab Philosophers'), and the works of Paracelsus

cosmic time. The terms astronomy and astrology were considered to be interchangeable in the Middle Ages – both were studied by *mathematici* – and they only began to be separated from one another during the late Renaissance. Astrology continued to interpret the meaning of the influence of the moving celestial bodies on life on earth, while astronomy increasingly became concerned with recording and calculating the movements of the heavens as a form of celestial mechanics. Rudolf's parents had had his horoscope cast by the famed Nostradamus in 1565 and he went on to employ many astrologer-astronomers at his court. While he constantly consulted them about his state of health, his prospects and the state of the empire, they in their turn began to lay down the foundations of modern astronomy.

During the Renaissance, alchemy and astrology were still central to medicine. Alchemy provided medicines and elixirs made from chemicals, minerals, metals and herbs, while astrology was important both in diagnosis and treatment. The horoscope of a person could indicate their underlying character: if Saturn was prominent in their chart, for instance, they would tend to have a saturnine, melancholic tendency. This in turn would help to understand their bodily weaknesses and strengths. In addition, the main organs of the body were associated with the different planets, reflecting the ancient Hermetic principles of 'as above, so below' and 'as within, so without'. Astrology would be able to tell what planets were having a beneficial or malefic effect on particular organs in the patient. It would also provide the correct timings to take the medicines, according to the most favourable disposition of the planets, so that they could have their maximum effect.

Most physicians still worked within the Aristotelian tradition of the four humours which were associated with the four elements: fire, earth, air and water. Disease was explained in terms of a serious inbalance of the humours in the body. But the followers of the revolutionary Swiss physician, alchemist and astrologer Theophrastus Bombastus von Hohenheim, otherwise known as Paracelsus, were beginning to gain ground, especially in Prague, which during Rudolf's reign became the European capital of Paracelsians.[9] In the first half of the sixteenth century, Paracelsus became the founding father of iatro-chemistry and pharmacy as well as a forerunner of homeopathic medicine. He believed that with his 'spagyric art', as he called alchemy (from the Greek words *spao* and *ageiro*, meaning 'tear apart and gather together'), he could produce the panacea for all ills; even Erasmus, the greatest humanist of the age, had faith in him. Although influenced by the Cabala and the

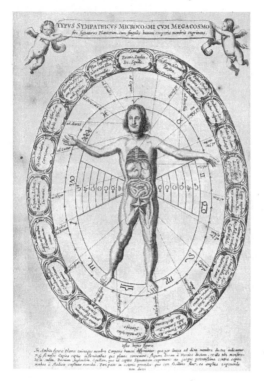

Astrological Man, showing the correspondence between human organs and the planets. Alchemists and astrologers both believed in the two principles: as above so below; as within, so without. Athanasius Kircher, Mundus subterraneus *(1678)*

Hermetic writings, experience was his great mentor. He insisted that his students throw away their old books and study the 'Book of Nature'. He broke with tradition by writing in German rather than Latin. He certainly lived up to his 'bombastic' name and reputation. He famously said: 'What light do you shed, you doctors of Montpellier, Vienna and Leipzig? About as much light as a Spanish fly on a dysentery stool!' On another occasion, he dismissed a critic as a 'wormy and lousy Sophist' and called himself a 'Monarch of Arcana'.[10]

According to Paracelsus (his name means 'Beyond Celsus', the Roman physician), in the beginning was *Iliaster*, a word he derived from the words *Ilias* (Troy) and *astrum* (star). This 'Great Mystery' was a kind of 'matter-energy' which had condensed to form the heavens and earth. It also gave birth to three main forces – the *tria prima* – that constitute the world, underlay all phenomena and are to be found in all substances. They are salt, sulphur and mercury, which correspond respectively to the body, soul and spirit. If the *tria prima* are not in balance, a person will be ill. The physician is therefore an alchemist of the body who seeks to re-establish the natural harmony of health based on the right proportions of the *tria prima*. Nature is always the foundation of medicine because man the microcosm is a quintessence of all creation and of all the forces flowing through the world.

Paracelsus also argued that since All is One and man is a microcosm of the macrocosm there are *astra* – planets – in the body as well as the heavens. The sun for instance rules the heart, the moon the brain, mercury the liver and so on. The task of the physician-astrologer is to restore the natural harmony between the heavenly and the bodily *astra* as well as between the *tria prima*.

Into his royal crucible, with its heady brew of Neoplatonism, Hermeticism, the Cabala, magic, alchemy and astrology, Rudolf welcomed some of the greatest thinkers and scientists of the day. These included the English magus John Dee, the German alchemist Oswald Croll, the Polish alchemist Michael Sendivogius, the Italian philosopher Giordano Bruno, the Danish astronomer Tycho Brahe and the German mathematician and astronomer Johannes Kepler. Because of the constant threat of persecution from Church and State, such original and subversive thinkers were often obliged to travel around Europe in search of a congenial place to continue their pioneering and potentially heretical work. They were men who were prepared to risk their lives in the search for knowledge wherever it might lead them, and despite their different nationalities, backgrounds and interests, they shared with Rudolf a readiness to go beyond the boundaries of permissible thought. Each one was, as Galileo addressed Johannes Kepler, a 'comrade in the pursuit of truth'.[11]

Rudolf was gripped by the Renaissance drive for knowledge as well as beauty. Indeed, he shared the widespread Renaissance view that the true is beautiful and the beautiful is true. As the world around him threatened to descend into the chaos of religious discord, he hoped to recreate a beautiful world of harmony based on the sacred science of the ancients. Yet for all his belief in miracles and wonders, Rudolf was far from being a relic of a bygone age. He was fascinated by the claims of magic, alchemy and astrology, but he was also interested in the emerging sciences of chemical medicine and mathematical astronomy.

While their work was rooted in the medieval world view, the late Renaissance thinkers who came to Rudolf's Prague developed new methods of experimentation and observation which saw the first glimmerings of empiricism and the modern scientific method. Steeped in alchemy, they were the fathers of modern chemistry and medicine; believing in astrology, they created the new astronomy.

9

THE MAGI

He that is grounded in Astrology,
Enriched with tongues, well seen in minerals,
Hath all the principles Magic doth require.

Christopher Marlowe, *Doctor Faustus* (c.1588)

It was not long after moving to Prague that Rudolf began inviting thinkers and experimenters from all over Europe to help him in his alchemical and occult researches. John Dee, the most celebrated magus of his age, turned up in 1586 and stayed in and around Bohemia for six years. During this time, he conversed with angels, undertook experiments to discover the Philosopher's Stone, probably spied for Queen Elizabeth and tried to persuade the Holy Roman Emperor to spearhead a moral and spiritual reformation of Europe.

Dee was an extraordinary man of an extraordinary age, one of the most learned individuals in Europe. Born in 1527, the son of a vintner who was a minor court official of Henry VIII, Dee had attended St John's College, Cambridge – where he had studied eighteen hours a day – and became a fellow at Trinity College. Aged twenty, he went to the University of Louvain in the Netherlands where he pursued his studies in mathematics, cartography and astronomy and wrote an alchemical work in twenty-four volumes called *Mercurius Coelestis* ('Celestial Mercury'). But he then went on to Paris where he gave lectures on Euclid to large and enthusiastic audiences. The young prodigy had arrived. He rejected offers of academic posts to pursue his own independent researches.

After receiving no reply from Queen Mary of England about his proposal to establish a repository of books and ancient manuscripts, he built his own library at home in Mortlake on the banks of the river Thames in Surrey which eventually housed the largest collection of books on natural sciences in England and possibly Europe. He also set up an astronomical observatory and alchemical laboratory. As a Renaissance adeptus of the first order, he believed in the power of amulets, talismans and angelic magic and was soon rumoured to be in communication with evil spirits.

Dee was steeped in the Neoplatonic and Hermetic tradition and the Cabala. He believed in cosmic harmony, in the dynamic web of correspondences between heaven and earth and in humanity as the microcosm of the macrocosm. The spirit world for him seemed to be more real than the world of appearances around him. He was a great admirer of Roger Bacon; he not only annotated his writings on the mysteries of nature but wrote an *Apologia* for his work. He even claimed the Spanish alchemist Ramón Lull as an ancestor. Like the Rosicrucians, whom he anticipated, Dee hoped for universal moral and spiritual reform of the world through the spreading of ancient wisdom.

DR. JOHN DEE.

Apart from being a great practitioner in astrology and alchemy, Dee was a brilliant mathematician. His influential preface (1570) to a new translation of Euclid by Sir Henry Billingsley earned him the title *Nobilis Mathematicus* and a significant place in the history of mathematics.

But he was no idle theorist and wanted to put modern discoveries to practical use. Dee studied cartography with Gerard Mercator while in the Netherlands and became involved back in London in planning overseas expeditions in search of a north-west passage to China. He was the archetypal Elizabethan Renaissance man, combining aspects of Shakespeare's magus Prospero with those of the seafaring adventurer Sir Francis Drake.[1]

John Dee wielded considerable influence at the English court. He was tutor at different times to Robert Dudley, Edward Dyer, Thomas Digges, Thomas Moffet (father to the little miss who sat on a tuffet) and the poet and diplomat Sir Philip Sidney. Above all, he was for some time the personal astrologer to Elizabeth I. He calculated the most favourable time for her coronation and she frequently asked him to attend her at court. She regularly consulted him about everything from naval affairs to her toothaches. When a small wax image of the queen with pins stuck in it was found in Lincoln's Inn Fields, it was Dee who was immediately summoned to court to ward off any evil by casting counter spells.

Elizabeth visited him with her retinue at his home in Mortlake several times. On one occasion, she came to see his library but, realising that he had buried his wife only a few hours earlier, refused to enter. She contented herself by seeing his magical crystal or 'shew-stone' used to conjure up celestial spirits. This resides now in the British Museum with an Aztec polished stone which he claimed could foretell the future. On hearing that Dee was about to sell some silver plate to raise money towards the end of his life, she sent him a gift of forty gold coins known as 'angels'.

Dee believed that the key to the mysteries of the universe and the riddle of existence could be found in numbers and symbols. In Antwerp, he came across a manuscript of Trithemius's *Steganographia* on ciphers and secret writing and spent ten days writing it out, calling it a 'boke . . . so nedefell and commodious, as in humanye knowledg none can be meeter or more behovefull'.[2] Standing in the same tradition, he published in Antwerp in 1564 his arcane masterpiece *Monas Hieroglyphica*, which presented a complex system of spiritual alchemy, Hermetic philosophy and Cabalistic numerology. The hieroglyph itself, which Dee called, the 'London Seal of Hermes', is a unified emblem of alchemical symbols which represent the underlying unity, or Monas, of the universe. In a crystallised form, it contained the whole of occult philosophy. Knowing his reputation as a Renaissance humanist, Dee made contact in 1563 with Rudolf's father Maximilian II in Hungary and dedicated his *magnum opus* to him.

The title page of the *Monas Hieroglyphica* is inscribed with the epigram: *Qui non intelligit, avt taceat, avt discat* ('He who does not understand should remain silent or learn'). Dee was following a long esoteric tradition in writing treatises which only the initiated could comprehend. It was intended to lead the few readers who could understand him to enlightenment through divine knowledge. It not only offered a ladder to reach the 'One and Only' but if digested properly would enable the magus to become invisible: 'He who fed [the monad] will first himself go away into a metamorphosis and will afterwards very rarely be seen by mortal eye . . .'[3]

Contemplating his 'shew-stone' or crystal ball, around 1581 Dee began to have visions and to hear angelic voices. One was of a girl of eight or nine who called herself Madimi and spoke in English and Greek. The Archangels Uriel, Galveh, Murifri, Michael, Gabriel and Raphael also appeared; writing down their messages, Dee recorded arrangements of numbers and combinations of letters as well as English script. Objects and scenes also appeared in the crystal, such as a bloody sword. Unable to remember all the visions, Dee employed a young notary called Edward Kelley who became the scryer or crystal gazer while Dee wrote down the messages.

Kelley soon acquired an extraordinary power over the English magus. From the day he appeared in Dee's study on 10 March 1582, they became inseparable, travelling with their families and working together in Poland, Bohemia and Germany until Dee returned to England from Prague in 1589 at the request of Elizabeth.

Kelley had the peculiar distinction of having no ears: they had been cut off for forging a document when he worked as a municipal scribe in his native town of Worcester and he wore his hair long or had a black cap with flaps to hide the mutilation. It seems that he had been an apothecary's apprentice and had briefly attended Oxford University. He soon earned a highly dubious reputation, being accused of necromancy and of exhuming a corpse from Walton-le-Dale Park for magical purposes. Although originally called Talbot, he changed his name to Kelley and passed himself off to Dee as an experienced alchemist. He claimed to have discovered in a bishop's grave

EDWARD KELLEY, "THE GOLDEN KNIGHT."

in the ruins of Glastonbury Abbey a 'red powder' or elixir possessing the properties of the Philosopher's Stone, together with a book by St Dunstan explaining the alchemical process to attain it.

Kelley was married to a woman called Joanna, who already had at least two children by a previous relationship, including possibly Elizabeth Jane Weston – who became a notable Latin poet under the name of Westonia in Bohemia and was hailed as the female Ovid or tenth Muse.[4]

For all his great learning and court connections, Dee seems to have been entirely won over by the charismatic Kelley. While it seems odd that such a young Mephisto should have had such influence over one of Elizabethan England's greatest intellectuals, it was probably due to his insatiable thirst for universal knowledge and his desire to communicate with the spirit world.

Kelley and Dee undertook 'angelic communications' together in séances using the 'shew-stones'. Kelley claimed that the angels spoke to him in a language called Enochian, named after Enoch, the Old Testament figure associated with Hermes. Dee took his personal spirits, the young girl Madimi and the Archangels Uriel and Gabriel, as spiritual guides. He kept a record which was published in 1659 as A *True and Faithful Relation of what passed between Dr John Dee and some Spirits*. It was an extraordinary account of his communications with spirits and his visionary experiences, mainly during the years 1583–6.

Dee first left England with his new assistant Edward Kelley in 1583 after an invitation from the Polish Count Albrecht Laski who had met them during his visit to the English court. Laski was the Palatine of Sieradz and a vast landowner. An unorthodox Catholic, he was a great patron of alchemists and paid for the first printing of an important work by Paracelsus. Dressed in purple velvet and with a great beard, he cut an impressive figure and was lavishly welcomed by Elizabeth with feasts and jousts. He was introduced to Dee by the Earl of Leicester. At a séance in Mortlake, the magus and his assistant predicted that the Count would become the king of Poland and obtain the Elixir of Life.

Laski was hooked and invited them to join him in Poland; both were in debt and agreed. They travelled with Laski with their two families and stayed on his estates near Cracow. After months of inaction, Laski grew impatient so Kelley arranged an experiment in which he produced a small quantity of gold which passed the tests of the Cracow goldsmiths. During his stay, Dee made contact with members of the University – giving them a rare fifteenth-century Greek translation of Boethius – and met Hannibal Rosseli who was to compile a vast edition of the Hermetic text *Pymander*.

Consuming more gold than they were making, Laski finally encouraged his two alchemists to travel on to Prague with letters of introduction and a safe passage. After an eight-day journey, they finally arrived at the European capital of alchemy on 9 August 1584. Dee wrote to Rudolf on 17 August asking for an audience. He had with him a letter of recommendation from the Queen of England and offered Rudolf a magic mirror in which the viewer was meant to be able to see whatever he desired.[5] Dee was also on an undeclared personal mission to strengthen the Hermetic resolve of the Holy Roman Emperor and to bring about the moral and spiritual reformation of Europe. As an astrologer, he was convinced that the configuration of the planets in the heavens in 1584 augured an immediate and important change on earth.

When Dee and Kelley arrived in Prague they first stayed with Rudolf's court astronomer Tadeáš Hájek at his house in the Old Town, which was called the 'House of the Green Mound'. It was a good choice: Hájek was not only Rudolf's physician but also in charge of his alchemical laboratories. Dee noted in his diary that the walls of Hájek's study were decorated with occult inscriptions and strange motifs: 'very many *Hieroglyphical* Notes *Philosophical* in Birds, Fishes, Flowers, Fruits, Leaves and Six Vessels, as for the Philosopher's works'.[6] High up on the wall of the south side was inscribed:

> This art is precious, transient, delicate and rare. Our learning is a boy's game, and the toil of women. All you sons of the art, understand that none may reap the fruits of the elixir except by the introduction of the elemental stone, and if he seeks another path he will never enter nor embrace it.[7]

Dee would have felt immediately at home here but Kelley quickly took the initiative and set down to work. At their first séance on 15 August 1584, he evoked a series of wild alchemical visions: an enormous furnace with an opening of four or five city gates belching a 'marvellous smoke'; a seething lake of black pitch from which rose a creature with the body of a lion and seven heads; and a great hammer with a seal embedded in its surface. Dee's angel Madimi then appeared, not in her usual guise as a young girl, but much larger and in an apocalyptic frenzy. She uttered a series of dire prophecies that the world would be turned upside down and Satan would reign supreme:

> Woe be unto the Kings of the Earth, for they shall be beaten into Mortar . . . Woe be unto the false preachers, yea seven woes be unto them, for they are the teeth of the Beast . . . Woe unto the Virgins of the Earth, for they shall disdain their virginity, and become concubines for Satan . . . Woe to the books of the earth, for they are corrupted.

Madimi not only declared that Satan sought the destruction of Dee's household and children but urged him to write immediately to the Emperor, 'saying that the Angel of the Lord has appeared unto thee and rebuketh him for his sins'.[8]

Over the next few days, Dee repeatedly asked his spirits for reassurance about his family and mulled over how he should best address the Emperor. Well schooled in etiquette at the court of Elizabeth, he finally took a profoundly obsequious tone and reminded Rudolf of his earlier connections with his family:

'To the serene and potent Prince and Lord, Rudolf by the grace of God, Emperor of the Romans ever august, and of Germany, Hungary, Bohemia, &c.' For his own part, he offered to present himself 'at the feet of your Caesarian Majesty abjectly to kiss them, extremely happy if in anything I shall be able to be pleasing and useful to so great an Emperor of the Christian republic'. He pointed out that he had met his forebears – Charles V at the court in Brussels and Ferdinand I in Pressburg, Hungary – and expressed 'a particular delight in the most clement Emperor Maximilian, the father of your Caesarian Majesty' whom he considered a man 'worthy of immortal glory'. This was no doubt because of his reputation for religious tolerance and because he had dedicated his *Monas Hieroglyphica* to him. Dee then hinted that during the composition of the work he had a presentiment that the House of Austria would produce one 'in whom, for the benefit of Christian polity, the best and greatest thing would, or might become actual'. This was probably a veiled reference to his hope that Rudolf might lessen the conflict between Protestantism and Catholicism and possibly to the real aim of Dee's secret mission in Bohemia. Suspecting correctly that Rudolf liked verbal games, he ended with: 'here am I, also the fourth letter of each of the three alphabets', that is to say, the letter D in Greek, Roman and Hebrew.[9]

In an unlikely choice, Dee asked the Spanish ambassador Guillén de San Clemente to deliver the letter to Rudolf. Although a staunch Catholic and envoy of Philip II, he was surprisingly well disposed to the Protestant Dee and dined with him regularly. He even ignored the counsel whispered by a Dutchman at his table that Dee was a conjuror, 'bankrupt alchemist' and spy sent by Walsingham to stir up trouble in the Holy Roman Empire. The two men shared common Hermetic interests, for the ambassador claimed direct descent from the Catalan alchemist and Cabalist Ramón Lull and knew his work well. Dee showed the ambassador the crystal ball he used to call up his angels and two of his notebooks describing the séances. San Clemente was suitably impressed.

On 3 September 1584 a response came to his epistle to the Emperor, written by one his secretaries. Addressing Dee as 'the noble and excellent master – master most deserving of respect', he informed him that if he came at two o'clock he would be admitted at once to the 'Noble Octavius Spinola, who is his Imperial Majesty's Stall-Master and Chamberlain' and who would introduce him to his Majesty.[10]

The invitation could not have come at a worse moment. The night before, Kelley had been involved in a drunken dispute with one of Laski's guards which rumbled on the next morning, so much so that the city watchmen warned Dee 'to have care of the peace keeping'. Leaving an enraged Kelley, he rushed across Charles Bridge and up to the Castle with his servant Emericus. The guard, confused about his identity, told him to wait. By the time Spinola arrived after spotting Emericus wandering around the courtyard, Dee was already an hour late for the audience with the most powerful man in Christendom. Leading him by gently pulling on his gown, Spinola took Dee through the inner courtyard, up stairs, along corridors full of marvels of art and nature, through a dining hall, until they reached the inner chamber of Rudolf. The Emperor was sitting behind a table, his hands by a wooden chest, some letters and a copy of Dee's *Monas Hieroglyphica*.

After an exchange of formalities in Latin, Rudolf commended the book, but admitted that he had found it too difficult for his 'capacity'. He then went straight to the point and said that the Spanish ambassador had told him that he had something useful to say.

'So I have,' replied Dee. Seeing that they were alone, he recounted how he had at great pain and cost spent forty years trying to gain 'the best knowledge that man might attain unto in the world' but 'that neither any man living, nor any book I could yet meet withal, was able to teach me those truths I desired and longed for'. He therefore decided to look elsewhere for enlightenment, to the angels, to God 'by whose commandment I am now before your Majesty and have a message from him to say unto you: and that is this:

> The Angel of the Lord hath appeared to me, and rebuketh you for your sins. If you will hear me, and believe me, you shall triumph. If you will not hear me, the Lord, the God that made heaven and earth (under whom you breathe and have your spirit) putteth his foot against your breast, and will throw you headlong down from your seat. Moreover the Lord hath made this covenant with me (by oath) that he will do and perform. If you will forsake your wickedness, and turn unto him, your Seat shall be the greatest that ever was, and the Devil shall become your prisoner: which Devil I did conjecture to be the Great Turk. This is my commission from God. I feign nothing, neither am I an hypocrite, or ambitious man, or doting or dreaming in this cause . . .'[11]

Rudolf was no doubt taken back by the audacity of Dee's criticism and his claim to be divinely inspired, but no less intrigued by his prophecy that he could defeat Sultan Murad III of the Ottoman Empire who had been threatening his borders once again.

The conversation then turned to Dee's famous 'shew-stone' which he claimed was of divine origin, having been given it by the Archangel Uriel. He further maintained that his angels had informed him of the secret of the Philosopher's Stone. The conversation then turned to astrology: Dee criticised a horoscope of the Emperor drawn up by a Bohemian and offered to cast one himself. But that was enough of the grandiloquent Englishman; Rudolf signalled for him to withdraw.

According to Dee's account, the Emperor was far from indignant at the Englishman's importunate threats. Rudolf said that he believed him and that he thought Dee 'loved him unfeignedly', adding that he would not willingly have had him kneel so often as he did. A week later he was told that the 'business' of their meeting was to be entrusted to 'the magnificent Master Dr Curtz' [Dee's spelling].[12]

The Jesuit Jakob Kurz von Senftenau was Rudolf's Court Councillor and later Imperial Vice-Chancellor. He was a keen botanist and took an active interest in astronomy. Dee spent six hours outlining his mission to Kurz on their first meeting, showing him his crystal ball and extracts from his 'books of actions' which contained a description of his unknown 'Enochian' language, which still remains undeciphered. At a subsequent meeting, however, when Kurz said that the Emperor wanted to see these books, Dee refused, saying that he could only provide copies which he would make 'at leisure'. This clearly was seen as a slight to the Emperor; later, Kurz reported that Rudolf considered his sins a matter for himself and his confessor and nothing to do with Dee. Although the Emperor said that he would act as his benefactor, the outcome meant that Dee was *de facto* dismissed.[13] Nevertheless, Kurz admired Dee's learning and arranged an honorary doctorate of medicine for Dee from the Jesuit university in Prague.

The reason why Rudolf turned against Dee may have been a report sent to him by the new papal nuncio Johannes Franciscus Bonomo, bishop of Vercelli. The report, which came into Dee's hands, mentioned rumours that he had summoned spirits 'with the aid of certain magical characters'. Since good spirits are not 'enchanted or moved to appear', then Dee must be working with evil ones. Moreover, Dee, being married, was not qualified to mediate between God and man.[14] The Catholic Church, which was trying to recapture Central Europe to the true faith, clearly saw the Protestant

Englishman as a serious threat to their plans, especially if he could gain the Holy Roman Emperor's ear.

Around Prague the rumours spread that Dee was prophesying the downfall of Catholicism. The Lutheran leader Václav Budovec, who had been Court Master at the Imperial Embassy in Constantinople and knew Dee personally, later recorded: 'A learned and renowned Englishman whose name was Doctor De [sic] came to Prague to see the Emperor Rudolf II and was at first well received by him; he predicted that a miraculous reformation would presently come about in the Christian world and would prove the ruin not only of the city of Constantinople but of Rome also. These predictions he did not cease to spread among the populace.'[15]

While he was in Prague, Dee's reputation as a magus spread far and wide and even the Tsar of Russia invited him to Moscow in 1586. He declined the offer but sent his son Arthur, who had been helping him in Prague, to Moscow where he wrote a work on alchemy called *Fasciculus chemicus*.

Dee and Kelley were joined during 1585 in their 'angelic communications' by the Italian humanist Francesco Pucci who had met them in Cracow. Educated for the priesthood in Florence, he chose instead the life of a wandering scholar. Believing in the natural goodness and immortality of man, he was widely considered by the Vatican to be a dangerous heretic. The massacre of Protestants on St Bartholomew's Day in Paris in 1572 led him to abandon Catholicism and develop his own millenarian and mystical creed.

After one of their séances in Prague, Pucci wrote to his mother in 1585:

> But then I heard from the angel most weighty propositions concerning the coming of Antichrist in a short space and received great confirmation of my hopes for an imminent renovation of all things, which God will accomplish through persons authorised by him and adequate to the task. Lamenting therefore my sin I will repair to the ministers of that [Papal] Seat, to give them satisfaction for my offence in the sight of God.[16]

He clearly considered himself and Dee two of the chosen few capable of reforming the world. Although Pucci went on to write a utopian work called *Forma d'una republica catholica* in which a dedicated and enlightened elite submit themselves totally to God, he was eventually executed as a heretic in Rome in 1597.

Fearful of his Protestant influence, the nuncios of the Vatican at Rudolf's court and the Catholic faction led by the chamberlain Jiří Popel of Lobkovic began to spread rumours that Dee was working as a secret agent on behalf of the Queen of England and the Protestant cause at a time when Rudolf's uncle, Philip II of Spain, was preparing his Armada to attack Britain. In late 1585, Robert Dudley, the Earl of Leicester, had left England with an expeditionary force to help the Dutch fight the forces of Philip. Elizabeth's government had thus formally aligned itself to a Protestant coalition against Catholic Spain and the Habsburgs.

In reality, Dee was not a militant Protestant but espoused a mystical form of Christianity beyond dogma and creed. But Rome was becoming increasingly edgy about his potential influence. The new nuncio in Prague, Germanico Malaspina, Bishop of San Severino, sent for Dee and Kelley in the spring of 1586 and tried to get them to incriminate themselves. Dee, however, was wary and declined to reveal the messages of his angels: 'It is not in our hands to give counsel.' Kelley was less circumspect. Although he had recently taken Catholic confession, in an outburst worthy of Luther he lambasted those ministers who were 'devoid of true faith and idle in their good works':

> May, therefore, the doctors, shepherds, and prelates mend their ways; may they teach and live by Christ by their word as well as their conduct. For thus (in my opinion) a great and conspicuous reformation of the Christian religion would be brought about most speedily.[17]

It confirmed the Vatican's worst fears. On 29 April 1586, Filippo Sega, Malaspina's successor, wrote to the Pope warning that Dee had managed to infiltrate the imperial court and was spreading a 'new superstition'. He had no doubt that Dee and Kelley posed a real threat: 'John Dee and . . . his companion have been in this court for some time, and setting out on the path to become authors of a new superstition, not to say heresy, they have come to the attention of the Emperor and all the court.'[18] It was even rumoured that he planned to assassinate Rudolf. With the Protestants in Prague increasingly asserting their power at court day by day, the Pope demanded that the Emperor arrest Dee and Kelley and send the two of them to Rome for interrogation.

There may have been good grounds for suspecting Dee to be an agent of Queen Elizabeth. On 6 May, Dee went to Leipzig to meet his servant Edmund Hilton who was probably acting as courier to the English court. When Hilton was delayed, Dee left with an English merchant a letter which was addressed to Sir Francis Walsingham, the Queen's chief spymaster: 'I am forced to be brief. That which England suspected was also here', he wrote cryptically. He did not elaborate but added that for the past two years he had been 'pried and peered into' by imperial spies.[19]

On his return to Prague, Dee heard that the nuncio had submitted evidence to Rudolf accusing Dee of practising necromancy and 'other prohibited arts'. On 28 May, Dee wrote to the Emperor, asserting his innocence. But it was to no avail. The next day a clerk of the court came with a decree signed by Rudolf banishing Dee, his family and Kelley from the Holy Roman Empire. They were given only six days to depart.

After two years in Prague, Dee left with Kelley and their respective families. They first went to Germany but then, in August, returned to the castle of Rudolf's fellow adept Vilém Rožmberk at Třeboň in southern Bohemia. Rudolf, who may have felt he had acted too precipitously, had allowed the two troublesome Englishmen to remain in his empire.

Rožmberk was the richest and most powerful noble in Bohemia. He belonged to an older generation of tolerant Catholics and three of his four wives were Protestant. His motto was *Festina Lente* ('More haste, less speed'). He had dedicated his life to the service of Rudolf's forebears Ferdinand I and Maximilian II and, from 1570, he had been the Supreme Burgrave, the highest official in the land. He was not only a fellow member of the Order of the Golden Fleece but had held the crown at Rudolf's coronation in 1575. And after Rudolf, he was the greatest alchemical patron in the land. He had six laboratories scattered around his domains. On the walls of his magnificent Český Krumlov, murals explored the theme of fertility using alchemical, astrological and Biblical motifs: for all his successive wives, he was unable to have children.

Rožmberk had a laboratory at Třeboň built specially for Dee and Kelley in a tower above the gatehouse of his castle. They quickly got down to work. On 19 December 1586, Dee noted in his diary: 'E.K. made a projection with his powder in the proportion of one minim (upon an ounce and quarter of mercury) and produced almost an ounce of best gold; which gold we afterwards distributed from the crucible.' It was enough to keep their generous patron happy for the time being. Kelley implied, as always, that total success was just around the corner.

The following year proved highly eventful, with the wily Kelley continuing to pull the nose of the gullible Dee, who had by now become entirely dependent on Kelley to translate the angelic messages in code which came via the 'shew-stone'. Under great pressure from his assistant, Dee signed a formal statement on 3 May 1587, declaring that they would own everything in common, including their wives, since this was the bidding of the spirits which spoke to Kelley. It was the supreme test of his faith in Kelley's angelic communications. Like Faust, he 'offered his soul as a pawn' in the pursuit of divine knowledge which he could not find in books. As for Dee's third young wife, she reluctantly acquiesced, avowing herself 'to be content for God's sake and his secret purposes'. At least she had the reassurance that Kelley had so far been unable to father a child.

A week later Dee wrote ecstatically in his diary: 'E.K. did open the great secret to me. God be thanked.' On 24 August, he recorded unusually in Latin: '*Vidi aquam divinam demonstratione magnifici domini et amici mei incomparabilis D Ed Kellei ante meridiem tertia hora*' ('In a demonstration by the magnificent Lord and my incomparable friend Dr Edward Kelley I saw divine water at the third hour before noon'). Then on 14 December, Dee recorded: 'Mr Edward Kelley gave me the divine water, earth and all!'

But the 'divine water' – probably an acid – was insufficient to transmute their *prima materia* into gold on a substantial scale. Dee became increasingly disillusioned. Kelley had not only failed to reveal the secrets of the Philosopher's Stone but his own scheme for the moral and spiritual reform seemed to be going nowhere. He had been banished by Rudolf and now even his new patron Rožmberk was becoming impatient at the lack of success.

Dee finally decided to leave for England. There were other reasons for his departure. In January 1589, Kelley passed on a letter from a frustrated Rožmberk saying that he wished Dee had not come to his dominions. There was also an urgent invitation from Elizabeth to return. Dee still had sufficient faith in his wily assistant to transfer his books and what was left of 'the powder' to him and to discharge any obligations in writing. He never saw Kelley again.

Dee's stay in Bohemia had been a key period in his life and he left with his family a comparatively wealthy man. Although the magus failed in his immediate mission to bring about a moral and spiritual transformation of the world through alchemy and the discovery of the Philosopher's Stone, he nevertheless had helped plant seeds that were to reach fruition in Central Europe in the Rosicrucian movement. Neither was he forgotten in Prague: the papal nuncio Alfonso Visconte wrote in 1589 that 'the man who has passed through nearly all the heretical sects is in England'.[20]

On his arrival in Mortlake, Dee was devastated to discover that his house had been pillaged and his library burnt by a mob who believed he was a necromancer. Although the Queen received him graciously at Richmond and at Christmas sent him two hundred, 'angels', he was never able to recover his property or rebuild his library. Sinecures eased his old age: in 1595, he was given the Chancellorship of St Paul's Cathedral and became Warden of Manchester College. But he died in poverty and neglect at the age of eighty-one in 1608. He still believed in his angels but had mixed memories of his alchemical adventures in Central Europe.

What became of Kelley? For a while he went from success to success in Bohemia. In one of his few surviving letters, Rudolf wrote on 27 October (no year is indicated but it was dictated around 1588) to Vilém Rožmberk asking him to release 'Eduard' temporarily from his service so that he could come to Prague to supervise a great alchemical work. The operation was a complex one and required expert help: 'The apex is missing, the mercury of the sun, and for this reason the matter cannot be resolved. It therefore was a good thing that Eduard came here himself, to help remedy this deficiency.'[21] Rudolf wanted him to work in his alchemical laboratory, well stocked with the latest furnaces, alembics, tubes, vases, and other instruments, which had been set up in the Powder Tower in the Castle.

Kelley was described at Rudolf's court as 'Eduard Kelley, born of an Englishman, of the knightly kin and house called Imaymi in the country of Conaghaku in the kingdom of Ireland'.[22] On his return to Prague in 1589, he was accepted as a citizen of Bohemia, granted a patent of imperial nobility and warmly welcomed by Rudolf who made him court alchemist with a large salary. Pleased with his contribution to the Great Work and his demonstrations of transmutations of small quantities of gold, the Emperor made him, on 23 February 1590, the *Eques Auratus* ('Golden Knight') of Imana.

He remarried a rich and well-educated Bohemian woman who gave him a daughter and a son. In 1590 his patron Vilém Rožmberk gave him the burgh of Libeřice, the estate to Nová Libeň and about nine villages. With his handsome settlement, he bought a brewery, a mill, a dozen houses at Jílové (famous for its gold mines), and two grand mansions in Charles Square in the New Town of Prague. On the marriage of one of his maid-servants, Kelley allegedly gave away rings, twisted with three gold wires, to the value of four thousand pounds.

One of Kelley's houses in Charles Square came to be known as 'Faust's House'. Kelley also allegedly lived, in 1590, in a house with a tower in Janský Vršek Street in the Malá Strana (Lesser Town) below the castle. A story still persists, recorded on a plaque nailed to the house, that a woman lived on the ground floor and one stormy night when her baby was ill she called up to the alchemist in his turret and asked for help. A sudden gust of wind blew up his long hair and revealed his severed ears. Infuriated, he shouted down: 'Go away, woman! Your child shall have the head of a donkey.' When she returned to see her baby in the cradle, it had indeed been transformed. Only by praying to the Madonna in a church opposite the house was the mysterious foreigner's magic undone.

Kelley went on to publish treatises on alchemy in his own name. These works were deliberately obscure, ostensibly to prevent the knowledge from getting into the wrong hands, but most probably because Kelley did not really know the true nature of the Philosopher's Stone. In the work *Theatre of Terrestrial Astronomy*, attributed to him, the author gives a characteristic description of the Chemical Wedding which finally gives birth to the Stone:

> Mercury and Sulphur, Sun and Moon, agent and patient, matter and form are opposites. When the virgin or feminine earth is thoroughly purified and purged from all superfluity, you must give it a husband to meet for it; for when the male and the female are joined together by means of the sperm, a generation must take place in the *menstruum*. The substance of Mercury is known to the Sages as the Earth and matter in which the Sulphur of nature is sown, that it may thereby putrefy, the earth being its womb.[23]

Kelley's fame spread throughout Bohemia. Matthias Erbinäus von Brandau claimed to have seen his tincture and recalled that he could make the *Mercurius Solis* in no more than a quarter of an hour. Another enthusiast in Hungary even maintained that the true wisdom of St Dunstan – the method of making the Philosopher's Stone – had been discovered by Kelley and passed on through Rudolf.[24]

It was not long before Kelley's reputation reached the court in England. Elizabeth's ambassador to Prague, Lord Willoughby, allegedly returned with a bedpan, part of which was made from Kelley's transmuted gold, to present to her. A string of hopeful young men set out to Třeboň in the hope of catching a glimpse of the Philosopher's Stone, including Sir Edward Dyer, one of Dee's former pupils. Lord Burghley sent agents to Prague to try to entice Kelley to return to practise his 'Royal Profession'. Burghley also wrote in May 1591 to Dyer for some of Kelley's 'mystic powder' to be delivered in a secret box so that he could demonstrate the possibility of alchemical transmutation to Elizabeth herself. Dyer pressed Kelley many times to return to England but to no avail.

Kelley, it seems, preferred to enjoy his exalted status and privileges in Prague and proudly boasted that he was Rudolf's personal alchemist. But the wheel of fortune eventually turned against the mercurial adventurer when the hot-blooded Kelley killed an officer in a duel, strictly forbidden in the city. He was seized in May 1591 as he was trying to escape to his erstwhile patron Vilém Rožmberk in southern Bohemia and was locked up in Křivoklát Castle.

During this time, Rudolf did his best to extract the secrets of alchemy from him. In a letter dated 8 February 1592, written by his secretary to the prison governor, it was made clear that the Emperor wanted to learn:

> First; in what way can the four pounds of tincture found at Kelley's house be purified and used in projections?
> Secondly; how is the potable gold prepared that Kelley gave [the Emperor] to taste?
> Thirdly; how is the apparatus called Tritrop used?
> Fourthly; how is white earth, or unripe silver, manufactured?
> Fifthly; how are certain precious stones made by artifice?
> Lastly; what is the signification of the secret characters in Kelley's note-book?[25]

While being interrogated about his knowledge and experiments, Kelley tried to escape by jumping from a window but he broke his leg on the rocks below. He may have been pardoned – Dee believed so in 1593 – but it seems that he earned Rudolf's displeasure once again. He was retained on his orders in 1596 at the castle of Most, where the German alchemist Oswald Croll visited him in the hope of learning more about the *Secretum solutionis*.

While in prison, Kelley wrote a treatise in Latin on 'The Stone of the Philosophers' which he dedicated on 14 October 1596 'To the most potent Lord of the Holy Roman Empire, Rudolf II, King of Hungary and Bohemia'. In the opening paragraph, he declared:

Though I have already twice suffered chains and imprisonment in Bohemia, an indignity which has been offered me in no other part of the world, yet my mind remaining unbound, has all this time exercised itself in the study of that philosophy which is despised only by the wicked and foolish but is praised and admired by the wise. Nay, the saying that none but fools and lawyers hate and despise alchemy has passed into a proverb . . . Hence I have written a treatise by means of which your imperial mind may be guided into all the truth of the ancient philosophy . . .[26]

Back in England, Dee heard in 1595 the news that Kelley was slain but it seems that he may well have muddled on to see in the new century. Again, he tried to escape from prison but fell, possibly on to his son's carriage below, and injured his remaining good leg. Facing life imprisonment, he apparently killed himself with poison. His family was deprived of all his property; his son John Adam was last heard of causing a fracas in Most. But his reputation lived on. In his *Theatrum chemicum Britannicum* (1652), Elias Ashmole gave his horoscope and published a work concerning the Philosopher's Stone allegedly by him. Two other tracts on the Philosopher's Stone attributed to Kelley were also published in Amsterdam and Hamburg in 1676.

In his extraordinary and eventful life, Kelley's most successful alchemical experiment was not the discovery of the Philosopher's Stone but the transformation of himself – from committed felon to one of the most-sought-after adepts of his age. While Kelley may have been the most successful of the puffers and charlatans who flocked to Prague, Dee was by far the greater intellect. He may have failed to bring about a moral and spiritual transformation in Central Europe, but was remembered as a great English magus long after his departure.

THE NEW HERMES TRISMEGISTUS

His Majesty is interested only in wizards, alchemists, Cabalists and the like, sparing no expense to find all kinds of treasures, learn secrets and use scandalous ways of harming his enemies . . . He also has a whole library of magic books. He strives all the time to eliminate God completely so that he may in future serve a different master . . .

Propositions to the Archdukes in Vienna (1606)

John Dee was one of many original thinkers to come to Rudolf's court to join him in his grand alchemical project. Often suffering persecution from Church and State in their own countries, alchemists flocked to Prague to enjoy the atmosphere of free enquiry and material security. At the height of Rudolf's interest in the 'Royal Art' as many as two hundred were at work in the alchemical 'kitchens'. While the promise of unlimited silver and gold attracted charlatans and puffers, among the alchemists there were some genuine scientists who were carefully observing the processes of nature and some real mystics who were interested in prolonging life only in order to have more time to become enlightened.

Prague became the Hermetic centre of Europe at the turn of the century. Rudolf's court attracted men of great learning who represented the magical world of the late Renaissance. Given the generosity of his patronage and the enthusiasm of his interests, it is not surprising that Rudolf came to be hailed within alchemical circles as the new Hermes Trismegistus. In the heady alchemical atmosphere in the castle, he was ready to inhale any new idea if it might lead to the discovery of the Philosopher's Stone.

But Rudolf's interest in alchemy was not driven by a desire to manufacture gold. He did not lack material wealth; indeed, after his death several million gold coins, partly an inheritance from his father, were found in his private chambers. As with all serious alchemists, he considered the discovery of the Philosopher's Stone to be an outer sign of inner enlightenment which could lead to the immortality of the soul. It was its unique combination of science and art, religion and philosophy, prophecy and beauty that made alchemy so interesting to him.

While Rudolf dreamt of a new golden era in his *Kunstkammer* and dabbled in experiments in his laboratory in the Powder House, some alchemists in Prague were beginning to produce real results which laid the foundations of modern chemistry and medicine. Outstanding among them was the German Oswald Croll who had been born in Hesse around 1563. With many of the other wandering scholars who turned up in Bohemia during Rudolf's reign, he followed Paracelsus's dictum: 'A doctor must be a traveller . . . Knowledge is experience.' After graduating as a Doctor in Medicine in 1582 at Marburg, he travelled to Heidelberg, Strasburg and Geneva universities. He then became a tutor first with the d'Esnes family in Lyon and then from 1590 with the family of Count Maximilian of Pappenheim in Tübingen.

On hearing of the congenial atmosphere for alchemists at Rudolf's court he came to Prague in 1597 where he worked on his principal treatise *Basilica chymica*. Although written in Prague, he did not dedicate it to Rudolf but to the Protestant Prince Christian I of Anhalt, Bernburg, Upper Palatinate, for whom he worked as a physician and secret agent for his Protestant Union. In it he expressed his belief in an imminent revolution which would not only overturn the old Aristotelian doctrines but bring about a new 'chemical' millennium for 'Elias the Artist, who is to restore all things' to their original purity.[1]

The title page of *Basilica chymica* contains portraits of Hermes Trismegistus, Geber, Ramón Lull, Roger Bacon and Paracelsus, clearly demonstrating the Hermetic tradition in which Croll stood. It also has an inverted triangle linking the triads of 'Animal, Vegetable, Mineral', with 'Mind, Spirit, Body' and 'Fire, Air, Water' which in the alchemical mind were all interrelated. They were placed within a larger circle giving the main sources of Croll's inspiration and that of the other alchemists at Rudolf's court: 'Cabala, Theology, Magic, Astronomy, Alchemy, Medicine'. The work was published in Frankfurt in 1609 with the subtitle: 'The alchemical church, containing a philosophical description, based securely on personal and practical experience, and containing directions for using very select and special alchemical remedies by the light of grace and of nature.'

Croll was called the German Paracelsus and, like his master, wished to establish alchemy at the heart of medical practice. He went beyond Paracelsus, however, in arguing that each being has its own *astrum* or star, constellation and even heaven. At the same time, he rejected the claims of astrology that said the stars directly influence events on earth: 'Through dew, rain and seasonal changes, the upper stars and the zodiac awaken and promote life and growth, but do not influence.'[2]

Croll used the Biblical account in Genesis to explain the existence of disease in the world. It was the Fall of Man, he said, that had brought about corruption in the world: God sowed the 'tinctures' of disease as a curse for Man's disobedience. And yet Croll also took the Gnostic view that the invisible inner spiritual nature of humans is pure if separated from its corrupt body: 'Man is a hidden world, because visible things in him are invisible, and when they are made visible they are diseases, not health, as truly as he is the little world and not the great one.'[3] It is, therefore, on the invisible, essential aspect of man, not on his body, that the alchemist-physician must operate.

By working on his spirit, he can cure his body: 'It is not the locall Anatomy of a man and dead corpses, but the Essentiated and Elemental Anatomy of the World and man that discovereth the disease and cure.'[4] In his view, in order to cure the sick the physician should first comfort the heart and then attack the disease. And by curing like with like, Croll was a forerunner of homeopathy. This did not mean, however, that he was cavalier in his treatment of patients. He carefully studied the relationship between causes and effects and prepared precise medicinal compounds.

Croll believed that God and Nature have put their signatures on all their works in the Creation, from the highest stars to the smallest pebbles. It is the task of the adept to read the divine book of signatures and to understand the correspondences, the sympathies and antipathies in all things. Unfortunately, modern human beings lack the grammar of this arcane language. It is to be found in the Hermetic hieroglyphs, in the sacred letters of Thoth, in the universal language of the *Logos*, which correspond to the laws of geometry, form, movement and equilibrium. The adept's job, therefore, is to seek to restore the lost wisdom of the ancients.

Croll combined alchemy, astrology and magic in his work. In order to make an amulet he recommended, for instance, the following ingredients: two ounces of toads dried in the air and sun and reduced to powder, 'the menstruum of young girls: as much as you can get, crystals of white arsenic, an ounce and a half of red arsenic, three drams of root of dittany or an equal amount of tormentil, one dram of unpierced pearls, one dram of coral, one dram each of Eastern sapphire and Eastern emerald, two scruples of Eastern saffron'. Croll suggests that several grains of musk or amber could be added to give a pleasant smell. Everything must be then reduced to a fine powder, mixed together, and added to 'gum tragacanth' dissolved in rose-water to make a paste. When the Sun and Moon are in Scorpio, or when the Moon is new, the paste should be fashioned around an amulet.

Croll recommended hanging the amulet around the neck by a silk cord or in the region of the heart, concluding that 'it not only preserves one from the plague but makes the body less susceptible to venereal or astral diseases. It draws poison from within, and consumes it from without.'[5] Rudolf was known to wear amulets close to his body and almost certainly used one of Croll's at some time.

Rudolf must have been irritated by his dedication of the *Basilica chymica* to Prince Anhalt. Croll was, however, allowed to visit Edward Kelley in prison at Most Castle and according to his treatise on signatures he was able to obtain some herbs from Rudolf's Brandýs estate. Rudolf was particularly pleased to obtain certain precious manuscripts and other 'secret matters' from Croll. When the physician and alchemist suddenly died in Prague in 1609, a document in coded writing was found on his person accusing Petr Vok Rožmberk of high treason against Rudolf. It disappeared mysteriously in the subsequent investigation – a sign of the growing religious and political intrigue at the court at the time between the Catholic faction led by the Spanish ambassador and the Vatican's nuncios and the Protestant Bohemian Estates.

Croll's European-wide reputation grew after his death. In *The Anatomy of Melancholy* (1621), Robert Burton referred to him as a physician and alchemist who was renowned for his alchemical gold which 'shall imitate thunder and lightning, and crack louder than any gunpowder'.[6] He also knew about the salt of corals 'to purify the blood for all melancholy affections'. Unfortunately, the salts of coral – a substance taken up by Isaac Newton in his own alchemical experiments – did not help Rudolf fight off his increasing attacks of melancholy as his obsession with the Philosopher's Stone intensified and the religious and political conflicts in his sprawling empire deepened.

*

Another personal physician to Rudolf, Michael Maier, was an alchemist and philosopher, a Doctor of Medicine as well as a Doctor of Philosophy like his master Paracelsus. Rudolf not only appreciated his medical knowledge and discerning advice but also his Hermetic interest in ancient wisdom. As a late Renaissance polymath, he spanned the arts and sciences. The Emperor was so pleased with him that he employed him as a private secretary and made him an Imperial Count Palatine and Free Knight of the Empire. He retained his confidence until his death.

Maier's healing skills were legendary. On one occasion when Rudolf was out hunting in the forest of Brdy with the English envoy Sir Thomas Smith, confidant of Queen Elizabeth, Smith's twenty-one-year-old niece Baroness Lucy Warren fell from her horse and broke her arm. Rudolf, who was smitten with her, immediately called Maier. After setting her arm, six times he sent forth a healing energy from his extended arm to the injury, each time for several minutes. She subsequently said it was as if she had had a dream from which some miraculous doctor had awakened her.[7]

An adept seeks to square the circle: 'Make of man and woman a circle, from that a square, then a triangle, then another circle, and you will have the Philosopher's Stone.' Michael Maier, Atalanta fugiens *(1618)*

Maier was born in Rendsberg, Holstein, in 1566, and practised medicine at Rostock and then Nuremberg and Padua. By 1592, he had already excited the interest of Rudolf. After receiving his doctorate in medicine from Basle, he moved to Prague and joined the Emperor's close entourage.[8] His many works were printed after Rudolf's death in a space of six years from 1614 to 1620 but he had been working on them in Prague and discussed their principles with the Emperor and his colleagues. As an alchemist and Lutheran, he insisted on the religious content of his art and saw the Eucharist as an alchemical transformation. He signed his name 'Hermes Malavici'.

His first published book, *Arcana arcanissima* ('Secret of Secrets', 1614), was a learned and speculative treatise on the real meaning of the ancient gods and the Egyptian and Greek myths associated with them. The protagonist undertakes a pilgrimage in search of the Phoenix which takes him to Egypt. In the Nile delta, he meets Mercury (the Roman equivalent of the Greek Hermes and the Egyptian Thoth), the 'god of culture and science' who shows him the dwelling of the fabulous bird.[9] The Phoenix itself is a symbol of the alchemical process, rising from the ashes, demonstrating the cycle of death and rebirth.

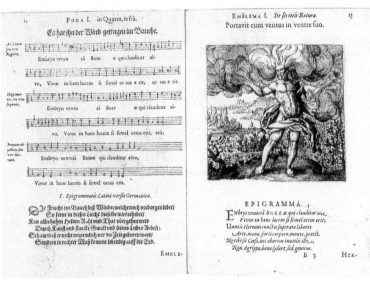

Michael Maier in Atalanta fugiens *(1618) wonderfully combines art, music and poetry. Wind here carries in his belly a baby who is said to be the future Philosopher's Stone*

Maier's most famous and imaginative work, however, was *Atalanta fugiens, hoc est, Emblemata nove de secretis naturae chymica* ('Atalanta fleeing: that is, new alchemical emblems of the secrets of nature'). It was published in 1618 with superb engravings by Matthew Merian. The title was inspired by Ovid's tale of Hippomenes who chases Atalanta and ravishes her in a temple, whereupon they are both turned into lions. In alchemical terms, it shows the rivalry between Sol and Luna, Sulphur and Mercury, who eventually join in a chemical wedding to produce the Philosopher's Stone. Maier's work intertwines images, music, poetry and epigrams to inspire the Hermetic seeker. The first emblem, for instance, depicts a naked man with smoke billowing from his head and arms – the Wind – with a baby visible in his stomach – the future Philosopher's Stone. The accompanying text states: 'The wind has carried it in its belly', probably meaning that Mercury (the wind) in its volatile form carries Sulphur (the infant).[10]

In this way, *Atalanta fugiens* uses symbols to show that the alchemical process and the search for the Philosopher's Stone involves a gradual realisation of truth. As visual representations of abstract thought, the emblems work on many levels: literal, figurative and allegorical. The fifty or so musical fugues in the text are to be sung and intended to help create a favourable atmosphere in the laboratory. *Atalanta fugiens* offers a marvellous summary of Renaissance alchemy with its unique combination of practical experiment and spiritual understanding, and demonstrates how the arts and sciences can combine to great effect. The whole could be seen, read, sung and contemplated with exquisite pleasure.

Maier became an important figure in the Rosicrucian Movement, which tried to bring about moral and social reform through Hermetic enlightenment. He defended their ideals in his *Verum inventum* (1619). On Rudolf's death in 1612, he visited Holland and then travelled to England where he met Sir William Paddy, the personal physician of King James I, the future father-in-law of the King of Bohemia. He may well have acted as a spy and ambassador. It was in London that he published his first book *Arcana arcanissima*. During his stay in England he also contacted Robert Fludd, author of *The History of the Macrocosm and Microcosm*, with whom he shared the same publisher in de Bry of Oppenheimer and similar Rosicrucian ideals. Maier died during the siege of Magdeburg in 1622 at the beginning of the Thirty Years' War. In many ways, Maier's work best sums up the unique combination of art, science, philosophy and religion which prevailed in Rudolfine Prague.

*

Another one-time Prague alchemist remembered as much for his magnificent illustrations as for his work is Heinrich Khunrath. Born in Leipzig in 1560, Khunrath studied in Basle and, given his wide range of intellectual interests, he aptly called himself a 'Doctor of this and that medicine'. He lived in Hamburg but was sufficiently well known to travel to Bremen on 27 June 1589 to meet John Dee. He was on his way home to England from Vilém Rožmberk and probably gave Croll an introduction to him; on 15 December 1591, Khunrath became the personal physician to the ailing noble. After Rožmberk's death, he moved to Prague where, on 1 June 1598, Rudolf granted him a comprehensive imperial *privilegium* or copyright to protect from plagiarism 'all work, both written and engraved, pertaining to medicine, alchemy, Cabala and very many other more secret matters'.[11]

Khunrath produced a series of books in the 1590s on alchemical emblems, including *The Catholic Magnesia of the Philosophers* and *Azoth*. The title of the latter was one of the many names used for alchemical mercury, deriving from the Arabic word for the substance '*al-zauq*'. The five letters A-Z-O-T-H were thought to have great magical power because they formed an acronym of the first and last letters of the Greek, Arabic, Roman, and Hebrew alphabets. As such, it embodied the wisdom of the ancients and pointed to the universal elixir of life.

Khunrath's masterpiece is his *Ampitheatrum sapientiae aeternae* ('The Amphitheatre of Eternal Wisdom', 1602). The subtitle defines its nature: 'a Christian-Cabalist, Divine-Magical, Physico-Chemical, Three-in-One Compendium'.[12] It admirably sums up the ingredients in the crucible of Rudolfine Prague. Its text is an extraordinary mixture of Hermetic philosophy and Cabalistic incantation while its images exploit delightfully the Mannerist vogue for distorted perspectives, figures and emblems.

On the frontispiece Khunrath declares his credo: 'Persevere, pray, work, without pride and without false modesty.' His message is that God is the Great Alchemist and that the cosmos is a creation achieved in his crucible. The illustrations conjure up a kind of alchemical Utopia, with Hebrew, Greek, Latin and German aphorisms and hieroglyphic obelisks scattered in the visionary tableaux. The four plates are entitled *Christ*, *Adam and Eve Conjoined*, *The Philosopher's Stone* and the *Laboratory*, representing four paths to knowledge and four stages of initiation: the path of Cabala, the path of Magic, the path of Alchemy and the path of Theurgy.

In one engraving, the cross-section of a mountain is inscribed in Latin and German with the text of the *Emerald Tablet* of Hermes Trismegistus. Originally coming to light in an Arabic work attributed to Geber, it dates to at least the eighth century. Written in typically cryptic language, it is a key text in the Hermetic tradition and offers the quintessence of spiritual alchemy:

> True it is, without falsehood, certain and most true. That which is above is like to that which is below, and that which is below is like to that which is above, to accomplish the miracle of the one thing. And as all things were by the contemplation of the one, so all things arose from this one thing by a single act of adaptation. The father thereof is the Sun, the mother the Moon . . . If it be cast on the Earth, it will separate the element of the Earth from that of Fire, the subtle from the gross . . . Thus thou wilt possess the glory of the brightness of the whole world, and all obscurity will fly from thee.[13]

A Renaissance alchemist prays before a tabernacle in his study-laboratory.
Heinrich Khunrath, The Amphitheatre of Eternal Wisdom (*1602*)

The most famous illustration of Khunrath's *Ampitheatre*, reprinted endlessly in works on alchemy, is that of the Renaissance magus in his richly furnished study-laboratory. He prays on his knees in front of a tabernacle. The Latin word *Laboratorium* is inscribed above the mantelpiece, combining the two essential aspects of the alchemist's endeavour: *Labor* (work) and *Oratorium* (prayer). The alchemist cannot hope to discover the Philosopher's Stone or attain divine wisdom without the two. It is the process which brings together the traditional distinction between inner and outer alchemy: success in the laboratory is not possible without the spiritual illumination of the soul. At the centre of the tableau are three musical instruments representing Paracelsus's *tria prima* – salt, sulphur and mercury – from which all nature is composed. Rudolf would have found all this deeply moving and a confirmation that his pursuit of the Philosopher's Stone was much more important than affairs of his earthly empire.

Khunrath, Maier, Croll and Dee were all extraordinary intellects but the most inventive and subversive thinker of the second half of the sixteenth century to make an appearance in Rudolf's theatre of the world was undoubtedly the Italian Giordano Bruno. His life and work embodied the mystical tendencies of Rudolfine Prague. Born in Nola, near Naples, in 1548, Bruno later liked to talk of the 'Nolan' as a prophet who would inaugurate a new golden age of peace in the world. At the age of fifteen, he became a Dominican friar but after being accused of heresy for supporting the Copernican view that the sun was at the centre of the universe, he abandoned his habit. He tended to see things in distinct black and white terms and, in an early work called *De umbris idearum* ('On the Shadow of Ideas') published in Paris in 1582, presented the world as divided between creatures of light and darkness. The former included the cockerel, phoenix, swan, lynx and lion which enjoyed the sunlit surface of the earth while the latter embraced witches, toads, basilisks and owls, banished into their lairs by the brilliant sun of divine knowledge.

Bruno, like Dee, embraced the life of a wandering scholar, attracted to the great centres of learning and sympathetic courts of the day. Lecturing at Paris, the volcanic Neapolitan caught the attention of King Henri III. He then travelled over the Channel to spread his prophecies and syllogisms in England.

Like Dee, he was constantly watched by agents of the Inquisition. During his stay in England, he may have worked as a spy, with the name 'Fugot', in the

French embassy to subvert the Catholic attempt to overthrow Queen Elizabeth's government.[14] He certainly expressed unbounded admiration for the Virgin Queen, calling her 'diva Elizabetta' who was 'inferior to no other monarch in the world'.[15] Wherever he went, his character and writings excited much interest and he attracted a secret sect of followers known as the Nolans.

At Oxford, he lectured in honour of Prince Laski's visit to the uncomprehending 'pedants' on the *Spaccio de la bestia trionfante* ('The Lair of the Triumphant Beast',1584). The work, a grandiloquent call for spiritual reform, was dedicated to the poet Sir Philip Sidney. In an address to the doctors of the University of Oxford in a work on the art of memory, he described himself without due modesty as 'the waker of sleeping souls, tamer of presumptuous and recalcitrant ignorance, proclaimer of a general philanthropy'.[16] The conservative dons, steeped in snobbish xenophobia, were not quite so impressed. One from Balliol College wrote of the performance of the 'Italian Didapper':

> Stripping up his sleeves like some juggler, and telling us much *chentrum & chirculus & circumferenchia* (after the pronunciation of his Country language) he undertook among very many other matters to set foot the opinion of Copernicus, that the earth did go round, and the heavens did stand still; whereas in truth it was his own head which rather did run round, & his brains did not stand still.

For his part, Bruno observed: 'The leader of the Academy on that grave occasion came to a halt fifteen times over fifteen syllogisms, like a chicken in the stubble.'[17]

Bruno believed the Hermetic philosophy to be the true religion with its worship of 'God in things' and its profound magic. He shared the view, expressed in the Hermetic text *Asclepius,* that 'A human being is a great wonder.'[18] That is, as he made clear in his dedication to Sidney, he espoused the Hermetic doctrine that 'in every man . . . there is a world, a universe'. The gods represent the virtues and powers of the soul. As for the universe, he declared that he worshipped the old religion of the Egyptians for revering the One in All: 'You see, then, how one simple divinity which is in all things, one fecund nature, mother and preserver of the universe, shines forth in diverse subjects, and takes divers names, according as it communicates itself diversely.'[19]

In Bruno's view, the 'Temple of Wisdom' was far older than Christianity and Judaism. It was first built among the ancient Egyptians and the insights of the Cabala came from the Egyptians (Moses, after all, was educated among the Egyptians). Bruno not only maintained that the Christian symbol of the Cross was taken from the Egyptians but implied that the Egyptian religion was superior even to Christianity. Indeed, in his poems *Eroici furori* published in England in 1585 and dedicated to Sidney, he prophesied the imminent return of the Egyptian religion through the revolution of the 'great year of the world' which will banish the prevailing 'dregs of science' and the 'dregs of opinions'.

In a splendid passage on sun-worship, Bruno dismisses those men who, like the 'dim-eyed mole', desire to remain in their native darkness and celebrates their opposites:

> Those who were born to see the sun, being full of thanksgiving when they come to the end of the loathsome night, dispose themselves to receive in the very centre of their eyes' crystal globe the long-expected rays of the glorious sun, and, with unaccustomed gladness in their hearts, they lift up hands and voices to adore the east.[20]

It was for such heretical statements and his readiness to encourage followers to bring about a spiritual revolution in Europe that the Vatican came to see Bruno as a real danger and a major threat. To make matters worse, in *De l'Infinito, universo e mondi* (1584) Bruno presented the living earth as revolving around the divine sun with other innumerable worlds in an infinite cosmos. Echoing Copernicus and against all Catholic dogma, Bruno affirmed that 'the earth did go round'. Nothing in the living world is immobile; everything moves in an inherent circular motion through a kind of magical animism. There is no death in the universe, only change. Inspired by the Hermetica and the Cabala, Bruno's cosmology could therefore do without the notion of the transcendent Creator God so dear to Catholicism.

On leaving England, Bruno returned to Paris with the French ambassador in 1585. He then travelled in the following year to Germany where he taught at Wittenberg university and may have founded a secret sect of 'Brunonians' or 'Giordanisti' working to bring about a miraculous transformation of Europe. During his stay, he wrote in 1587–8 several works on the art of memory, a technique he had already developed from the writings of the Catalan alchemist Ramón Lull. The Silesian Hans von Nostiz later recalled the excitement he evoked in his lectures: 'I can still remember how, thirty-three years since, Iordanus Brunus of Nola first demonstrated his magnificent Lullian and Mnemological arts in Paris and drew many disciples to him privately.'[21]

Bruno believed that the magus could uncover the secrets of the universe within his own memory. The Egyptians were able to capture with marvellous skill 'the language of the gods' because the 'sacred letters' of their hieroglyphs were based on images taken directly from 'things of nature'. When the modern European phonetic alphabet was invented, however, it brought about a 'great rift both in the memory and in the divine and magical sciences'.[22] But all was not lost. Bruno proposed an original method of retraining the memory based on the imagination. Since the mind of God is present in the mind of humans, it is possible to rediscover divine truths. By engraving on the memory celestial images which are 'shadows' close to the 'ideas' of the divine mind, one can become godlike.

Having failed to make much headway in England and Germany, Bruno would have been naturally drawn to Prague in the hope of impressing a sovereign who might be sympathetic to his ideas. He would have known of Rudolf's reputation as a great patron and also probably met Czechs while staying in Wittenberg who urged him to visit their capital. Bruno and Rudolf shared many beliefs: he could expect a warm welcome.

While living in Prague for six months in 1588, Bruno printed two of his most important works. The first was entitled provocatively *One Hundred and Sixty Articles against Mathematicians and Philosophers*. It was partly written in response to Rudolf's mathematician and astronomer Fabrizio Mordente, whom Bruno had met in Paris and called a 'Triumphant Idiot', but also intended to urge the Holy Roman Emperor to become the new Hermes Trismegistus of the late Renaissance and to inaugurate a new age. To this end, Bruno penned a fulsome dedication to Rudolf.

The work itself is full of geometrical diagrams and develops Bruno's own idiosyncratic version of magical numerology which he called 'mathesis'. Some diagrams have the shapes of lutes and serpents, but three involve overlapping circles. The first represents the universal mind (*figura mentis*); the second symbolises the intellect (*figura intellectus*); and the third is the figure of love

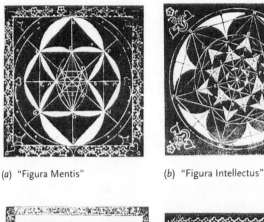

(a) "Figura Mentis"   (b) "Figura Intellectus"

(c) "Figura Amoris"   (d) "Zoemetra"

Figures from Giordano Bruno's One Hundred and Sixty Articles against Mathematicians and Philosophers *(1588)*

(*figura amoris*), harmonising contraries and uniting the many in one. The last has the word MAGIC written on the diagram. The three are also given in the text the astrological symbols for the sun, moon and a five-pointed star, probably Venus.

Bruno not only railed against analytical and discursive reason as a source of knowledge but expressed his belief in a single universal religion and his hope for the salvation of humanity through an enlightened elite. While acknowledging in his dedication to Rudolf that it was a time of darkness afflicted by quarrelling sects, Bruno maintained that true religion should be without controversy and dispute since it was a movement of the soul based on the universal law of love. Rudolf would have entirely agreed and, as a sign of his appreciation, personally granted the visiting Italian philosopher a sum of 300 thalers.

Bruno dedicated his second book published in Prague, *On the Calculations and Combinations According to R. Lull*, to the Spanish ambassador at Rudolf's court, San Clemente, with whom the Emperor always had cordial relations. Inspired by the work of Ramón Lull, the alleged ancestor of San Clemente, Bruno developed in the book an original method of training the memory which involved placing different 'memories' or ideas on an imaginary wheel. By revolving six concentric wheels with their ideas, it was possible to form original combinations and thereby create new knowledge. The method was later taken up by the German philosopher Leibniz and inspired him to construct one of the first calculating machines – the prototype of the modern computer. In addition, by arguing that truth emerges by combining two opposites in the 'point of union', Bruno anticipated Hegel's dialectical method. In this way, the beginnings of modern science and philosophy emerged from a mystical and occult form of medieval mathematics.

After his stay in Prague, Bruno returned via Switzerland to Germany. He was welcomed by the learned Protestant Duke of Brunswick, patron of artists, astrologers and alchemists, who stood by Rudolf until the very end and served as the last President of his Privy Council. Less attractive was his reputation as an active persecutor of witches: convinced like Rudolf in the reality of the spirit world, he believed that witches could genuinely raise evil forces and use them against their enemies. Bruno met Brunswick at the University of Helmstedt in 1589 when he gave a funeral oration for the duke's father. Bruno later dedicated two of his last published books to Rudolf's close friend and ally.

Bruno returned to Italy in 1591 in goodwill, bearing a manuscript on the seven liberal arts which he intended to dedicate to Pope Clement VIII. But after being denounced by one of his students, he was arrested in Venice by the Inquisition the following year. Bruno's first great heresy was to believe that the Hermetic philosophy was the true religion. He had not only presented a vision of the cosmos as a living being but admired the Egyptians for worshipping the One-in-All. His other great heresy was to promulgate Copernicus's view that the Earth moved around the Sun. Although rooted in his Hermetic beliefs, his advocacy of the new cosmology made him appear thoroughly scientific.

Bruno seems to have recanted these heresies at his first trial but he was sent for a retrial in Rome. This time he refused to recant, and after eight years of imprisonment and interrogation he was burnt at the stake, his mouth stuffed with a gag, on 17 February 1600. The method of execution could not have been more symbolic at the dawn of the new century in which religious intolerance was to gain ascendancy.

After his death, Bruno was acclaimed as a hero of modern science who preferred to die rather than renounce his belief in Copernican theory.[23] But he was more than a martyr to the cause of science. With his celebration of the ancient religion of the Egyptians, he had made it his life's task to bring about a peaceful cosmological revolution throughout Europe which would bring an end to its wars and persecutions. As the Jesuit Father Joseph Pittau, the Chancellor of the Academy of Science at the Vatican, has observed: 'Certainly Giordano Bruno was not condemned because of science. Mostly it was because of superstition – the fear of alchemy and all those things.'[24] It was primarily as an 'Egyptian' and as a Hermetic magus that Bruno was doomed. Rudolf might well have suffered a similar fate had he not been the Holy Roman Emperor.

In addition to Bruno, there were other Hermetic thinkers and alchemists who came to Prague and made real contributions to the history of science. In the 1590s Rudolf warmly welcomed the alchemist Pole Michal Sedivoj, better known as Michael Sendivogius. Born in 1556, he studied in Cracow where Faust of the *Faustbook* is said to have studied Chaldean, Persian and Arabian spells and conjurations. Like so many other alchemists, he then took up the life of a wandering seeker of the Stone.

In the 1590s, he lived intermittently in Prague in a Gothic residence adapted into an early Baroque style. It still stands today in the Old Town and is known as the 'House of the Three Plumes' as well as 'The Wolf's Throat'. It seems that while he was in Prague he was twice thrown into jail for failing to pay his debts. On the first occasion in 1597, he appealed to the Emperor to be released.

Michael Maier probably introduced Sendivogius to Rudolf. Maier was sufficiently impressed to choose him under the pseudonym 'Anonymous Sarmata' as the most recent of his twelve heroes or 'sophic apostles' which appeared in his *Symbola aureae mensae* ('Symbols of the Golden Table', 1607). Sendivogius wrote several works on alchemy which were published anonymously between 1604 and 1614 and often reprinted. In keeping with the alchemists' playful love of secrecy, they were usually prefaced by obvious anagrams of his name.

Sendivogius said that he gained his alchemical knowledge from an alchemist called Alexander Seton. Of Scottish origin, Seton claims in 1602 to have visited the pilot Jacob Huassen in the Netherlands whom he had saved the year before off the Scottish coast. In an alchemical experiment, he showed the seafarer how to transform lead into gold. He then travelled around Europe, visiting Italy, Switzerland and Germany. In Fribourg, he convinced the sceptical Professor Dienheim of the possibility of manufacturing gold with the help of a magic powder. Several documents claim that he performed the transmutation in Germany; in Cologne, he even used lapis lazuli as his first substance in the alchemical process. When Christian II, the Elector of Saxony, heard of his skill and knowledge, he had him arrested and tortured but the Scot refused to reveal any of his secrets.

MICHAEL SENDIVOGIUS.

Allegedly, Sendivogius helped Seton to escape from prison. He survived only another couple of years but it was long enough for him to bequeath some of his magic 'red powder' to his saviour. Sendivogius is said to have not only married Seton's widow but to have borrowed some of his writings in his most celebrated work *Novum lumen chymicum* ('New Chemical Light'), published simultaneously in Prague and in Frankfurt.

In Prague, Sendivogius was reputed to have transmuted gold for Rudolf in his laboratory. Suspecting that the 'red powder' might contain the 'seed of gold', Rudolf had some of it tested and was delighted to find that it contained none: it was, indeed, a catalyst. But as with all known alchemical experiments which claimed to produce gold, the experiment could not be exactly repeated as the conditions were so variable. Sendivogius claimed that Seton had not given him the right formula to create more powder before he died.

The experiment itself was enough to fire Rudolf's alchemical dreams and he had a marble plaque placed on the walls of the castle to inspire his other puffers: *Faciat hoc quispian alius /Quad fecit Sendivogius Polonus!* ('Let anyone else do/ What Sendivogius the Pole has done!').[25] This *Tabula marmorea Pragensis* was still in place as late as 1740.

Rudolf may have sent Sendigovius on a mission east in order to gain Hermetic secrets from a Greek adept and certainly gave him the title of Counsellor of State and a gold medal for his services. When Sendigovius was ambushed on one of his trips between Cracow and Prague by a Moravian knight who wanted to know his secrets, Rudolf allegedly imposed a heavy fine on the opportunist. Despite being the envy of German and Bohemian alchemists, Sendivogius was retained by Ferdinand II after the death of Rudolf and probably died in Poland in 1636.

Sendivogius's reputation among alchemists was mainly based on the *Novum lumen*. In the preface, he entices the reader by offering with obvious sexual overtones a view of 'Diana unveiled' and to open the 'gates of Nature' and 'to lift the veil, and enter her inmost sanctuary'. It was addressed to 'all genuine seekers of the great Chemical Art, or sons of Hermes'.[26] Newton was one of them, for he studied his carefully annotated copy for years.

In characteristic alchemical fashion, Sendivogius says that his knowledge was drawn from the fountain of nature and hands-on experimentation: *'naturae fonte et manuali experientiae'*. He warns that there are only a few true alchemists around, and that to understand their hidden meaning the reader must go beyond the 'outer husk' of their words. The would-be adept should humbly listen to nature, and even study so simple an operation as 'natural generation'. Modern learning, he argues, is greatly superior to the ancients, except in one respect: 'they knew the secret of preparing the Philosopher's Stone'. He defines the Philosopher's Stone as Tincture; that is, nothing other than 'gold digested to the highest degree'.[27] Despite the title of his book, Sendivogius adds little to Paracelsus and argues that the key to success is to combine the three principles of Mercury, Sulphur and Salt in the right proportion in a favourable place in nature and at an astrologically favourable time. What is new is his prediction of the imminent coming of the New Age:

> The times are at hand when many secrets of Nature will be revealed to men. The Fourth or Northern Monarchy is about to be established; the Mother of Knowledge will soon come . . . Mercy and truth will meet together; peace and justice will kiss each other; truth will spring up from the ground, and righteousness will look down from heaven . . . and all knowledge will be the common property of all.[28]

As was the case with much Renaissance science, among the dross there is some genuine gold. Although Joseph Priestley is usually credited with discovering oxygen in the late eighteenth century, it now seems almost certain that Sendivogius discovered the gas during an alchemical experiment a century and half earlier. The Dutch inventor Cornelius Drebbel of Alkmar, who had visited Prague at the turn of the seventeenth century, took up the discovery later.

In 1624, Drebbel built the first known working submarine, made from wood and greased leather and powered by twelve oarsmen, and travelled along the River Thames from Westminster to Greenwich at a depth of five metres. He found that by heating a flask of saltpetre (potassium nitrate), he could produce enough of the 'elixir of life' (oxygen) for the oarsmen to breathe. The experiment was later verified by Robert Boyle. This was almost exactly the same method used by Joseph Priestley 153 years later, although he produced oxygen from heating a compound of mercury. Once again, the experimental work of the alchemists made a real contribution to the progress of science.[29]

Among other serious alchemists at Rudolf's court were the Martin Rulands, father and son, of Bavarian origin. The elder was not only a Paracelsian and author of medical and theological works in his own right, but compiled several important dictionaries. His son, who was a physician during the 1590s at Regensburg, moved to Prague and took over from his father when he died in 1602. Much appreciated as one of his physicians, Rudolf ennobled him in 1610. He was far from modest and signed himself grandly: 'Doctor of Philosophy and of Medicine, and Physician and Alchemical Healer-Chamberlain of the most sacred person of His Imperial Majesty'.[30] He not only wrote a defence of alchemy which was dedicated to Rudolf's adviser Andreas Hannewaldt in 1607, but claimed he knew the *Lapidis philosophici vera conficiendi ratio* ('The True Method for completing the Philosopher's Stone', 1606).

The Rulands' library was full of occult works, including a treatise on the locations of hell. They were no doubt drawn upon in the remarkable *Lexicon alchemiae sive dictionarium alchemistarum* ('Lexicon of Alchemy or Alchemical Dictionary'), dated 10 April 1611. It contains many useful definitions as well as being a mine of information, ranging from the elixir of life to the treatment of metallic ores. The various stages in the alchemical process, such as calcination, putrefaction, solution, coagulation, sublimation and projection, and the various methods, such as extraction, distillation and sublimation, are all carefully defined. It was of theoretical and practical use, with sensible entries on metals, minerals and stones. On the other hand, the entry on the Philosopher's Stone had five pages with veiled definitions. We are told, for instance, that it is 'the most potent virtue concentrated by art in the centre. Outwardly, it is a Tincture. Or it is the Universal Medicine by which age is renewed in youth, metals are transmuted, all diseases cured. It was made by Theophrastus. It is the Stone of the Wise whereby the imperfect metals are improved.'[31]

The most famous Czech alchemist to work for Rudolf was Bavor Rodovský of Hustířany. Born in 1526, he soon squandered his estates for his passion for the golden game and for the rest of his life had to live off the largesse of the wealthy Bohemian patrons of alchemy. In 1578 he worked in Rudolf's laboratory in Prague Castle but clearly was unable to achieve a successful transmutation for he was imprisoned for debt. Two years later, he found refuge on the estate of Jan Zbyněk of Házmburk where he was able to study, write and experiment in comparative peace for the next twenty years. This prolific author not only translated into Czech the Hermetic classic *The Emerald Tablet* but just before he died completed the alchemical textbook *Philosophical Languages* and a book on the *Culinary Arts*.

Outside the inner circle of Rudolf's alchemist-physicians were less well-known characters who come and go in the records of the imperial and city administration. One of the more prominent was the Dutchman Theobald (Ewald) Hoghelande who tried to make the arcane science more accessible in *De Alchimiae difficultatibus* (1594). Echoing St Aquinas, he stressed both the intellectual and experimental aspects of alchemy: 'Alchemy has fixed her seat for herself in intellectual ability and in experimental demonstration.' In his *Historiae aliquot transmutationis metallicae* (1604), he further described various transmutations, including Bohemian ones, and attached a life of the Spanish alchemist Ramón Lull.

Hoghelande mentions Hieronymus Scotus, who is sometimes confused with Odoardus Scotus, Alessandro Scotta and Jerome Scoto. The shadowy alchemist came from Italy via Germany and dedicated to Rudolf the manuscript of his *Speculum alchemiae*, beautifully written on both sides of a single strip of vellum. He claimed that the Emperor rewarded him well: 'Thanks to just this occult wisdom, granted me some time past by God, and today passed on to you, Rudolf II, the greatest of the Caesars, has adorned me with the highest offices and with the greatest honours.'[32]

Alessandro Scotta was reported to have arrived in 1590 from Italy in a magnificent coach with three carriages of retainers and set himself up in a luxurious residence in the Old Town. His greatest claim was the possession of a magic mirror. By looking into it the Spanish ambassador in Prague was apparently able to see Philip II in the act of writing. When the ambassador was asked what had been written, he replied that he had no right to reveal the secrets of the imperial correspondence. Unable to make ends meet, Scotta travelled on to Cologne where he persuaded the Archbishop-Elector Gebhard to look in the mirror to see the most beautiful woman of the town. When he saw the Protestant Countess Agne of Mansfeld, he fell madly in love with her, converted to her religion and nearly caused a war about his succession.

Another story has Rudolf sending Jerome Scoto as an envoy to Prince William of Hesse and Duke John Casimir of Saxe who were two lovers of the 'Royal Art' of alchemy at the centre of the Protestant camp opposed to the Counter Reformation. During his stay with the Duke, Scoto allegedly persuaded his host's young wife to participate in an experiment of sexual magic. The experiment did not go unnoticed. Scoto managed to escape but the gullible Duchess spent the last twenty years of her life imprisoned in a nunnery.

The veracity of the many tales and rumours associated with this elusive opportunist cannot be verified but they give a composite picture of the kind of cunning charlatan who masqueraded as an alchemist in the courts of Europe. While in Prague, he may have attained some éclat there but was reported to have ended his days exhibiting his magical tricks in a little wooden booth in Old Town Square.[33]

A more infamous character who turned up in Prague was the Greek alchemist who called himself Count Marco Bragadino. His real name was Mamugna and he was little more than a brigand in stylish black clothes decorated with counterfeit gold. He had already gained notoriety in Venice and in Vienna. Wherever he went he was accompanied by two black mastiffs that some took to be familiar spirits. He left for Munich after a couple of years where he was eventually hanged for swindling a large sum from the Duke of Bavaria and buried with his hounds in a common grave.

Despite the vast amounts of money Rudolf spent on supporting his alchemists and thinkers and the time he spent in his own alchemical studies and experiments, it does not seem that the Habsburg Hermes Trismegistus ever achieved the supreme goal. Of the almost three thousand entries made in the inventory of his collections in 1607–11, there is not one reference to the Philosopher's Stone. Nevertheless, his project was no failure in the long run for by encouraging his scientists to pursue their wildest dreams in a tolerant and supportive environment he helped lay the foundations of the Scientific Revolution of the seventeenth century. This was especially true in the field of astronomy.

THE STARRY HEAVENS

Given that I am perfectly informed by men worthy to judge this science, I know that you have formulated important hypotheses to facilitate its study and that one cannot find a man in our epoch who is your equal.

Rudolf II to Tycho Brahe

By the turn of the seventeenth century, Prague had become the foremost centre of scientific learning and endeavour in Europe. Astronomy and astrology had not yet gone their different ways: aspects of the former were used to understand the mind of God and calculate the calendar of the Church while the latter was important for predicting the future, whether it meant the state of the weather and crops or the fate of an individual and the nation. In an uncertain world, anyone who claimed to see into the future was taken seriously, especially by the most powerful secular representative of Christianity.

Rudolf took a great interest in the study of the heavens. The German manuscript of his horoscope drawn up by Nostradamus consisted of no fewer than 238 pages of commentary, ample for Rudolf to mull over in the intimacy of his study. The horoscope covered everything from his health, religion, pleasures, marriage, voyages, secret enemies and friends. Its general conclusion was that Rudolf would attain a 'great exaltation of reign and empire'.[1]

During his upbringing, Rudolf avidly read books on astrology in the libraries of his father in Vienna and his uncle in Spain. His theoretical interest had been deepened by the appearance of the new star in the constellation of Cassiopeia in 1572 in the year he was crowned King of Hungary. The star faded and disappeared two years later, one year before he attained the Czech crown. His concerns were further fired by the controversy over the meaning of a comet which appeared in 1577. It was considered, according to the rubric of a contemporary engraving as 'a most terrible and most mysterious comet'.[2] It proved a scientific *cause célèbre* of the day, with pamphlets written on both sides of the question of whether comets as particular events determine human affairs.

Given his interest in the subject, Rudolf warmly welcomed astronomers to Prague. He particularly championed the polymath Johannes Jesenský (Jessenius), who later became a close friend of Brahe and Kepler. He was of Slovak background but liked to call himself an *eques Ungarus* ('Hungarian knight').[3] Born in 1566 and educated in Breslau, as a student of medicine in Padua he dedicated his first philosophical tract to Rudolf in 1590. On the strength of it, he was awarded a degree from the Carolinum University in Prague. While living in Wittenberg afterwards as a professor of anatomy at the university, he became friendly with the German mathematician Johannes

Nostradamus, within a magic circle, showing Catherine de Médicis a procession of the future kings of France in a magic mirror. Nostradamus drew up Rudolf's horoscope

Kepler and intervened on his behalf at Rudolf's court. When Brahe and Kepler fell out, he was the first to heal the rift; when Brahe died, he gave a fulsome oration at his funeral.

Like Brahe, he tried to reconcile the earth-centred system of Ptolemy with the new sun-centred view of Copernicus. Like Kepler, he believed in the underlying harmony of the universe. Like both of them, he accepted the correspondence between heaven and earth which underpinned a belief in astrology. His most important philosophical work was entitled *Zoroaster* (1593), a work of universal philosophy which attempted to recover the lost wisdom of the ancients: 'We have named our little book Zoroaster because the oracles which we followed as guiding principles were the magic of Zoroaster and the theology of the Chaldeans.'[4]

Apart from his astronomical interests, Jesenský performed the first public human dissection in the history of the Carolinum University in June 1600. The corpse, which had been taken from the gallows, was already rotting and the festive members of Prague high society who attended the ghoulish demonstration appreciated how the unseasonably cool weather reduced the stench. Jesenský included in his Latin treatise on the subject some hexameters in praise of Rudolf and Bohemia, calling Prague not only a city but a 'world'. The Emperor immediately asked the prince-elector of Saxony to let Jesenský come to Prague where he lived for six years and became one of the city's most sought-after medical practitioners.

Another outstanding polymath at Rudolf's court was his personal physician, Tadeáš Hájek of Hájek (Thaddaeus Hagecius). Born in the city to a prosperous family, he had served as doctor to three Habsburg emperors. After the death of Maximilian II, Rudolf kept him on and greatly valued his opinion. For many years he occupied a central position at the court and had wide contacts outside the country before being ennobled in 1595 for his services.

Hájek was not only an astronomer and mathematician but also a physician, alchemist, surveyor and botanist. He was the most distinguished Prague scholar in the 1570s and 1580s. He investigated the use of clocks to measure celestial positions, published a series of ephemerides – tables indicating the future movements of the Sun, Moon and the planets – and drew up a report on alternative calendars after the introduction of the Gregorian system in 1582. As an astronomer, he advocated the new solar-centred cosmology of Copernicus and was the founder of the so-called meridian school of astronomy which sought accurate observations and calculations of the paths of planets. As a surveyor, he was the first person to try to triangulate the environs of Prague; he would have liked to have mapped the whole of Bohemia but was unable to raise sufficient funds. He even wrote on metoposcopy, the study of the character and fortune of a person from his face.

As a practising alchemist, his interest in distillation extended to writing a book on beer in Czech and he also translated into Czech the celebrated *Herbarium* by the Italian writer Pietro Andrea Mattioli. Following in his father's alchemical footsteps, Hájek examined for Rudolf the alchemists who came to Prague and advised him on the state of the Great Work undertaken in his laboratories in the Castle.

Hájek's most important work was a treatise called *Dialexis*, published in Frankfurt in 1574, on the new star that appeared in 1572 and he further engaged in the polemic over the comet of 1577. But while he was open to the theory of Copernicus, he retained a profound belief in the role of celestial events as manifestations of an organic and dynamic universe. He not only edited a tract on astrology but drew up horoscopes for Rudolf and his circle.

Hájek knew or corresponded with many of the astronomers of the day, including Georg Joachim von Lauchen (Rheticus) who supported Copernicus and devised a new house system in astrology, and Girolamo Cardano, the most outstanding mathematician of his day whose book on the games of chance offered the first systematic computation of probabilities. It was Hájek too who brought to Rudolf's attention the importance of the work of Tycho Brahe, whom he had met at Rudolf's coronation at Regensburg in 1576. He had given him a folio of Copernicus's *Little Commentary*, copied from a manuscript kept in his father's library in Prague, and they went on to correspond about Brahe's observations of Mars.

It was in large part thanks to Hájek that the great Danish astronomer Tycho Brahe came to settle in Prague in 1599 to become Rudolf's court astronomer and close companion. Brahe was born on 14 December 1546 into the aristocratic family of Otto Brache and Beate Bille in Knutstorp (Knudstrup) near Helsingborg, now in south-west Sweden, then part of Denmark. His twin brother having died, he was christened Tyge, which he later Latinised to Tycho which had fine associations with the Greek god of destiny Tyche. When he was two he was taken, apparently without any protest from his parents, by his Lutheran uncle Joergen and aunt to their castle in Tostrup to be brought up in princely fashion. At the age of twelve he was sent to study philosophy and rhetoric at the University of Copenhagen, one of the best in Europe at the time. But by the age of thirteen his interest in astronomy and astrology was fired by an eclipse of the moon on 21 August 1560. Henceforth, he began studying mathematics as well as law and spent his nights observing the night sky. As he later wrote, from boyhood he knew almost perfectly all the stars and was familiar with the annual movement of the heavens.[5]

Brahe would have been taught at Copenhagen that the heavens were divided into two levels: the *primum* and *secundum mobile*. The former consisted of what an observer on Earth sees while looking at the night sky and included the changes over a day and a year as the stars and planets moved in regular cycles. The latter was more mathematical and involved the use of trigonometry in calculating the positions and movements of the planets. It had long been observed that while events occur in an unpredictable way on Earth, they appeared regular and orderly in the heavens. All celestial movement, it was believed, described perfect circles and spheres, reflecting the perfection of God's Creation. On the outermost sphere were the stars, while the inner spheres were made up of the planets, five of which were visible to the human eye. No heavenly body could leave its sphere. On the other hand, astronomers had great difficulty in explaining the observably erratic movement of the Sun, the Moon and the planets, which sometimes appear to an observer on earth to move backwards, a phenomenon known as retrogression.

Moreover it was assumed that the Earth was at the centre of the universe and everything revolved around it. This view had prevailed since Aristotle had first insisted on the immutability of the spheres in the fourth century BC in Athens and it had been taken up by the great astronomer Ptolemy in Alexandria in the second century AD. By helping to destroy this carefully wrought world view Brahe and Kepler revolutionised astronomy.

At the age of fifteen, Brahe was sent to the University of Wittenberg to continue his studies in law and medicine but instead he began to buy astronomical books to read. These included Sacrobosco's *On the Spheres*, Peter Apian's *Cosmography*, Regiomontanus's *Trigonometry*, as well as an up-to-date ephemeris, a table showing the position of the celestial bodies throughout the year. He studied the constellations from star maps drawn by Albrecht Dürer and soon realised that existing tables, both the earth-centred one of Ptolemy and the recent sun-centred one of Copernicus, were flawed.

Not long after, in 1565, his uncle, the vice-admiral of the Danish fleet, died. Brahe did not inherit his estate but he had enough funds to move to Rostock to continue his studies where a quarrel broke out with one of his countrymen that was literally to mark him for life. It may have been sparked off by some student ragging about a Latin poem Brahe had composed. It prophesied that the eclipse of the Moon on 28 October 1566 would predict the death of the Turkish sultan, Suleiman the Great, only for news to arrive that he had died six months before. Another astrological computation made by the young Brahe further warned him that some accident might occur on 29 December. At dinner in a tavern that night a quarrel erupted with his distant cousin Manderupa Parsberga which became so serious that the two students went outside into a churchyard and fought a duel in total darkness. Brahe was cut across the forehead and lost the middle part of his nose.

The experience of recovering in Rostock that winter strengthened his interest in alchemy and medicine. The disfigurement was only partially

Tycho Brahe

hidden by a metal nose made from electrum – a mixture of silver and gold – which Brahe fashioned for himself and held in place with an adhesive salve which he always carried in a small box. It earned him the title of 'The Man with the Silver Nose'. When it was destroyed by a pet dog one night while he was sleeping, he had fourteen made to wear on different occasions. One of them fell into the possession of Voltaire, who later offered it as a gift to Frederick the Great, presumably well cleaned and polished.

After nine years at different universities, Brahe finally settled in Augsburg in the spring of 1569 where he became friendly with Paul Hainzel, the burgomaster of the city. Together, they constructed a great wooden quadrant to determine the altitude of celestial orbs, so big that it required forty men to set it up in Hainzel's garden. They also built a sextant and other instruments which surpassed those available at the time. With them, Brahe began making observations which earned the respect of contemporary astronomers. His horoscopes also attracted the attention of the powerful and wealthy.

On the death of his father in 1571, Brahe inherited half the income from the ancestral estate at Knutstorp. By this time, he had grown into a barrel-chested, polished courtier, without a nose but with flowing reddish-blond hair. Returning to Denmark from Augsburg, he set up in the following year an observatory and an alchemical laboratory in his uncle's castle at Herrevad near Copenhagen and began to live with Kirsten Jørgensdatter, the daughter of a clergyman at Knutstorp. Since she was not a noble, he was unable to marry her formally. They had a happy, life-long relationship and she bore him eight children.

The first work Brahe published was an astrological and meteorological almanac for the year 1573. He wrote it not for money, which he did not lack, but out of interest. It reveals his pious Lutheran faith as well as his astrological beliefs. There is no better teacher of theology, he argues, than the universe itself: God created humans and put them on the Earth at the centre of his Creation. But where all is constant and perfect in the heavens, on earth all is change, growth and decay. As an astrologer, he did not doubt that celestial events, especially the Moon, had a strong influence on the weather. But since there are local conditions on earth, the effects will vary from place to place. His intention was therefore not so much to predict the weather as to study the discrepancies between the actual and predicted weather and thereby to investigate the nature of the relationship between heaven and earth.

Brahe first came to prominence among astronomers with his fifty-two-page pamphlet entitled *De stella nova* (1573). In the previous year, at the age of twenty-five, he had seen on 11 November from his observatory an exploding star to the north-west of the constellation of Cassiopeia which shone brighter than Venus for more than a year. It was what is today known as a supernova, resulting from the explosion of a 'white dwarf' star. This anomaly was yet another blow to the medieval world view of the Aristotelians who believed that the heavens beyond the Moon were fixed. 'Let all philosophers, new as well as ancient, be silent!' Brahe exclaimed in exultation. 'Let the very theologians, interpreters of the divine mysteries, be silent! Let the mathematicians, describers of heavenly bodies, be silent!'[6]

Brahe moved next to Copenhagen and was invited to give a course of lectures at the university in which he defended the principles of astrology. All his life, Brahe believed in the influence of the celestial bodies on earth: 'To deny the power and influence of the stars', he declared, 'is to detract from divine wisdom and influence.' He was convinced that the ruling planets in a horoscope shaped the person's character. Though he did not deny that people can be changed by 'lesser causes such as upbringing, education, conversation, foreign travel and things like that', he insisted that the reasons for the fundamental differences between people can be sought nowhere better than in astrology.

Clearly well versed in the subject, he addressed the main traditional objections to astrology: that it is not always easy to determine the exact moment of birth; that twins born at the same time often have different fortunes; and that many people can die at the same time in a war or a natural catastrophe when their horoscopes do not indicate identical deaths. To these objections, he replied that astrologers do not claim that the sky acts in precisely the same way upon all those born at the same time but 'that they are subject to diversity and are altered in different ways by heavenly influences'. Aware of the concerns of theologians and philosophers that astrology appears too deterministic, he further argued that thanks to human consciousness and freedom we can rise above the influence of the stars: 'Nor is man's free will in any way made subordinate to the stars but through it, under the guidance of reason, he can do very many things beyond the influence of the stars, if that is what he wishes.' Indeed, 'if people wish to live as true and supramundane human beings, they can conquer whatever malevolent inclinations they may have from the stars'.[7]

The core of Brahe's argument was the medieval principle that the stars incline individual lives and human events in a particular direction but do not determine them: *astra inclinant, non determinant*. He also adopted Thomas Aquinas's view that *sapiens homo dominatur astris* ('the wise man is master of the stars'), in so far as he is master of his passions and capable of rising above a brutish life through education and enlightenment.

In the course of his lectures on astrology, Brahe mentioned the theory of the Sun and the Moon according to the Copernican model. The Polish astronomer Nicolaus Copernicus first described his sun-centred model mathematically in 1512 but did not publish his magnum opus *De revolutionibus orbium caelestium* ('The Revolutions of the Celestial Spheres') until a month before his death in 1543 for fear of being attacked by Aristotelian traditionalists and theologians such as Martin Luther. He argued that the Earth is merely one of the planets, revolving around the Sun and rotating on its own axis, a view which greatly simplified the geometry of the planetary system. He boldly made clear his inspiration from ancient Egypt and Greece:

> At the centre of all things resides the Sun. Could we find a better place in this most beautiful of all temples, from whence this light illuminates all things at once? Rightly is it called the lamp, the spirit, the ruler of the universe. For Hermes Trismegistus it is the invisible god, Sophocles' Elektra calls it the all-seeing. Thus, the Sun sits on its royal throne and guides its children, which circle it.[8]

Although dedicated to Pope Paul III, this beautiful and profound work was banned by the Catholic Church and remained on the Index of forbidden books until 1835.

Brahe did not entirely endorse the implication that the Sun was at the centre of the universe, thereby overthrowing traditional Christian dogma; instead, he maintained that Copernicus's theory could be adapted to the idea that the Earth did not move – something that he went on to try and establish in his own system.

For all the reasoned argumentation in his works, Brahe was famously superstitious. He would avoid an old woman in the street, a hare in a field or swine on the road, fearing them as evil omens. An inverted slipper or three lighted candles would upset him. To be lucky in gambling he would carry part of a hangman's halter and a *lapis alectorius*, a bean-sized stone of the sort sometimes found in the stomach of a fowl. His astrological studies had convinced him that thirty-two days of each year were particularly unlucky to undertake a journey, get married, make a transaction or to fall ill.

While travelling through southern Germany, Switzerland and Venice in search of a suitable site for a new observatory, Brahe happened to pass through Regensburg to see the magnificent coronation festivities for Rudolf as the King of the Romans on 1 November 1575. He was invited to dine with the new Holy Roman Emperor and was asked to cast his horoscope. He counselled him not to marry as his sons would only bring him misfortune – advice which Rudolf followed much to the horror of the House of Habsburg and the Vatican.

Aware of Brahe's growing European reputation and fearful of losing him to other monarchs, Frederick II, King of Denmark and Sweden, offered Brahe for life the use of a small island called Hven off the coast of Denmark, visible from Hamlet's castle of Elsinore. He was also given a handsome pension in order to build a castle-observatory. Brahe was delighted. The cornerstone was laid on 7 August 1576 on the astronomer's thirtieth birthday at the most astrologically propitious time. The final structure was a palatial and well-equipped observatory on a hill called the Uraniburg, the 'City of the Heavens', named after Urania, the classical muse of astronomy, and Uranus, the Greek word for the heavens. Partly inspired by the Italian architect Andrea Palladio, it was designed on the Pythagorean principles of musical harmony and geometrical symmetry. The palace even had running water, unknown at Hampton Court or the Louvre at the time, with a mechanical fountain at the geometric centre of the building.

One day in 1577 a comet was reflected in the newly filled ponds in the gardens at Uraniburg. Brahe studied its parallax carefully, that is, its position against the backdrop of stars taken from different angles at different times. He concluded that it was higher than the Moon and was following an unusual orbit, quite out of harmony with the regular circuits of the planets. It proved yet another blow to the Aristotelian concept of an unchanging universe. Forever the astrologer, Brahe wrote in his report to Frederick that it augured 'great disunity among reigning potentates' and 'an exceptionally great mortality among mankind'. As such, it might mean 'well-deserved punishment for inhumane tyranny'. Unjust monarchs were intended to take note.[9]

During his time at Uraniburg Brahe started to work out his own cosmological system, a compromise between the geocentric one of Ptolemy and the heliocentric one of Copernicus. His observations had shown up anomalies in the Ptolemaic system but he was still reluctant to follow Copernicus in placing the Sun at the centre of the universe. Instead, he maintained that all the planets revolve around the Sun while the Sun and Moon orbit the Earth. It did not depart from the geometry of the Copernican system but retained the Catholic dogma of an unmoving Earth. As such, it was used by Jesuit scholars to attack Galileo while Brahe had to defend it, with increasing paranoia and frustration, against the growing band of Copernicans.

Brahe used his resources well at Uraniburg and built up a pan-European reputation for his improvements to lunar theory and his vast collection of observations. A workshop was set up that produced the most advanced astronomical instruments of the day, including quadrants to measure the altitude of the stars and armillary spheres to determine the positions of the stars. He designed a beautiful star map, with all the signs of the zodiac, engraved on a three-metre globe which became the centrepiece of his library. To house his instruments he built a partly subterranean observatory called Stjernborg ('Star Castle'). Tycho Brahe was the last great astronomer to work without a telescope.

Brahe enjoyed entertaining lavishingly and opened his doors at Uraniburg to the rich, powerful and eccentric, including James VI of Scotland in 1590 during his visit to marry a Danish princess. Keen to pass on his knowledge, Brahe trained young men in reasoning and observation so that they could work as his assistants. At Uraniburg there was a dwarf called Jepp employed as a jester and Brahe's assistants and guests would entertain each other with stories over the long dinners.

Throughout this period, Brahe continued to practise astrology. He had attributed the great plague that decimated Europe in 1566 to the unhappy conjunction of Jupiter and Saturn three years earlier. Some of his predictions were confirmed while others were less successful. He once predicted that a noble lady would be killed by a horned beast; one year later a countess was murdered by her husband. If his predictions proved erroneous, he would often make an excuse. After predicting that Frederick II would pass away in 1593, he merely observed when the king died in 1588, 'death was too previous'. His horoscope of the King's son Prince Christian ran to sixty-one pages. Although he predicted he would have few offspring, the future king eventually sired eighteen illegitimate children. And he singularly failed to predict the difficulties he would encounter with Christian when he ascended to the throne.

Brahe was also a keen practitioner of alchemy which he called 'terrestrial astronomy'. Next to astronomy, it was his greatest intellectual passion.[10] By the age of eighteen he had designed a huge solar mirror to help him make alloys of precious stones. At Uraniburg, he set up in the cellar a large laboratory which had sixteen furnaces in order to give the correct degree of heat for his alchemical experiments. He even installed five furnaces in the main dining cum working cum sleeping room on the ground floor so that experiments could continue during meals and through the night. But he chose not to divulge his findings to the general public so they would not get into the wrong hands: 'On consideration and by the advice of the most learned men, I thought it improper to unfold the secrets of the art to the vulgar, since few persons are capable of using its mysteries to advantage and without detriment.'[11]

Nevertheless, he was mainly interested in alchemy in order to produce medicines rather than gold. His elixir based on 'Venice treacle' (*theriaca Andromachi*) which contained traditional alchemical substances, was sold under his name by almost every apothecary in Germany as a remedy against epidemic diseases. When he sent some to Rudolf, he wrote:

> When properly prepared it is better than gold. It may be still more valuable by mixing with a single scruple either of gold, tincture of corals, or sapphire, or garnet, or solution of pearls, or of potable gold, if this can be obtained free of all corrosive matter. In order to render the medicine helpful for all diseases which can be cured by perspiration, and which constitute a third of those which attack the human frame, it should be combined with antimony.[12]

Unfortunately for Brahe, Frederick died in 1588 and he was succeeded by the eleven-year-old Christian IV. Jealous of his privileges, the king's entourage turned the boy against the master astronomer and a new royal ordinance condemned morganatic marriages such as Brahe's. The new king then removed some of his fiefdoms, refused to allow his children to inherit Uraniburg and criticised him for the way he maltreated his peasants. There was some truth in the last accusation for he had forced the islanders to do a great deal of unpaid labour for his City of the Heavens. He even tried to seize the improved land of a tenant farmer, and when his dwarf jester tried to escape the island, he had him beaten. Certainly during the 1590s Brahe became increasingly autocratic, jealous of his reputation and unwilling to brook any opposition. The final straw for the teenage Christian was news of Brahe's failure to maintain the Chapel of the Magi in the cathedral of the mainland Roskilde estate which contained the tombs of Christian's father and grandfather. Moreover Brahe never bothered to attend church services there.

Realising that his political and financial situation was deteriorating fast, Brahe decided in 1596 to leave his beloved Uraniburg and its Renaissance gardens. He packed up his superb instruments, unique library of 3,000 books and his alchemical laboratory and boarded a specially commissioned ship accompanied by his wife, five children, servants, assistants, his personal secretary Longomontanus and his future son-in-law Franz Tengnagel.

In need of a new patron Brahe now took up Rudolf's long-standing invitation to come to Prague. The astronomer had earlier sent Rudolf some of his books in the hope that he might allow them to be printed in the Holy Roman Empire. On 13 June 1590, Rudolf authorised the printing of his works in Hamburg. He wrote to him in his own hand, a rare distinction:

> Given that I am perfectly informed by men worthy to judge this science, I know that you have formulated important hypotheses to facilitate its study and that one cannot find a man in our epoch who is your equal . . . You employ your time well by consecrating yourself to these faraway and celestial things. You know them so well that we await from you new hypotheses on the movements of the sky. In no way would we want to fail to distinguish you by our imperial favour and to encourage you in your work.[13]

Rudolf felt that they were destined to meet and saw a hidden meaning in the fact that the Dane's first name Tycho was associated with Tyche, the Greek goddess of fortune.

After leaving Denmark, Brahe and his train took refuge in a castle at Wandsburg near Hamburg lent by his friend Viceroy Heinrich Rantzau of Schleswig-Holstein. He realised that his greatest chance of patronage would come from the magical theatre of the world in Prague. Brahe decided to complete a book called *Astronomiae instauratae mechanica* and dedicated it to Rudolf. Making full play of the new art of perspective and with handsome woodcuts, it described his instruments and gave an account of his life and his work at Uraniburg. He also sent his sixteen-year-old son Tycho in the New Year of 1598 to Prague with a magnificent manuscript version of a star catalogue for the Emperor.

To press his case, he contacted his old correspondent Tadeáš Hájek and the imperial librarian Ottavio Strada who had been an acquaintance since his student days. After receiving a copy of the *Astronomiae instauratae mechanica*, the Archbishop Elector Ernst of Cologne further wrote to Rudolf assuring him that 'the whole German fatherland' would bless him if he granted generous patronage to Brahe, the 'unique and most laudable restorer of the sciences'.[14]

There was only one impediment, namely Nicholas Raimarus Bär (who also Latinised his name to Ursus, the Bear). Using false credentials, he had become Rudolf's Imperial Mathematician and had plagiarised Brahe's ideas after a visit to Uraniburg. With a penchant for the mysterious and mystical, Ursus combined an unoriginal understanding of mathematics with a belief that the end of the world was nigh. When he published the 'Tychonic system' as his own in *Fundamentum astronomicum* in Strasbourg in 1588, Brahe was understandably furious and told him so. Ursus replied in the following year in a work published in Prague called *De Astronomicis hypothesibus, seu systemate mundane tractatus*. It contained a vitriolic diatribe against Brahe, not only mocking his disfigurement (he could 'discern double-stars through the triple holes in his nose') but asserting that Europe's greatest observer of the stars was more of an astrologer than an astronomer. The work even reprinted a letter from a young scholar in Graz – Johannes Kepler – who had inadvisedly written to Ursus: 'the bright glory of your fame . . . makes you rank first among the *mathematici* of our time like the sun among the minor stars'.[15]

By an extraordinary coincidence, on the same day that he received Ursus's attack, Brahe received a copy of Johannes Kepler's slim volume called *Prodromus dissertationum cosmographicum*. Who was this unknown stripling who had such high esteem for his enemy? On opening the pages, Brahe was not only intrigued to find a brilliant mind at work but delighted when he read in the accompanying letter that he, Brahe, was 'the prince of mathematicians not only of our time but of all times'. Praise indeed but then Kepler was the first to admit that he had 'a childish or fateful desire to please princes' and that had 'in every way a dog-like nature. His appearance is that of a little house dog.'[16]

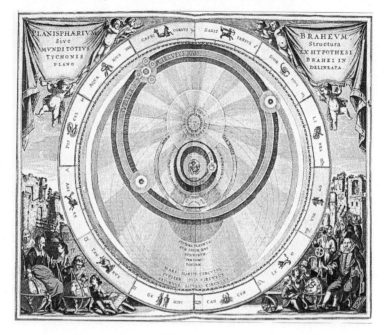

Planisphere based on Tycho Brahe's cosmological system, with the Earth at
the centre of the universe and the five planets orbiting the Sun.
A. *Cellarius*, Harmonia macrocosmica (1660)

Privately, Kepler did not think much of the 'Tychonic system' – he called
his ideas 'little paper houses' – but he was itching to get his hands on the
Dane's unique collection of celestial observations. Furthermore, he was
beginning to develop a new harmonic theory based on the analogy of music
to replace his earlier theory based on Plato's five solids. In the late summer
of 1599, Kepler wrote to his old tutor that he had the theory like 'a bird under
a bucket'.[17]

Delighted with Brahe's books and worried that other copies had been sent to
the courts of Europe, Rudolf followed the advice of his physician Hájek, his
counsellor Johannes Barwitz (Barvitius) and the gem artist Caspar Lehmann
to invite Brahe to visit him in Prague. The eager astronomer left his family
and train at Wandsburg where he had wintered and set out for Prague with
his two sons. As they approached the city, Ursus departed ignominiously.

Unlike many ambassadors who had been languishing for months seeking an audience, Brahe was ushered in straight away. The Holy Roman Emperor gave the Protestant Dane the rare honour of seeing him alone in his audience chamber. He stood down from his throne, bare-headed, and extended his hand in welcome. It was a gesture of respect normally extended only to a king.

According to Brahe, the Emperor answered all his questions in Latin. He promised to support him and his research, 'all the while smiling in the most kindly way so that his whole face beamed with benevolence. I could not take in everything he said because by nature he speaks very softly.' When Brahe presented him with three books fetched by his son Tycho, who was waiting in the antechamber, Rudolf reviewed the contents briefly and decided to read them later. The Emperor 'again responded with a splendid speech saying most graciously that they would please him greatly'.[18] He stayed up all the following night to finish the books and the following day told Brahe to have his family join him to Prague.

The books included an elegant manuscript version of a catalogue of 1,000 stars and a beautifully printed copy of Brahe's *Astronomiae instauratae mechanica*. Both were dedicated to the Holy Roman Emperor. The date of dedication of the latter was January 1598 but it was not published until four years later. He also gave him a secret recipe for a plague elixir, which no doubt greatly endeared him to Rudolf.

As Brahe left the room he was taken aside by Rudolf's secretary Barwitz:

> The Emperor wished to have a mechanical device [for measuring distances] on my carriage shown to him (for he had seen it from the window when I drove up to the castle). I therefore had my son fetch the mechanism from the carriage, gave it to Barwitz, and showed him how to explain the construction to the Emperor. When Barwitz had done this and returned to me, he said that the Emperor said he had one or two similar devices but none so large or made in exactly the same way. He did not want to accept mine from me but would have one made for himself by his astronomer, from the pattern of mine.[19]

Against the advice of his counsellors, Rudolf offered Brahe the promise of an estate and a yearly pension of three thousand crowns. When it came to it,

Rudolf gave Brahe the choice of three castles, including his own favourite hunting lodge at Brandýs nad Labem. It was a Gothic fortress, some 20 kilometres north-east of the city, which had been turned into a Renaissance chateau with a high tower, complete with a huge sgraffito mural of an elephant on a wall of its inner courtyard.

Brahe stayed there for a short while but finally chose the splendid and comfortable Renaissance chateau Benátky nad Jizerou. It was built facing south on a cliff top 60 metres above the river Jizerou 36 kilometres north-east of Prague. It dominated the rolling landscape and had a free horizon on all sides – a perfect platform for observing the heavens. There was not only an adjoining church in the late Gothic style but on the exterior wall of the interior courtyard there was a huge sgraffito mural which still exists, depicting the Emperor engaged in the hunt. Its distance from Prague – about six hours by coach – gave Brahe relief from the prying attentions of the Emperor. After all his troubles in Denmark, he had at last landed on his feet and had firm ground from which to view the heavens. 'Thank God', he wrote to his friend Erik Lange, 'everything seems to be turning out right, and I hope it may soon be even better . . . ' To make sure that Brahe could settle in Bohemia as a citizen for good, Rudolf wrote to the Bohemian Estates asking for 'Tycho and his progeny to be included in the country's rolls, according to the old custom'.[20]

Brahe moved his family into Benátky (Czech for 'Venice') in August 1599 and occupied the west wing of the castle. He began immediately to set up an observatory and established an alchemical laboratory. A careful division of labour was arranged: Brahe's son Georg directed the experiments while his assistant Longomontanus observed the Moon and its phases. One of his first tasks was to determine astronomically the geographical position of Benátky: he carried out his observations on the 1 and 2 January 1600 and determined the latitude on 23 January. Near one south-facing window a line indicating the local meridian can still be seen on the floor. It was probably the first astronomically determined point in Bohemia.

Benátky soon filled up with Brahe's assistants, pupils, servants and equipment. As at Uraniburg, he opened its doors to those with a genuine interest in astronomy and lavishly entertained his guests who came from all over Europe. Each night Brahe and his assistants would observe each of the five visible planets in the same way, recording their position in longitude, in latitude, their height in the sky, and the approximate variations in their distance from the Earth. The same techniques were applied to most of the stars in the night sky. The Jewish astronomer David Gans from Prague, who visited them on three occasions, wrote enthusiastically:

> Yes, I was there among them in the rooms used as an observatory, and I saw with my own eyes the marvellous work that was carried on there . . . three instruments, each operated by two scholars, took the astronomical determinations of the star at the very moment it passed the line of midnight . . . For this purpose [Tycho Brahe] used a clock of a new and marvellous conception . . .[21]

Being Rudolf's personal astrologer was the price Brahe had to pay for his patronage. The Emperor insisted that Brahe come to Prague so that he could draw up astrological predictions for him on a regular basis. He was worried about the Turkish front, the choice of generals, even the possibility of his own assassination. He increasingly began to rely on Brahe not only for his predictions but for his advice on the affairs of state. For his part, the move was not entirely unwelcome as he was having trouble with the imperial official supervising the building of the observatory and he enjoyed the attention at court.

When Brahe's instruments finally reached Prague in October 1600, Rudolf had them mounted on the balconies of the Belvedere in the Castle gardens. But it meant that he had to continue to dance attendance on Rudolf rather than lord it over his castle at Benátky. In addition, there was an important technical drawback: from the south-facing balconies the view of a large part of the south-western sky was blocked off by the Castle.

Brahe first took up temporary residence in a house called the Golden Griffin on the Hradčany next to the monastery of the Capuchins. But he soon found the cloister bells, which rang regularly throughout the day, intolerable. Rudolf had invited the monks to Prague but now issued an order to banish them from the city because he thought they were responsible for giving him cramps in the heart. The enraged monks attributed their expulsion to the evil machinations of the 'alchemist' Tycho Brahe next door. In the records of the cloister, it is written:

> The Emperor wished to drive the Capuchin monks out of Prague owing to the complaint of the alchemist who because of their presence could accomplish nothing with his sorcery. This alchemist came from a noble Danish family. His name was Tycho Brahe. This alchemist complained

of the Capuchins, saying that their prayers and services disturbed him, and the Emperor, who was gullible, thereupon ordered the monks to leave Prague . . . In the meantime, the Emperor, whenever the Capuchins held prayers, began to have cramps of the heart and had really serious attacks. He knew, however, of no reason for such attacks, which were caused by the sorcery of the aforementioned alchemist, and the matter went so far that the Emperor believed he saw the monks actually in front of him and so he often cried out that their banishment would be enforced.[22]

The noise of the cloister bells meant Brahe was delighted to move to the grand residence of Rudolf's former Vice-Chancellor Jakob Kurz von Senftenau above the Castle, just a short walk from the palace. The house has disappeared but fine bronze statues of Tycho Brahe and Johannes Kepler stand on the site. Brahe turned the room at the top of the house into an observatory and installed some of his instruments. He painted on the walls four tableaux to illustrate the history of astronomy. The first was of a distant ancestor of the Emperor, Alphonse X of Castille, who had ordered the *Alphonsine Tables* of celestial movements. At his feet were Ptolemy and Al-Battani, also known as Albanenius the Arab. The second depicted Charles V with Copernicus and Apian, the German astronomer who studied the movement of the moon. The third was of Rudolf and Tycho Brahe and the last was of Frederick II of Denmark and the castle of Uraniburg. Rudolf would have appreciated the compliment.

Typical of their time, both men shared an interest in the miraculous and in the rational; in astrology and astronomy; in religion and mathematics. Furthermore, Rudolf valued Brahe's counsel because he was not attached to any clique or faction in his entourage. As part of his position as court astrologer, Brahe had to advise him not only on appointments but on the continuing campaign against the Turks. He told him that there were good and bad days for certain actions and decisions. As a result, Brahe came to be known at court as 'the evil spirit of the Emperor'.

Not mincing his words, he predicted that Rudolf would be assassinated like Henri III of France early in the new century. The revelation from such a respected source had a devastating effect on the Emperor: it not only intensified his paranoia but made his ingrained melancholy worse. He increasingly refused to give audiences and barely left his *Kunstkammer* and private chambers, seeing in any unknown face a potential assassin. For his part, Brahe was still bitter about his forced departure from Denmark and his instinctive pessimism took a turn for the worse.

There was, however, a young Lutheran mathematician and teacher who was to have a profound effect on both their lives. He would ensure that their names would never be forgotten in the history of science. His name was Johannes Kepler.

THE NEW ASTRONOMY

I have congratulated myself on the exceptional good fortune
of having such a man as a comrade in the pursuit of truth.

Galileo Galilei to Johannes Kepler, 4 August 1597

With the approval of Rudolf, Kepler came to join Brahe in 1600. He was to stay in Prague for twelve years until Rudolf's death. During this time he wrote about thirty treatises, including his 1609 masterpiece *Astronomia nova* which, as the title implies, laid the foundations of the new astronomy.

When they first met, Brahe was fifty-four and Kepler was twenty-nine. It was not an easy collaboration. Kepler called his master 'the phoenix among astronomers' but Brahe soon began to treat him like a servant. Where Brahe was an elegant, extravagant aristocrat who believed that the Sun orbited the Earth, Kepler was an impoverished, introverted teacher who believed the Earth orbited the Sun. It was not long before they had a row which led Kepler to withdraw from Benátky Castle. But it was only temporary: the pull of making a great impact in science was stronger than personal differences.

Yet for all their differences and tensions, their respective skills proved a perfect match. Brahe was probably the best observational astronomer of all time, whereas Kepler, with poor eyesight, had mathematical abilities second to none. Brahe was able to measure the movements of the planets while Kepler was able to formulate their laws. By bringing the two men together, Rudolf inadvertently made a huge contribution to astronomy in particular and to science in general.

Kepler was born on 27 December 1571 in Weil der Stadt, a small village near Stuttgart at the edge of the Black Forest. He came from Lutheran burgher stock, but his parents were uneducated and argumentative and their marriage was fraught with strife. His father disappeared for long periods fighting as a mercenary and his mother eventually followed, despite being beaten and abused, leaving Kepler to be brought up by relatives. It was not an easy childhood – he was puny and nearly died of smallpox – which left him near-sighted and multiple-visioned. But he was lucky enough to be sent to good free schools where he excelled in mathematics, became fluent in Latin and acquired some Greek. He soon found that he always saw both sides of every question – 'There was nothing that I could state which I could also not contradict' – which proved an asset and a disadvantage for the rest of his life.[1]

After schooling in Adelberg, Kepler received a fellowship to train for the Protestant ministry first at Maulbronn and then at Tübingen where he engaged in two academic debates supporting the heliocentric system of Copernicus. Although the university still officially taught Ptolemaic astronomy, his teacher of astronomy and mathematics, Michael Mästlin,

Johannes Kepler

believed that the Copernicus system was probably true. Kepler also read Nicolas de Cusa, sometimes called the first modern astronomer, who argued that the universe is infinite, has no centre and that the Earth is a sphere. These two astronomers as well as his own reasoning led Kepler to consider all the mathematical advantages which Copernicus had over Ptolemy. The student who had planned to become a Lutheran minister decided instead 'to honour God through astronomy'.

At the same time, he remained convinced, like the Pythagoreans and the Neoplatonists, that there is an underlying harmony and order in the universe. In his view, geometry, music, medicine and astronomy are all related at a fundamental level. For Kepler, cosmic harmony resulted from the combination of beauty and simplicity, the very attributes of God.

But there was one other crucial element in Kepler's make-up which eventually made him such an original thinker. Unlike previous generations of astronomers, he was not content simply to describe the heavenly bodies; he wanted to know the causes of their movements in certain patterns and at certain speeds. In other words, his great innovation was to seek out the physical explanations for celestial phenomena.

It was Kepler's 1596 work *Mysterium cosmographicum* that had first attracted the attention of Rudolf and Brahe. The short volume was published with the long title *Prodromus dissertationum cosmographicum* ('Introduction to the Cosmological Essay'), and the subtitle *Containing the Cosmographical Mystery of the Marvellous Proportions of the Celestial Spheres, and of the True and Particular Causes of the Number, Size and Periodic Motions of the Heavens, Demonstrated by Means of Five Regular Geometric Bodies*. Drawing up the pattern of the Great Conjunctions of the planets Saturn and Jupiter (an exceptionally powerful combination in astrology), he noted that they did not always fall into the same places in the zodiac. He concluded that the spatial relationships between the orbits of the five different planets mirror the five Platonic solids which were taken up by Euclid – the tetrahedron (four-sided), hexahedron (six-sided), octahedron (eight-sided), dodecahedron (twelve-sided) and icosahedron (twenty-sided). The solids correspond respectively to Aristotle's five elements: fire, earth, air, water, and the quintessence which was identified with the heavens. Kepler believed that each solid nests inside a sphere of a planet into a harmonious whole, with every corner touching the inside surface. The tetrahedron, for instance, separates the spheres of Saturn and Jupiter. Kepler was convinced that such simple patterns lie behind the surface diversity of the world and that number governs every aspect.

Combining pagan wisdom with Christianity, he further maintained that God created the five regular solids the day before he created the heavens. The symmetry for Kepler was clearly divine: 'God is also glorified in astronomy through my work', he wrote to Mästlin.[2] He further suggested that a planet speeds up as its orbit brings it closer to the Sun because of the Sun's whirling force, a view which his old tutor thought would lead to the ruin of astronomy.

It was an inspired work for a twenty-four-year-old. Galileo was so impressed after reading the preface that he wrote to the unknown author from Padua on 4 August 1597, saying how he congratulated himself on the exceptional good fortune of having such a man as 'a comrade in the pursuit of truth'. He confessed that he had been a Copernican for many years but had not dared to publish his views for fear of sharing the same fate as Copernicus and earning the ridicule of his colleagues. Kepler replied on 13 October urging him 'to come out publicly' but received no reply.[3] In a letter written to his friend Johann Herwart on 16 March 1598, he wrote that he was 'utterly convinced of the truth of the Copernican theory' and that he planned to concentrate on the ideas of physics concerning the origins of the relationship between the Earth and the centre of the universe 'for one must first determine the "what" from which the "why" is derived'.[4] This deceptively simple question was to transform astronomy.

Since 1594 Kepler had been living a modest existence with his wife Barbara Mühleck and stepdaughter as a teacher of mathematics at a school at Graz on the edge of the Black Forest in Austria. His wife, from a well-off family, had been widowed twice. She was prone to depression and miserliness, and in Kepler's own words was 'simple of mind and fat of body'. At Graz, he bore the grand title of District Mathematician which meant that he had to compile an almanac, an annual calendar with astrological predictions for the following year. These concerned the weather, harvests, war, disease, as well as the most likely times when the Turks might attack or religious and political strife break out. For 1595, he prophesied a particularly cold winter, an attack by the Turks from the south and a peasant uprising: all took place.

On 11 January 1600 one of Rudolf's advisers, Ferdinand Hoffmann, Baron of Grünbüchl and Strechau, happened to be passing through Graz from Vienna to Prague and he remembered that the young teacher Kepler lived there. He had admired his recent work and decided to offer him a lift in his carriage to Prague. The journey took ten days and, after arriving, another couple of weeks went by before a letter of invitation came from the illustrious prince of astronomers: 'You will come not so much as a guest', Brahe wrote to Kepler on 26 January, 'but as a very welcome friend and highly desirable participant and companion in our observations of the heavens.'[5]

Kepler was thrilled and went to see him at Benátky Castle. Brahe was feeling his age at fifty-four; Kepler, from poor beginnings, was now a thrusting 29-year-old. It was to be a great meeting of minds. After moving into Benátky Castle, Kepler immediately began to help Brahe's assistant Longomontanus calculate the movement of the 'red planet' Mars. He also did his best to gain access to Brahe's closely guarded observations. The older astronomer hoped that they would confirm his system, not Copernicus's, and his paranoia was such that he obliged Kepler to pledge in writing that he would never reveal any of his secrets. The memory of Ursus's betrayal still smarted.

For his part, Kepler thought that the Mars observations might at least confirm his hypothesis that a force from the Sun moved the planets. But as a quiet scholar used to tranquil domestic life, Kepler did not like the boisterous life at Benátky with its noisy communal meals. Since Danish was the lingua franca, the castle came to seem to him like 'a reigning loneliness of people'.[6] To make matters worse, Brahe's assistant, the haughty Wesphalian nobleman Tengnagel, called him a '*domesticus*' – a hired servant. And then there was the matter of his pay; only following a row after which Brahe departed from Benátky for Prague did he deign to arrange a small stipend for Kepler from Rudolf; when this was not forthcoming, he agreed to pay him out of his own funds.

But the lure of the celestial observations overcame any personal reservations and Kepler travelled with Brahe's cousin Frederick Rosenkrantz to Graz to collect his family. Rosenkrantz was going to join the Austrian forces fighting the Turks who were once again advancing through the Balkans and even threatened the southern border of Austria. He was the same Rosenkratz who was to be immortalised with another of Brahe's cousins – Knud Gyldenstierne (Guildernstern) – in *Hamlet*. Kepler arrived in Graz just in time. Archduke Ferdinand himself was attending a commission which demanded that non-Catholic citizens either convert to Catholicism or leave. The deeply Lutheran Kepler left in the nick of time.

When Brahe moved from Benátky Castle to Prague, Kepler followed him. The Dane was not discontent but the pressure of work and the court was beginning to show on the fifty-four-year-old. Kepler wrote of his master: 'He always resembles a lost man, but always somehow extricates himself. His success at this is to be wondered at.'[7] Brahe felt that old age was creeping up on him and that his spirits were becoming enfeebled.

Kepler moved with his family into Brahe's new residence and was asked by him to write a short account of the 'Quarrel between Tycho and Ursus over Hypotheses' for posterity. He was still unable to get his hands on Brahe's observations; the frustration led Kepler to become a staunch advocate of the open and free sharing of ideas and knowledge within the community of scholars. How else could science progress? Although the crucial tables were never published in Brahe's lifetime, by comparing the Copernican and Tychonic models, Kepler could at least clarify his own view that it was essential to seek the physical causes for the motion of the planets.

After his daughter's marriage to Tengnagel, Brahe at last in October 1601 introduced Kepler to the Emperor. He told Rudolf that with his new assistant he would compile a magnificent set of astronomical tables based on his observations that would be more accurate than any other in the world. They would be called the *Rudolfine Tables*, if only he would permit it, and would be a lasting monument to the Emperor and a testament of his generous support for learning. There was just the little matter of Kepler's salary. Rudolf was delighted with the idea and immediately made the necessary arrangements. As an early biographer of Kepler wrote, Rudolf in such matters was 'distinguished by a delicate and big-hearted manner'.[8]

At last all seemed in order, but disaster was quickly to follow. Only three days after the meeting Brahe was taken ill during the banquet given in his honour at the palace of Petr Vok Rožmberk. Courtly etiquette prohibited one from rising from the table before one's host had risen, and Brahe declined to relieve himself. Thereafter the astronomer was unable to urinate and quickly succumbed to uremic poisoning. Kepler described the intimate details of his illness; forever the astrologer, he even noted down the position of the Moon, Saturn and Mars on the night of the banquet. In his words, the great Danish astronomer felt 'less concerned for the state of his health than for etiquette'.

Unable to pass urine, suffering from uremia, experiencing insomnia, intestinal fever and little by little delirium, Brahe died eleven days later on 24 October 1601. His final wish, although he knew Kepler was of the Copernican persuasion, was that his assistant might present 'all his demonstrations in conformity with his hypothesis'.[9] On the last night, Kepler recorded that Brahe repeated over and over again in flawless Latin: *'ne frustra vixisse videar'* ('Let me not seem to have lived in vain'). He need not have worried. He could not have had a better successor to ensure his reputation.

On hearing the news of Brahe's death, Rudolf was inconsolable. He arranged for the Protestant Dane to be buried lavishly with great pomp and circumstance in the Church of our Lady Before Týn in the centre of the Old Town of Prague. A life-size brass relief of Tycho Brahe, complete with metal nose, was ordered by the Emperor. It still stands in the church. The bronze panel depicts Brahe in armour as befitting a knight, with one hand on a globe and the other on the hilt of a sword. On his tombstone is written in Latin: 'Neither power nor wealth, only Art and Science will endure.'

Overwhelmed with grief after the funeral, Rudolf allegedly resorted to necromancy. He conducted a magical ceremony to raise the spirit of his departed friend but, like so many of his attempts at the supernatural, it failed. He did not leave his bed chamber for a week afterwards. When at last he recovered, he began to turn his attention to Tycho Brahe's successor elect, Johannes Kepler.

Two days after Brahe's death, Rudolf sent his secretary Barwitz to tell Kepler he had been named Imperial Mathematician. He invited him to take responsibility for Brahe's instruments and manuscripts and for the completion of the *Rudolfine Tables*. Rudolf offered the Brahe family 20,000 florins for them, more than Kepler could have hoped to earn in a century on his old Graz salary as a mathematics teacher. As far as Kepler was concerned, it was a dream come true; at last, he had access to the closely guarded astronomical data. And thanks to Rudolf's perspicuity and generosity, he was able to work in Prague without the fears that Galileo had experienced in Padua and Florence.

Kepler's years in Prague under Rudolf's protection proved to be the golden years of his intellectual life. He compared his patron to a fixed star around whom the planets moved, but the increasingly depleted imperial treasuries meant that he was often not paid. Nevertheless, he moved into a spacious house with his family in the New Town, an hour's walk from the Castle. It was a splendid time to live in Prague. Kepler called it 'a gathering of nations'; indeed, under Rudolf's policy of religious tolerance and his generous patronage of the arts and science, it had become the cultural centre of Europe. But as Kepler's star rose, his domestic life darkened. His relationship with his wife was far from ideal: she did not understand his work and could be miserly and quarrelsome at home. About this time, he also lost his favourite son to smallpox.

*

As Court Astronomer, Kepler was expected, like Brahe before him, to provide for Rudolf regular predictions regarding the affairs of empire as well as the development of his private life. Kepler has been called the first of the modern astronomers, yet all his life he practised astrology to supplement his salary and regularly published astrological calendars predicting future events.

A seventeenth-century cartoon of an astrologer receiving money for his services. Tycho Brahe and Johannes Kepler were both practising astrologers and made astrological predictions for Rudolf

As far as astrology was concerned, Kepler was both a believer and sceptic. He did not deny the validity of astrology and never abandoned its central belief that the conformation of the heavens influence the character of a person at birth. In a letter to his friend Johann Herwart in April 1599, he wrote that it influences a human being 'in no other way than that in which the peasant haphazardly ties slings around pumpkins; these do not make the pumpkins grow, but they determine its shape. So do the heavens; they do not give a man morals, experiences, happiness, children, wealth, a wife, but they shape everything with which a man has to do.'

Like Rudolf, Saturn figured prominently in Kepler's horoscope, traditionally associated with melancholy. In the same letter, he wrote, in a remarkable piece of self-analysis:

In my case, Saturn and the Sun work together in the sextile aspect (I prefer to speak of what I know best). Therefore my body is dry and knotty, and not tall. My soul is faint-hearted and hides itself in literary corners; it is distrustful and fearful; it seeks its way through harsh brambles and becomes entangled in them. Its habits are similar. To gnaw bones, to eat dry bread, to taste spiced and bitter things is a joy to me. To walk over rugged paths, uphill and through thickets, is a holiday treat to me. I know no other way of seasoning my life than science.[10]

While recognising that the divisions of the zodiac are man-made and that the stars are signs rather than determining causes of human behaviour, his confidence in astrology was based on the fact that it seemed to work: 'The belief in the effect of the constellations derives in the first place from experience, which is so convincing that it can be denied only by people who have not examined it.'[11] Kepler therefore tried to justify astrology in an irreproachable scientific manner as to both its method and goal.

In a 1598 letter to his old tutor Michael Mästlin about his most recent astrological almanac he wrote: 'As to all the prognoses, I intend to present . . . a pleasant enjoyment of the grandeur of nature along with the statements which appear true to me . . . If you agree with this you will, I hope, not be angry with me if, as a defender of astrology in word and action, at the same time I try to implant the opinion in the masses that I am not an astrological buffoon.'[12] Mästlin was openly critical of his former pupil's astrological activities, but the young man replied: 'If God gave each animal tools for sustaining life, what harm is there if for the same purpose he joined astrology and astronomy?'[13] Hitherto, astrology and astronomy had been considered virtually synonymous but Kepler's remarks and Mästlin's disapproval show how the two branches had already begun to part company at the beginning of the seventeenth century.

Kepler composed four almanacs in the years 1603–1606 in Prague, of which only those for 1604 and 1605 survive. In one of them, he expressed his wish to decipher the secrets of nature by using the clear light of reason: 'I may say with truth that whenever I consider in my thoughts the beautiful order, how one thing issues out of and is derived from another, then it is as though I had read a divine text, written into the world itself, not with letters but with essential objects, saying: Man, stretch thy reason thither, so that thou mayest comprehend these things.'[14]

Kepler also wrote a number of serious treatises on astrology. In 1602, he published The Principles of Astrology, in which he criticised the vanity and worthlessness of astrology as ordinarily practised, but he still claimed that it was fundamentally valid. He famously wrote: 'Astronomy, the wise mother; astrology, the foolish daughter selling herself to any and every client willing and able to pay so as to maintain her wise mother alive.'[15] Kepler, however, never thought astrology was foolish in the sense of being the pursuit of fools. He confessed that against his best reasoning and deepest doubts, it provided 'a most unfailing experience (as far as can be expected in nature) of the excitement of sublunar natures by conjunctions and aspects of the planets instructed and compelled my unwilling belief'.[16] In A Third Person Intervening, he further warned 'certain Theologians, Physicians and Philosophers . . . that, while justly rejecting the stargazers' superstitions, they should not throw out the child with the bath water'.[17]

But while believing in the fundamental principles of astrology and defending his almanacs, he was sceptical about the claims of most contemporary astrologers and could see the damage they could inflict on the weak and the gullible, particularly those in power.

In a letter of 3 April 1611 about his patron Rudolf, Kepler made a distinction not only between astronomy and astrology but between two kinds of astrology: 'Ordinary astrology . . . can easily be used to please both parties [in political controversies]. I believe that in such weighty reflections one should not only exclude ordinary astrology but also the one which I have recognised as being in accordance with nature.'[18] He loathed the former, practised by charlatans who exploited human gullibility and wishful thinking for their own gain. He was particularly concerned about the effect Rudolf's court astrologers were having on his ability to make decisions. As Imperial Mathematician, he therefore tried as much as possible to keep them at bay. In the same letter he argued that

Astrology can do enormous harm to a monarch if a clever astrologer exploits his human credulity. I must watch that this should not happen to our Emperor . . . I hold that astrology must not only be banished from the Senate, but also from the heads of all those who wish to advise the Emperor in his best interests; it must be kept entirely out of his sight.[19]

In fact, Kepler developed an original view of astrology that did not find widespread recognition. It was part of his Hermetic world view which assumed the existence of the harmony of the spheres, the World Soul, the correspondence between the macrocosm and the microcosm, and the existence of universal sympathy. He believed that it was through 'radiations' that the planets influence life on earth. As the rays strike the Earth at different angles, they form harmonious patterns similar to those of music. The soul intuitively recognises the patterns since it is an image of God, the ultimate source of all geometric truths.

In Kepler's opinion, there is no evil or dark star in the heavens since 'it is the nature of man as such . . . that lends to the planetary radiations their effects on itself; just as the sense of hearing, endowed with the faculty of discerning chords, lends to music such power that it incites in him who hears it to dance'. This might imply that humans project meaning into the planets but in a sentence which anticipates Jung's notion of archetypal ideas, Kepler wrote: 'the soul bears within itself the idea of the Zodiac'.[20] This is because every individual soul is part of the World Soul and because eternal ideas, forms and numbers are innate in the human mind.

When Tengnagel returned to Prague on October 1602, he persuaded the Emperor that he should take over the compilation of the *Rudolfine Tables* – at twice Kepler's salary. Kepler had to hand over the manuscripts, but he kept secretly for himself the Mars observations. When Tengnagel found out they were missing, Kepler was obliged to relinquish them in the following year. Two years later, Brahe's son-in-law, deeply involved in Habsburg diplomacy, finally agreed to share the responsibility for looking after the manuscripts and completing the tables.

Kepler tried to keep some distance between himself and the Emperor, bridling at the thought that he was just a kept servant. He wrote to his old teacher Mästlin on 5 March 1605 from Prague: 'I am living here on the stage of the world as a single private person, glad if I can squeeze out part of my salary from the Court. Besides I fancy myself and conduct myself as if I did not serve the Emperor but the whole of mankind and posterity.'[21] Nevertheless, he still had to justify himself to Rudolf as Imperial Mathematician. When Rudolf asked him in the autumn of 1602 what he planned to publish in the near future, he replied that he would complete a book called *The Optical Theory of Astronomy* as well as commentaries on Mars. In the former, Kepler was the first to realise that the image of the outside world is projected by a lens onto the surface of the retina. He was also the first to discover the inverse square of light: from a candle light, he observed that the intensity of light is inversely proportional to the square of the distance.

Back at work on Brahe's Mars observations, Kepler was interrupted by the sight of a new star on 17 October 1604. As bright as Jupiter, it appeared near Saturn and Jupiter, which were in conjunction. The conjunction of Jupiter and Saturn occurred every twenty years but this conjunction marked the beginning of a two-hundred-year cycle during which the conjunction would take place in the 'fiery trigon', that is to say, in one of the four areas containing three signs (trigons) of the zodiac associated with the element fire. A conjunction of Saturn and Jupiter was bad enough; one at the beginning of the fiery trigon was even more worrying. To calm down the Emperor and the citizens of Prague, Kepler published a small report insisting that all would be well in this particular case.

It was the appearance of the new star that really fascinated Kepler. After observing it from a specially built wooden tower until it faded in the night skies, he wrote *De stella nova in pede Serpentarii* ('The New Star in the Foot of Serpentarius',1606) and dedicated it to Rudolf. As its subtitle states, it was 'A book full of astronomical, physical, metaphysical, meteorological and astrological discussions, glorious and unusual'. He rejected the widespread view that it was set alight by planets by arguing that it was much more distant than the planets. As for the idea that it was a chance combination of atoms, he suggested that it was as 'if a pewter dish, leaves of lettuce, grains of salt, drops of water, vinegar, oil, and slices of egg had been flying around the air for all eternity, it might at last happen as if by chance that a salad would result'. And its astrological import? Kepler urged the good citizens of Prague to consider their sins and repent. He still held firm to his Hermetic belief that the universe was an organic, living being and that 'the whole world is full of life'.[22] Such reasoning was bound to appeal to the Emperor.

Again, when a brilliant comet appeared in the sky in 1607 (since known as Halley's comet), Kepler sought to reassure Rudolf who feared, like most of his fellow countrymen, that it was an ill omen. He reminded him that the comet had been seen in 44 BC during the funeral procession of Julius Caesar and had appeared at seventy-five-year intervals ever since. It was not a bad omen but a confirmation of the regularity of the universe: 'Each of the myriad of stars is a shining witness of the incontestable truth that everything in nature is in motion, progress is life, rest is death.'[23]

Forever eager to be paid for his work and frustrated at the intermittent delivery of his imperial salary, Kepler sent a copy of his *De stella nova* in October 1607 to King James of England. He dedicated it 'To the King-Philosopher, the serving philosopher; to the Plato, the ruler of Britain, Diogenes at Prague asking Alexander for a gift sends . . . from his hired barrel this, his philosophical writing'.[24] For all its shameless toadying and self-deprecatory allusion to the Cynic Diogenes of Sinope who was said to have lived in a barrel, the dedication evoked no gift from the English king. Rudolf, for all his importunate demands and rackety administration, was still a better bet.

Disappointed, Kepler pressed on. After eight years of observations of the orbit of Mars from his observatory in Prague and poring over Brahe's data, he published in 1609 his masterpiece – *Astronomia nova*. Dedicated once again to Rudolf, it was a book written for astronomers and mathematicians rather than for the general public.

The problem of Mars, which he had been mulling over ever since he met Brahe, was that it had the greatest 'eccentricity', that its position was too far off centre from the Sun for Copernicus's theory, and from the Earth for Ptolemy's. With the use of Brahe's observations, Kepler resolved the problem by imagining that he was a Martian astronomer looking down at the Earth. Kepler gradually realised that the Earth was acting like a planet and, moreover, that it travelled around the Sun in an elliptical way, speeding up and slowing down with a predictable mathematical regularity. He further calculated that the speed of the Earth was inversely proportional to its distance from the Sun. It was a superb combination of theory and observation, rarely surpassed in the history of science. This ground-breaking work was his greatest contribution to astronomy. He went on to demonstrate his hypothesis by comparing his own calculations for planetary positions with Brahe's accurate data.

From the earliest times it had always been assumed that planets travelled in circles, as a sign of the harmony of the cosmos and of God's divine order. But armed with incredulity, Kepler was prepared to think the unthinkable. His analysis was, as he remarked, a voyage of exploration in the skies equivalent to those of Columbus and Magellan across the oceans. He at last had managed to give a physical explanation to the movements of the planets. He had shown that terrestrial and celestial physics were one and the same: the laws influencing the Earth are no different from those affecting all the other bodies in the heavens.

The problem of Mars proved the catalyst for Kepler to work out his two famous laws of planetary motion which so influenced Newton: firstly, that a planet moves in an elliptical orbit, and the Sun is at one focus of the ellipse; and secondly, that the further a planet is from the Sun, the longer it will take to orbit. The Sun rotated a field of magnetic-like emanations which in turn rotate the planets. The theory not only accounted for the available data but satisfied his deep-felt insight into the geometrical symmetry of God's Creation.

It would have been impossible to calculate that the Earth moves as a planet in an elliptical orbit around the Sun without Brahe's painstaking and meticulous observations. Kepler had ensured that Brahe would not be forgotten. But it was left to Newton to explain the physics behind his two laws and to develop fully his notion of magnetic force into the concept of gravity.

Kepler's masterpiece did not get off to a smooth start however. When it appeared in the summer of 1609, Kepler had to forfeit the entire edition to the printer in Heidelberg in order to cover the costs. Worse still, Tengnagel had control of his father-in-law's observations and was still trying to defend his system. He was not pleased by Kepler's *Astronomia nova* and he wrote a preface warning readers 'not to be swayed by anything of Kepler's, especially his liberty in disagreeing with Brahe in physical arguments'.

Rudolf, though, was more discerning. He lavished praise on the former schoolmaster from Graz and declared that he would give him a bonus of two thousand thalers – a wonderful windfall, if only it had been paid. Kepler's triumph seemed an empty one. Apart from the money worries, his wife was suffering from ill health and depression.

But then on 15 March 1610, the imperial counsellor Wacker von Wackenfels came with electrifying news: Galileo Galilei, with his new telescope, had discovered four new moons orbiting Jupiter. Kepler enthusiastically agreed with the Italian master that it confirmed Copernicus's theory for it was clear that not everything orbited the Earth. On 19 April, he wrote a letter to Galileo, later published as a thirty-five-page book entitled *Conversation with the Starry Messenger*, in which he defended the use of telescopes and the 'plausibility' of Galileo's findings.

Four months later Galileo replied: 'I thank you because you were the first one, and practically the only one, to have complete faith in my assertions.'[25] Kepler replied that Galileo had aroused in him 'a passionate desire' to see his instruments and hailed him as 'wise Pythagoras' who had 'opened the holy of the holiest of the skies'.[26] But despite his broad hint, Galileo did not send Kepler a telescope, examples of which he was sending to rulers all over Europe.

Kepler eventually managed to borrow one, however, from the Elector Ernst of Cologne, Duke of Bavaria, and confirmed Galileo's observation of Jupiter and its moons. The clockmaker Heinrich Stolle later made for Rudolf a telescope based on Galileo's design; it had a royal crown engraved on its casing.

Kepler soon completed a work on optics called *Dioptrice* which appeared in 1611. It described the physics of the eye and the actions of lenses. It included the description of a telescope which later bore Kepler's name and is still in use today. It improved on Galileo's by inserting two convex lenses which gave a much larger field of view. None of Kepler's own telescopes have survived, but his *Dioptrice*, together with the earlier *Optical Theory of Astronomy*, formed the basis for optical theory in the seventeenth century.

Kepler at this time also published a short treatise entitled *A New Year's Gift or The Six-cornered Snowflake*. Walking across the Stone Bridge to a house in Jesuit Street, he had noticed a six-pointed snowflake land on his coat. The next one had a different shape but was six-pointed, as were the next and the one after that: all the snowflakes that fell out of the sky were six-pointed. The number was highly significant for Kepler for it corresponded to the six sides of a cube. He further noted that 80 per cent of the stars he had observed were six-pointed: as above, so below. The observation confirmed for him yet again the underlying mathematical elegance of the universe. The little publication, almost a piece of whimsy, proved to be a fundamental work of crystallography and one of the first attempts at a mathematical theory of the origin of organic and inorganic shapes.

It was not a good period in his private life: Kepler lost one more of his three remaining children to smallpox (two had died earlier) and his wife Barbara sank deeper into depression and ill health before dying of fever. Kepler's application for a post at Württemberg University was rejected because he had earlier declared that a Calvinist could be a 'brother in Christ' and had advocated 'a priesthood of all believers'.[27]

Kepler remained loyal to his old patron who needed him as never before, dividing his time between the gloomy palace and his despairing home. Contrary to his own astrological calculations, he consoled Rudolf that the stars still predicted a long life for him. At least he could count on his patronage for the time being.

THE EMPEROR OF DARKNESS

His Majesty has now reached the state of abandoning God entirely; he will neither hear nor speak of Him, nor suffer any sign of Him. Not only does he refuse to attend any sermon, public service, procession or the like, but he hates and curses all who participate in them, being never more impatient of God and every good work than on such holy occasions.

Propositions to the Archdukes in Vienna (1606)

At the end of the sixteenth century, Rudolf and his empire were entering an uncertain period. Despite the elusive nature of the Philosopher's Stone, he continued to welcome to his court anyone professing knowledge of alchemy, astrology, the Cabala and magic. But while Rudolf's scientists were laying down the foundations of the Scientific Revolution and his artists represented a last flowering of Renaissance art, his own emotional life and political and religious affairs were going from bad to worse.

Throughout Rudolf's reign, he had been beset by twin problems. The first was the struggle for supremacy between the Protestants and the Catholics. The second was the threat of the Turks of the Ottoman Empire on his ever-shifting southern and eastern borders. Not only did the Catholic Counter Reformation oppose the forces of the Protestant Reformation throughout his dominions, but there was talk of a new Crusade against Islam. For his part, Rudolf refused to participate in the campaign outlined to him by the papal ambassador Bonomi which aimed at the 'systematic extirpation of heresy'.[1]

Compared with the possibility of discovering the secrets of nature and of extending life indefinitely, local matters of politics and religion paled into insignificance. Yet Rudolf still dreamed of his Grand Plan to build an alliance between European principalities and states based on a moral and spiritual regeneration brought about by Hermetic wisdom which would allow freedom of conscience and thought. Without informing his own ministers, he increasingly used his artists and adepts as special envoys to establish cordial relations with sympathetic rulers in Europe to this end. But the execution of his plan was piecemeal and erratic and he made little progress with it.

Despite persistent skirmishes between the Catholics and Protestants, the Augsburg parliament agreed in 1582 to levy a Turkish war tax on Rudolf's behalf. Two years later, he managed to renew a truce with Sultan Amurat III who had lost control of the Mediterranean Sea at the Battle of Lepanto and was now preoccupied with fighting the Persians. Ever since the time of Ferdinand I, the Holy Roman Emperor had been obliged to pay an annual tribute to the 'Commander of the Faithful', as the Sultan liked to call himself. Rudolf, forever keen to maintain the peace, made sure that the customary 45,000 thalers were paid, adding as a gesture of good will a marvellous silver clock plated with gold, in the form of a castle. When it rang the hour, a little door opened and silver figures representing the Sultan and his suite emerged to turn a half circle and disappear through another door. The Sultan was delighted. But it was never more than a temporary truce in a stalemated war.

With the Ottoman Empire fighting the Persians, it seemed a favourable time for Philip II to launch his 'Invincible Armada', carrying well-trained inquisitors and well-tried instruments of torture, against the Protestant Queen Elizabeth. His vision of a universal Catholic monarchy in Europe was in sight. Rudolf, although no friend of England, refused to participate in the preparations since like his father he sought a reconciliation between the two main branches of Christianity.

The signs for 1588 had not been good. Imperial astrologers had predicted a solar eclipse, two lunar eclipses and the passage of a comet; then there was to be a conjunction of Jupiter and Mars. It seemed as if affairs on earth would be as perturbed as those in the sky. It came therefore as no surprise to Rudolf to hear that the Invincible Armada had floundered, thanks to bad weather: eighty ships were lost, fifteen thousand men killed, four thousand taken prisoner. Philip put it down to the will of God and never fully recovered.

Rudolf, in the meantime, was still trying to achieve the release of his brother Maximilian in Poland who had been captured in 1587 during an ill-conceived attempt to invade Poland and have himself crowned king. Philip refused to come to his aid. The new Pope Sixtus V also stood aloof, declaring: 'The sins of the House of Austria and the passivity of the Emperor are the real causes of this misfortune.'[2]

The Vatican eventually sent the cardinal Aldobrandini as an intermediary who reported back to the Pope that the Emperor was pious and well-intentioned; but this did not prevent him from conspiring against him. Writing to Sigismund Báthory, the new King of Poland, he declared that he thought that Jiří Popel of Lobkovic, the staunch Catholic and High Steward of Bohemia, deserved to be the king of Bohemia more than Rudolf.

At a banquet in his honour, Lobkovic toasted Aldobrandini with the words: 'Long live the future Pope!' Aldobrandini, letting down his guard, replied enthusiastically: 'Long live the future king of Bohemia!'[3]

Rudolf was furious but he abided his time. The negotiations in Poland dragged on and in the end in 1598 he ignominiously had to sign away any claim to the country in return for his brother. Worse was to follow: a year later, Aldobrandini became Pope Clement VIII.

The religious situation in Prague had long been complex and fragile.[4] Although Rudolf was the Holy Roman Emperor, he lived in Prague on the frontier of the orthodox Catholic world. The Protestants were in the majority – about 85 per cent – and the Catholics an influential minority, especially at court. On the Protestant side there were the Utraquists and the Czech Brethren. The Utraquists were so called because they practised 'in both kinds', that is they felt able to take Catholic and Protestant communions. They were increasingly split into two factions, with the more extreme being influenced by Lutheranism. The Czech Brethren, on the other hand, were followers of the fifteenth-century radical John Huss who had argued, like an anarchist *avant la lettre*, that the authority of divine grace was higher than secular or ecclesiastical power. They formed the principal religious body in Bohemia and espoused principles of equality and fraternity.

At the same time, the Catholics were being supported by the Jesuit and the Capuchin orders. The former valued literature, art and science and enjoyed a degree of luxury, while the latter adopted a life of austere poverty, but both were equally militant in promoting the Counter Reformation. Although Rudolf as the Holy Roman Emperor was meant to defend Catholicism, he resented the interference of the Vatican in his personal and imperial affairs, especially concerning the succession and the appointment of officials. He was inclined neither to support actively the Catholic cause nor take action against the Protestants.

The forces of the Counter Reformation were, however, increasingly making inroads in the Holy Roman Empire. In Styria, Archduke Charles put himself entirely in the hands of the Jesuits and obliged the Protestant burgers either to convert to Catholicism or leave. On Charles's death in 1590, Rudolf nominated his brother Ernst as regent of Styria but he was eventually replaced by Charles's son who, as Ferdinand II, became the ruthless Catholic leader in the Thirty Years' War. Rudolf's appointment of his brother Maximilian as governor of Lower Austria and his brother Matthias as governor of Higher Austria and Vienna further inflamed the disputes between Protestants and Catholics; as soon as Matthias was in office, he began ousting Protestant ministers from several towns.

In the early nineties, the Vatican redoubled its efforts to ensure that Rudolf remained a good Catholic and that he carried out measures against the virulent Protestant disease. The strong Spanish delegation in Prague, which had been strengthened by successive Spanish ambassadors through the lavish distribution of favours, honours, promises and pensions, lent its support. Rudolf, however, asserted his independence by nominating as his Vice-Chancellor of ecclesiastical affairs Kryštof Želinský of Sebuzín, a talented man who, according to the horrified nuncio Antonio Caetano, was not only a Calvinist *manqué* but, far worse, a Czech Brother.

In the growing religious discord, Rudolf began to fear for his life. Sir Henry Wotton reported back from Vienna in 1591 to Lord Edward Zouche in London that a Flemish priest had been found in the Emperor's privy chamber with an instrument in a wide sleeve, after the form of a cross-bow. 'It is strange', he commented, 'that a Papist should seek the life of the temporal head of all Papists, as great things are feared, and no man dares speak much; yet some even of great place spare not to say that his Majesty is lately half converted in religion.' Wotton thought that Rudolf would have to grant complete religious toleration to save his empire:

> He now seems rather to bear the title of Emperor for fashion's sake, than authority to command by virtue of it. The Emperor may mend the matter when he will, by yielding every man his conscience at liberty, which either he must do shortly, or peradventure Rodolph the Second

will end the Empire after three hundred years continuance in the house of Austria.[5]

But while Rudolf hated the interference of both the Vatican and Spain in his affairs and the machinations of the Counter Reformation, he had no real sympathy for the militant Protestants either: he disliked their doctrinal wrangles and their readiness to assert their political rights. Like his father, he liked to rise above the theoretical disputes to contemplate the essence of Christianity and to stand above the tawdry mêlée of religious and political dissension: 'We are arbitrator, intermediary and judge', he wrote, 'we must not take sides in any case.'[6]

In reality, he had little choice. The Protestants in the Bohemian Estates held about 85 per cent of the seats, roughly reflecting their number among the population. Although Rudolf had kept to the Basle Agreements allowing the Utraquists to follow their religion, under great pressure from the Vatican, the Spanish ambassador and the local Catholics he renewed the old edicts against the Czech Brethren.

Paradoxically, Rudolf's inertia and procrastination probably saved his empire from being torn apart by the religious conflicts between the Lutherans, Calvinists and Catholics, particularly in the German lands. His weakness as a king was often the salvation of his subjects. If like his uncle Philip he had moved against heretics with decisive action, he would have upset the delicate balance of the Habsburg house of cards. Instead, his tolerance, liberalism and apathy postponed the inevitable by three decades.

In the meantime, Philip's forces had occupied Paris; Henri of Navarre, leader of the French Protestants, managed to repulse them and then converted to Catholicism in 1593. He was crowned Henri IV in the following year. With the Treaty of Vervins, he ended nine years of war with Philip and with the Edict of Nantes of 1598, which guaranteed the rights of the Huguenot minority, he brought to an end more than forty years of religious wars.

Relationships with the Ottoman Empire, however, took a turn for the worse. In 1590, the Sultan's Grand Vizir Sinan Pacha doubled the annual tribute paid by the Holy Roman Empire without warning or explanation. Rudolf sent his Chancellor with more gifts but no money; his coffers, ransacked for the purchase of rare works of art, were virtually empty. His Chancellor died in prison, and the heads of six Christians were paraded on spears before the imperial embassy in Constantinople. Turkish raids and incursions were made all along his borders. Rudolf readily put on his imperial armour for his portraits but he was quite incapable of leading his forces against the infidels like his grandfather Charles V. Then in 1593 the impatient Sultan declared war on Rudolf and under the orders of Sinan Pacha a vast army rolled across the Hungarian plain towards Vienna, soon seizing two powerful fortresses at Gran and Raab, the main defences on the route there.

Rudolf had no choice but to convene the Bohemian and imperial parliaments in order to raise funds to cover the costs of the war. But the Catholic leader Popel of Lobkovic, frustrated at not becoming the Supreme Burgrave, tried to rally the Protestant voices against Rudolf. The parliament ended in disarray. With a rare burst of energy, Rudolf reconvened the parliament, persuaded the members to provide the funds and had Lobkovic arrested. He was charged with plotting against the Emperor and of amassing riches at the expense of the Crown, and condemned to death. Rudolf, ever clement, was ready to pardon Lobkovic as long as he confessed his errors. When he refused, the Emperor felt he had no choice but to give him life imprisonment.

At the imperial parliament convened at Regensburg on 13 May 1594, Rudolf fared little better. As soon it was opened, the Catholics and Protestants were at each other's throats. There were months of negotiations and delays, but by raising the spectre of the Turks occupying and pillaging Vienna, Rudolf eventually obtained the necessary funds.

Rudolf was very pleased with his Czech and Protestant Vice-Chancellor Kryštof Želinský of Sebuzín, who since the fall of Lobkovic had won his complete confidence. He was happy to leave to him the everyday management of the government so that he could pursue the more important tasks of collecting works of art, overseeing his alchemists and studying the stars. For his part, Želinský established an efficient and centralised bureaucracy. But the Vatican did not approve. The papal nuncio Tommaso Contarini was complaining in 1596: 'All secrets are open to the majordomo, all business is in his hands, by him hearings are given, to him ambassadors address themselves, by his means favours are granted, at his request justice is obtained.'[7]

Once Aldobrandini had become Pope Clement VIII, there was constant tension: the Vatican was concerned about the succession to the throne and the growing Protestant movement while Rudolf saw the papal interference as an infringement of his imperial privilege. The Pope sent the cardinal Filippo Spinelli to counteract the influence of Želinský. In his report, Spinelli said:

'The government of the realm is in the hands of the Vice-Chancellor and his secretaries are hardened Calvinists . . . Želinský has the diabolical design to extirpate Catholicism in Bohemia.'[8]

Spinelli then set about undermining his position by telling Rudolf that there was a plot between the German and Bohemian Protestants against him led by the Palatine Elector and Želinský. Rudolf was not at first convinced, but then Spinelli accused Želinský of high treason. The Emperor, Spinelli wrote to the Pope with indignation, only judges his functionaries according to their capacities.

Rudolf seems to have been temporarily persuaded by Spinelli to allow a radical shake-up of the Bohemian Chancellery, the supreme office of the land, which led to the dismissal in 1599 of non-Catholic officials. These included the Chancellor of the Exchequer, Ferdinand Hoffmann, a loyal supporter of the Habsburgs for twenty years. The vacant post of Chancellor was filled by a dogmatic and ardent advocate of the Counter Reformation who had been brought up by the Jesuits. Rudolf further agreed to strip the Chancellery of its supervision of church matters and alienated the Protestants by renewing a mandate against the Czech Brethren which placed them in a state of illegality. It was the final straw for Vice-Chancellor Želinský and he resigned.

The Vatican pressed home its advantage. The question of Rudolf's excommunication was taken up on more than one occasion by the Pope and cardinals in Rome. To excommunicate the temporal anointed ruler of Christendom, however, was seen as far too destabilising for the Holy Roman Empire, especially in these troubled times. Instead of excommunicating Rudolf, the Vatican eventually decided to pack the court and the city of Prague with agents working for the Catholic cause. Archbishop Berka of Prague substituted the Jesuits – who worked among the rich and educated and were considered too subtle – with the Capuchin monks who proselytised among the poor and were notoriously hard and austere. The forces of the Counter Reformation were amassing both within and without the Castle walls.

Rudolf could still act impetuously on his own. He was convinced that alchemy had implications for politics. Would not the 'Chemical Wedding' of Sol and Luna, the male and female principles symbolised by Sulphur and Mercury, create a new era of harmony on earth? Locked in his study in the Belvedere Summer House in the Royal Gardens or turning over a priceless object in his *Kunstkammer*, in his wildest moments Rudolf still envisioned a world in which Protestant and Catholic, Muslim and Christian, even East and West would come together, bury their differences and coexist in perpetual peace.

In 1600, Rudolf gave his blessing to the English adventurer Anthony Sherley to form a European coalition and to unite with Persia and attack Turkey on two fronts. But despite protracted negotiations, which led to Rudolf making Sherley a Palatine of the Empire in 1607, the grand coalition failed to materialise, mainly because the Vatican and Spain did not want the Emperor to be its head. Typically Rudolf wanted all or nothing, total victory or continued war.

As part of his diplomatic offensive, he gave two rare audiences in July 1600 to the French ambassador, the Maréchal de Boisdauphin, who offered on behalf of the new King Henri IV to join the Holy League against the Ottoman Empire. Whatever his own courtiers might have thought, the French visitors were impressed by the Emperor. They found him to be 'of middle height, in good condition for his forty-eight years, with a red face, a bristly beard, dressed in grey velvet, the Golden Fleece around his neck and on his head a black velvet brooch decorated with a grey feather'. Boisdauphin observed: 'He talks like an Emperor.'[9]

While remaining personally humane and generous, Rudolf became increasingly frustrated with the growing discontent within his empire. As events grew more menacing, his method of dealing with a crisis was Hamlet's 'wise hesitation'. Johannes Kepler had an exalted view of Rudolf's inaction at a time when his own court and ministers were despairing of him. In 1598, the young teacher from Graz in Austria wrote:

It looks as though the emperor possesses a certain Archimedean manner of motion. It is so gentle that it barely strikes the eye, but in the course of time puts the entire mass into motion. There he sits in Prague, understands nothing about the military profession, but yet, without authority (as one previously believed) accomplishes wonders, keeps the princes submissive, makes them accommodating, obliging, liberal, checks a monarch who for so many centuries had been so formidable, makes him pliable by the long drag of war, without himself suffering such a great injury as to outweigh the ravages to the enemy. In this manner he lays the foundation for a position of full power, so that only the subjection of the Turks still seems to be missing.[10]

Kepler was not alone; it was a widely held view among Protestants that his passive presence on the throne kept countless disasters at bay.

As his hope to discover the Philosopher's Stone began to fade like the smoke from his alchemists' kitchens, Rudolf's bouts of melancholy deepened. They laid him low for weeks on end, during which time he was unable to attend to his laboratory and collections, let alone to affairs of state. The beginning of the new century saw the second major crisis in his life when he seems to have suffered a serious nervous breakdown from which he never fully recovered. His grasp of everyday reality had been weak at the best of times, and the artificial environment of the court and his passion for the occult sciences had only encouraged his interest in the marvellous and the magical. The breakdown seems to have been provoked partly by his failure to assert his authority over his counsellors and administrators. Then there was his failure to achieve his grand plan of perpetual peace: the war with the Turks was stalemated and Europe remained as divided as ever. The endless dispute with the Vatican over the succession and his encouragement of potentially heretical thinkers only made matters worse.

The new century coincided with Rudolf's mid-life crisis: he was forty-eight in 1600 and had long feared that he would die before his fiftieth birthday. It was widely thought that he was under the sway of a prophecy that predicted he would be plotted against by members of his own family. Rudolf was deeply affected by the general air of uncertainty and fear at the turn of the century. There was an atmosphere of violence, intrigue and mistrust stalking the narrow, cobbled streets of Prague. The plague epidemic of 1599 understandably caused widespread alarm.

As the new century approached, there were many apocalyptic publications, including one by Rudolf's court astronomer Hájek, which predicted imminent doom or revelation. The new star of 1572, the comet of 1577 and the conjunction of the 'fiery trigon' of 1588 had created a climate of foreboding. The introduction of the Gregorian calendar in 1582 had further fostered a feeling of uncertainty. Although supported by Brahe and Kepler, it created difficulties for astrology and aggravated the split between the Catholics, who supported the change, and the Protestants, who generally opposed it.

The crisis in Rudolf's life only reflected a wider malaise in society and culture. The optimism and idealism of the Renaissance were giving way to a sense of doubt, anxiety and disappointment. These years saw a shift in the cultural framework with the older organic, holistic way of looking at the world giving way to the mechanical and instrumental way which culminated in the Scientific Revolution. For the time being, the two world views, the magical and the utilitarian, existed side by side at Rudolf's court, but the tensions were growing. The seekers of esoteric truths and the advocates of free enquiry, including Rudolf himself, were under threat in a world of growing intolerance and social conflict. In these circumstances, it is not surprising that Giordano Bruno, who managed to combine the new science with the old metaphysics, was burnt at the stake by the Inquisition in 1600.

For the Vatican's diplomats and spies at his court, Rudolf's mental illness, the paralysis of his will and his continued involvement in magic and alchemy were further signs that he was possessed by satanic forces. Cardinal Filippo Spinelli, the papal ambassador at the court, finally wrote to Pope Clement VIII in 1600:

> It is generally agreed amongst Catholics in Prague that the Emperor has been bewitched and is in league with the devil. I have been shown the chair in which His Majesty sits when holding conversations with the Prince of Darkness himself. I have seen the little bell His Majesty uses whenever he wished to summon the spirits of the departed to do his bidding.

On another occasion, the Cardinal advised the Pope of Rudolf's strange behaviour on his way to mass:

> When he enters the chapel, he stays close to the exit, and appears to be trembling all over. His Majesty seems afraid of the sign of the cross. I understand he has ordered his private chaplain not to make signs of the cross in his presence. As far as his Holiness is concerned, the Emperor has been overheard referring to Him in terms I could not possibly commit to a letter. It appears to me that His Majesty is possessed by the devil himself.[11]

It was the uncompromising view of Spinelli that Rudolf had become insane: by definition his morose rejection of sound Catholic advice was an act of a demented mind.

Other rumours circulated: the president of the Chamber of Finances, Wolf von Unverzagt, wrote to Archduke Ferdinand of Styria that the Emperor would feel the clothes of those who approached him to assure himself that they did not carry a cross or a relic. When a chamberlain slipped an Agnus Dei (a wax medallion stamped with a lamb as an emblem of Christ and blessed by the Pope) in the doublet of the Emperor, it was reported that as soon as he put it on, he rolled on the ground, groaning and shouting.

Rudolf's family offered no consolation or support. His inherent melancholy had been made worse by the news in 1598 of the death of his uncle, Philip II of Spain, with whom he had spent his early years, and his replacement by his son Philip III who preferred bull-fights to politics and art; he would reign over the spectacular decline of Spanish power and influence.

Rudolf was constantly harried about providing a successor for the House of Habsburg. Maria de Medici of Florence had been proposed to him as a potential bride in the 1590s, but as with his cousin Isabella, the Infanta of Spain, he was unable to commit himself. Yet he was furious at the news of Isabella's impending marriage to his younger brother Albrecht, whom the dying Philip had made Viceroy of Portugal and the Governor of the Low Countries as the dowry of his daughter. They married in 1598.

Two years later, Albrecht wrote to Rudolf: 'They say you are an alchemist, an astrologer, and that you are given to necromancy. If this be true and Your Majesty has fallen into the habit of using the services of the dead and other supernatural sources to attain his ends, pity the House of Austria.'[12] Despite his concern for his dynasty, Albrecht followed Rudolf in being a great advocate of peace. He successfully negotiated successive treaties which wound up three wars in the north with France, England and Holland.

In the meantime, Rudolf also fell out with his youngest brother, Maximilian, the Grand Master of the Teutonic Order, who had succeeded their uncle Ferdinand as regent of Tyrol in 1597. They were similar in many ways, as patrons of artists and of adepts in alchemy and magic, but when Rudolf tried on a whim to assert direct control over the Tyrol, they understandably became estranged.

Rudolf was not only being criticised by his family but the Vatican soon stepped up its attack. He liked to act independently and hated being told what to do or to believe, especially by the papal nuncios who were becoming increasingly exasperated by his failure to give unconditional support to the Catholic cause. Rudolf's revulsion grew to such a degree that after 1600 he refused to have any Roman sacraments. He felt the need for absolution but demanded that his confessor drop the words '*auctoritate apostolica*' – referring to the authority of the Pope – while giving it.

Rudolf's swing between apparent support and then violent rejection of the Counter Reformation merely reflected his inherent weakness of will and his deep spiritual malaise. Yearning for security and fearing the future, he found it difficult to make a clear decision. As a result, he often postponed any decision until it was almost too late and then would suddenly decide in an arbitrary fashion. Circumstances were changing fast at the turn of the century, and Rudolf was unable to adapt to them.

It was at this juncture that the papal nuncio Spinelli decided on a new approach. He abandoned his policy of persuasion and tried to dominate the Emperor through threats of excommunication. The more evasive and fluid Rudolf was, the more exasperated he became.

On 25 September 1600, Spinelli at last managed to attain an audience with the Holy Roman Emperor, serving only to confirm Rudolf's worse fears that there was a plot against him. When the Cardinal left, Rudolf complained to his servants about his bad breath: it was widely thought that the breath expressed the state of a person's soul and Rudolf felt sullied by Spinelli's too intimate presence.

After the interview, Rudolf remained in a great state of agitation. The president of the Chamber of Finances wrote:

> Night and day the Emperor is tortured by the idea that he is abandoned, that he can have confidence in no one, that his subjects have lost their respect for him, that one wants to take his power and his life from him, that one wants to poison him, that one is bullying him, that he is obliged to bend to the will others.[13]

In this troubled and paranoid state, Rudolf suddenly identified his long-serving minister Wolf Rumpf von Wullross as the instigator of the plot against him. He had been Chamberlain and as High Steward and President of the Privy Council had come to control most of the important decisions. Was he not, after all, the agent of his hated brother Matthias? In the middle of the night, the Emperor was consumed by panic and ferocious anger. He called for

Rumpf immediately. When his old and bewildered minister entered, sleep still in his eyes, he accused him of treason and attacked him ferociously with a dagger. Only a sudden clap of thunder stayed his arm momentarily. Rumpf fled.

Far from calming down, Rudolf, in a frenzy, turned the dagger against himself; since the heavens were against him as well as the earth, there was nothing left to live for. Just in time manservants sent in by Rumpf grabbed the demented Emperor and prevented him from plunging the dagger into his own breast. Tearing himself from them with superhuman energy, he then broke a window and tried to cut his throat with one of the pieces of glass. Again, the servants managed to pull him down. At last Rudolf's energy was spent. Sobbing, he collapsed.

Two captains were thereafter posted at the doors of his chamber with strict orders to admit no one except his servants. Rudolf fell into deep despair, often remaining immobile for hours on end. He still insisted on Rumpf leaving Prague immediately and when his counsellor Paulus Sixt Trautson tried to intervene on his behalf he banished him too. He ordered a clean sweep throughout the administration, only retaining his secretary Barwitz and his two trusted secret agents, the Lords of Liechtenstein and of Hornstein.

Despite all the nuncio's pleas, Rudolf adamantly refused to see a priest. During the nights of insomnia which followed his breakdown, the idea suddenly came to him that it was the Capuchins who were to blame for all his troubles, those austere and militant monks whom the Pope had sent to reverse the Protestant rot in the kingdom of Bohemia and who had so disturbed Tycho Brahe by their bells. And had not Brahe prophesied that the Emperor would die 'at the hands of a monk'?[14] He felt that their very presence had an evil effect on him. He therefore sent a messenger to the Archbishop of Prague ordering them to leave the city immediately. The Archbishop Berka refused point blank. Rudolf insisted; Berka wrote two letters to the Emperor imploring him to leave the pious and obedient monks in peace. Then with Jesuitical cunning, the Capuchins managed to dispel his wrath: they called from Venice the painter Cosmus de Castelfranco and commissioned him to paint the *Adoration of the Holy Kings*. The remedy worked; Rudolf softened; they could stay after all.

Art, not threats, was the cure for all the Emperor's ills. He was further cheered by a gift from Cardinal Torriani of the *Danae* by Titian and by the acquisition of the bust of his illustrious ancestor Charles V by Leoni. He sat in front of this imposing visage and found new strength within himself.

Then, as luck or providence would have it, Pope Clement VIII sent Father Johannes Pistorius of Nidda as his confessor. At one time Lutheran, Calvinist and Catholic, Pistorius was an able physician as well as a learned theologian and Cabalist. He understood illnesses of the mind as well as of the body. Rudolf realised that he was dealing with a man of learning, not a blind fanatic. After talking with the Emperor, he wrote back to Rome: 'He is not possessed, as certain people judge, but he works with melancholy. However, despite the long passage of time, this has hardly taken root.'[15]

Thanks to his benign care, Rudolf gradually recovered from his worst delusions. During Holy Week in 1601, Pistorius even persuaded the Emperor to fulfil his religious duties – the sacraments of communion and confession – which usually caused him great anguish.

Even so, rumours that Rudolf was possessed by the Devil continued to circulate. Some suspected his valet de chambre Hieronymus Makofsky of Machau because he read occult books. Others said that he had sold his soul to Satan in his alchemical studies in pursuit of the Philosopher's Stone. The Margrave of Ansbach reported back to the Calvinist Elector Palatinate that the Emperor hated priests, especially the Capuchins who bullied him, and preferred the Lutherans whom he considered 'more faithful and frank'.[16]

At the beginning of the seventeenth century, when affairs of empire had to be addressed, Rudolf was still comparatively lucid. For questions of art and science, he had lost none of his habitual discernment. But when it came to issues of religion, the new Renaissance learning and his occult studies had left him painfully anxious and perplexed.

THE RECLUSE OF PRAGUE

Tis all in peeces, all coherence gone
All just supply, and all Relation . . .

John Donne

D id Rudolf descend into madness at the turn of the century? Certainly there was madness in the family: both his great-grandmother, Juana la Loca, and his Spanish cousin Don Carlos had succumbed and his own son Don Giulio was to follow suit. Rudolf had suffered a period of depression in the late seventies and possibly a nervous breakdown around 1600. But depression is not the same as madness. The suggestion moreover made by Melchior Goldast von Haiminsfeld in 1612 that Rudolf had become mentally diseased through dissipation seems to have been based more on court gossip than any recorded medical diagnosis of the *morbus gallicus* – the contemporary phrase for syphilis.[1]

Rudolf was not even the 'the sanest madman' in Christendom as he has been described by the historian R.J.W. Evans.[2] To claim that Rudolf was insane is far too simplistic. Certainly his behaviour became stranger at the turn of the century and perhaps he was a little unhinged for a time. He certainly suffered from paralysis of the will, he underwent periods of deep depression, but it does not follow that he was mad. His deepening melancholy resulted neither from possession by the Devil nor his genetic make-up, but rather from the painful gulf between his aspirations to discover the Philosopher's Stone and to bring about universal harmony, and a tragic sense of his own decaying self and crumbling empire.

In truth, he was most likely a man who suffered from manic depression – occasionally incapacitating him or exciting sudden outbursts. He was undoubtedly eccentric and insecure and saw himself on a different plane to most other human beings. But he was not mad in the clinical sense of being completely out of touch with reality. However ill and erratic in his behaviour, he was no fool when it came to recognising talent in art and science. And in politics, which he despised, his apparent indecision proved to be a form of wise hesitancy.

There was even a certain method to his apparent madness. It was well known that Rudolf would often abuse his ministers publicly, and in a sudden fit of violent rage, he banished his chamberlains Rumpf and Trautson. But Rudolf's long-nurtured suspicion that they had been plotting against him was probably well founded. As for his hatred of the fanatical Capuchins, it was partly justified by their desire to foment religious discord and spearhead the Counter Reformation. Equally, Rudolf was quite right to distrust the motives of his courtiers who were all jostling for power, and to be more at ease with his comrades in truth – his artists, scholars, craftsmen, alchemists and astrologers. As his sympathetic confessor Pistorius put it, Rudolf's illness was not madness but a case of extreme melancholy. Melancholy had a specific meaning at the time. It was one of the four humours distributed in a person associated with the four elements and planets. Physically the result of an excess of black bile, melancholy was identified with earth, the dullest of the elements, and Saturn, the most sombre of the planets.

While it was generally accepted that one's personality type was largely determined at birth according to the stars, there was a theory in the Renaissance, made fashionable by Marsilio Ficino, that melancholy could be transformed from the lowest of the four conditions to the highest, to become 'the humour of great men, great thinkers, prophets and religious seers'.[3] Scholars, for instance, who were prone to melancholy could transform themselves by surrounding themselves with stones, plants, animals and people who were associated with the life-affirming planets – the Sun, Venus and Jupiter.

Dürer's engraving *Melencolia 1* (1514) is a vivid illustration. The sitting and pensive woman, surrounded by a disordered array of instruments and tools and with the wings of Time on her back, is usually depicted as a tragic genius overwhelmed by frustration and despair. But on closer scrutiny she appears to be in an intense visionary trance. She is inspired and protected by the spirit of Saturn. The starved dog at her feet is not necessarily a symbol of a depressed state but rather of the physical senses brought severely under control in the first stage of inspiration.

Engraving of Albrecht Dürer's Melencolia, I. *Rudolf suffered all his life from melancholy and sought relief by collecting and encouraging the arts and sciences*

Rudolf, who was born under Saturn, seems to have moved on occasion in the opposite direction, from melancholy's transformation into genius to a descent into morbidity. It was an alchemy of personality recognised by Robert Burton in *The Anatomy of Melancholy* (1621). The more Rudolf strove to become a great prophet, the more he realised his incapacity, which made him feel only more lugubrious. Yet as Burton pointed out there was a way out of the apparent impasse. Melancholy might be ingrained in his personality from birth, but its symptoms could be alleviated through certain medicines and elixirs, by a peaceful and pious life and by the contemplation of the beauty of God's Creation.[4] Despite his deepening problems, Rudolf's sombre disposition did improve somewhat through these means after the crisis of 1600.

Unfortunately for Rudolf, as Holy Roman Emperor he was an isolated and lonely figure at the apex of the great pyramid of empire. He was unable to trust his ministers and courtiers and had no faith in the word of diplomats, especially those from the Vatican and Spain. Now that his favourite brother Ernst was dead he had no one in his family in whom he could confide.

Although his long-serving mistress Katharina, daughter of the court antiquary Ottavio Strada, was always there, she does not seem to have reached his innermost being. He was more interested in art and science than conjugal love and warmth; he sought to penetrate the mysteries of nature rather than to enter the heart of another mortal. Although she occupied an apartment in the Castle, bore him several children and had remained a faithful and supportive companion for seventeen years, he rarely saw her. Jealous courtiers spread rumours that she had conspired with a butler to steal from the collections, but this was hardly likely from the daughter of their chief curator. She offered unwavering loyalty and silence; in return, the Emperor ensured that she and her children were cared for at court. Nevertheless, his everyday companions were mainly his valets who occasionally brought him an imperial courtesan.

The exact number of children Rudolf had with his long-suffering companion is not clear. One source says six, of which three were girls and three boys, and another says eight, of which four were boys and four girls.[5] They had mixed destinies. The oldest daughter Carolina seems to have married into a bourgeois family but her two sisters retreated to nunneries in Vienna and Madrid. Of the younger sons, one was killed by a friend in an alley in Vienna in a dispute over a prostitute. Another died in the Thirty Years' War.

None of the children seem to have been remarkable, except for Don Giulio, who was also known as Julius Caesar and Don Juan of Austria. He seems to have been Rudolf's favourite and shared with him a fascination for clocks and mechanical instruments. But he was cursed with an unfortunate horoscope and the Habsburgian Portuguese inheritance, and soon started to show signs of the same malady which afflicted Don Carlos, the son of Philip II. At nine, he started having epileptic fits; at sixteen, he began scandalising the court with his arrogance and his cruelty to animals and servants. In 1606, Rudolf had to send him away from the court to Krumlov Castle in southern Bohemia. As a savage huntsman, Don Giulio lived there among weapons, fierce dogs and uncured skins, preying on the local girls.

Rudolf could have turned to his mother Maria, like the children of Catherine de' Medici in France, if only she had not been so rigid, domineering and so intransigently Catholic. She had returned to Spain not long after the death of her husband and in her final years had entered a convent of barefoot Carmelites near Madrid. When she died in 1603 at the age of seventy-five, Rudolf did not attend the obsequies in Prague nor did he seem particularly affected by her death. It just provided another excuse not to see anyone.

Rudolf had still not given up the idea of marrying and having a successor – anything to keep his thrones out of the grasp of his hated brother Matthias. Disguised as ambassadors, he sent his painters to the small courts of Europe in search of a suitable match: Julie d'Este, niece of the easy-going Cardinal Alexandre d'Este; Archduchess Anne, daughter of his uncle Ferdinand of Tyrol; the Princess of Württemberg and Princess Marguerite of Savoy. The portraits of these young, accomplished and beautiful women adorned his *Kunstkammer* like members of an imaginary harem; but Rudolf enjoyed contemplating them rather than touching them in the flesh. Yet even if he never made a move, he still felt a certain proprietary right to them. When Maximilian approached him to ask permission for Matthias to marry his cousin Anne, it only deepened his resentment against his brother, though he eventually sent the Archduchess a magnificent set of diamonds and rubies as a wedding present.

At the very time that he was losing his grip on power, Rudolf continued to commission new works of art and buildings. In the grounds of the Strahov Monastery above the Castle, he had his architect Giovanni Battista Bussi lay out the Church of St Roch in the shape of a cross in 1602 in gratitude to the saint for sparing Prague from the plague of 1599.

In 1602 Rudolf also had made for himself a magnificent new crown as a symbol of his glory. The Dutch goldsmith Jan Vermeyen supervised the making of a highly wrought crown made from enamelling, gold, diamonds, rubies and pearls with a huge pear-shaped sapphire in pride of place. The large pearl in the central panel was the property of Charles V, stolen by the Spanish conquerors from a native diver in the Gulf of Panama, while the other pearls were given by the Persian ruler Shah Abbas. Based on designs made by Dürer for Maximilian I, the crown had four convex triangles decorated with reliefs: three depicted Rudolf at his Hungarian, Bohemian and imperial coronations and the fourth represented him as conqueror of the Turks. The name 'Rudolf' was engraved on the inside. It became his most precious and magnificent possession. The wealth was real; the workmanship, superb; the sentiments, tragically ill-founded.

Despite his failing health and collapsing empire, his artists continued to produce works of art exalting him not only as the Augustus-Imperator but as the conqueror of the Turks, the liberator of Hungary and the mediator of Europe. In 1603, he commissioned Adriaen de Vries to make two bronze busts: one of his grandfather Charles V and one of himself. The meaning was clear: he wanted to present himself as the natural heir to his illustrious ancestor. Yet de Vries was not entirely an abject Habsburg propagandist. Rudolf's bust is quite realistic, showing him to be full-faced. Another bust of Rudolf made by de Vries in 1607 offers an even more intimate portrayal, presenting him as dignified but somewhat sad.

Rudolf continued to intervene in his studios and suggested ideas – which he called 'impressions' – to his artists. He recommended to Adriaen de Vries a cycle of allegories on the Turkish wars. It included the depiction of Rudolf in armour wielding a lance on a rearing stallion although he had never participated in a battle in his life and had never gone to the Turkish front. Such imperial propaganda was intended for popular consumption. Unfortunately, the myth could not be further from the truth and wishful thinking was not enough to hold back Rudolf's enemies. The brush at this stage was not mightier than the sword.

In 1603, von Aachen also produced a triumphant portrait of Rudolf. The central bust of the *Romanorum Imperator Augustus*, clad in armour and crowned with laurel on his head, is surrounded by heavy neo-classical architecture supporting three male figures representing military Victory, Knowledge and Virtue. At the top is Rudolf's devise ADSIT – *a Domino salus in tribulatione*, meaning 'In trouble, deliverance comes from the Lord'. It is placed above the fish-tailed goat representing the zodiac sign Capricorn (the sun sign of Augustus) and the Habsburg imperial eagle. At the bottom are two half-naked figures with their arms tied behind their back symbolising the conquered infidel. Dedicated to the '*augustissimo, invictissimo, sapientiss, et feliciss Rom: Imperatori, Rudopho II*', it became as printed by Aegedius Sadeler the most widely circulated portrait of the Emperor.

While Rudolf entirely approved of von Aachen's work, he may have had mixed feelings about a triple portrait of himself, his grandfather Ferdinand I and his father Maximilian II by the Galician painter Paulus Roy. Rudolf would have appreciated the ingenuity of the grid-based portrait, painted on a wood panel covered with little grooves. Looking from one side, the portrait of Rudolf appears; from the other, Ferdinand and Maximilian. It is the oldest known painting of this particular kind of *trompe l'oeil*. To see his illustrious ancestors depicted next to him no doubt underlined his own sense of inadequacy and ineffectiveness at the time.

Rudolf would have preferred the elaborate *Allegory of the Reign of Rudolf II* (1603) which seems largely an excuse for cavorting, half-naked nubile women by Dirk de Quade van Ravesteyn. Full of emblematic devices, it depicts Justice with a sword between her legs, flanked by Abundance and Peace with a dove on her shoulder.[6] Between them sits Knowledge, who pushes away a soldier representing Mars, behind whom is a shadowy Turk in a turban. The Ottoman threat is always there in the background. The mighty Eagle of the Habsburgs is painted with outstretched wings. The whole was clearly

Allegory of the Reign of Rudolf II (1603) by Dirk de Quade van Ravesteyn.
Justice, with a sword between her legs, is flanked by Abundance and Peace,
while the Ottoman threat skulks in the shadows

intended as an allegory of the fruits of Rudolf's reign which allowed
knowledge to flourish and maintained a difficult peace.

In reality, there was growing bigotry and conflict in Rudolf's empire as well as
in the rest of Europe at the beginning of the seventeenth century. The imperial
myth of peace, harmony and abundance had never been more distant. Despite
Rudolf's attempt to unite Europe, individual states ignored his pleas and
continued to pursue their own interests. Having ended forty years of religious
civil wars, Henri IV of France had signed the Treaty of Vervins with Philip II
but maintained friendly relations with Turkey to keep Germany and Spain in
check. Catholic Spain distrusted Rudolf, whom they considered little short of
a heretic. Venice was careful not to antagonise the Turks so that its merchant
fleet could operate in the Eastern Mediterranean. Only the Protestant princes
of Germany gave the Holy Roman Emperor political support and financial aid
but again it was only to further their own cause.

Abandoning his hope to bring together East and West, Rudolf still
believed in his grand plan to create a pan-European Christian League, uniting
Protestant and Catholic against Turkish expansionism. But unlike his uncle
Philip II who sought absolute control over his dominions, Rudolf wanted
passive control and preferred persuasion to force. Even so, he had little desire
or time for discussion and a great reluctance to see diplomats.

Although a tiny majority in the land, the Catholic nobility had come to
dominate the administration of Bohemia after the cabinet changes at the turn
of the century. In many Austrian lands, including Upper Austria and Styria,
Rudolf's brothers were persecuting the Protestants. In his unstable state of
mind Rudolf was increasingly given to impetuous and ill-considered
decisions.

At Strasbourg, a civil war threatened between Catholic and Protestant
factions over the election of a bishop. When Henri IV supported his
illegitimate son as a candidate, then aged twelve, Rudolf reacted violently.
Feeling his own authority and the traditions of the House of Habsburg once
again challenged, he wrote – a rare occurrence – to the Pope whom he usually
wanted to keep at bay:

> This is not only an offence against the Emperor and his House, but a
> violation of the privileges of the bishops of the Empire by which the
> bishops and the canons must have a double princely ascendance since

several generations. It would be a mortal danger for the Church of Germany if the bishop of Strasbourg were to go to a man 'born of a cursed kiss'.[7]

Under intense pressure from the papal nuncio Cardinal Spinelli, Rudolf had agreed in 1602 to re-establish the mandate against the Czech Brethren, with medieval pageantry and court fanfare, which in effect outlawed them. The decree annulled earlier freedoms granted to them and ordered the confiscation of their property and the closure of many of their schools and chapels. This sudden and uncharacteristic *volte face*, which he was later to regret seriously, was a sign of Rudolf's illness.

The Protestant Bohemian Estates decided to forget their differences and form a united front. It only added fuel to the religious discord in the land. Shocked by his apparent change of heart and distrustful of his growing isolation, the people of Bohemia began to turn against him.

Rudolf soon grew disillusioned with the new Catholic orientation of his crumbling administration and resented the increased power of the Spanish and Vatican factions at court. Only Matthias's attempt to win support from the Protestant estates of Austria, Hungary and Moravia made him retain some contact with the Vatican and its nuncios in Prague. Nevertheless, his European reputation as a humanist had not dimmed. In 1609 James I of England dedicated to him, as the greatest prince of Christendom, his defence of a secular monarchy against the claims of the Pope.

Rudolf did not like his personal initiative to be blocked by the established administration. As a result, the Privy Council floundered while he preferred to deal with his own chosen advisers. The administration had gone into steady decline and, by the turn of the century, it was in a state of near collapse. The resumption of the war with the Turks in 1604 only increased the pressure. Throughout this time, Rudolf made matters worse by refusing to make prompt decisions or to delegate his authority. In reality, while he embodied the mystique of the House of Habsburg, he had little real power. His policy of 'wise hesitation' which had proved effective now looked more like serious neglect. His absolutist tendencies and his refusal to compromise contributed greatly to the worsening of the situation.

Rudolf increasingly turned to his valets for reassurance and help. One was Blahel, the shadowy keeper of Rudolf's stoves, an essential task in the draughty rooms of the Castle in the Bohemian winter. Another was Hieronymus Makofský of Machau. He was an Utraquist, that is, he accepted the communion of both the Catholic and Protestant Churches, which made him doubly suspect at court. And then there was an ambitious new valet, Philip Lang, a converted Jew from the Tyrol. While overcoming Rudolf's natural suspicion, he began stealing works of art from his *Kunstkammer*.

There was considerable rivalry between the three men. Blahel informed Rudolf that Lang had bewitched him; Rudolf dismissed the idea. When Makofský was mysteriously killed, Lang became even more impudent and indispensable. Rudolf's worst fear seemed about to be realised: his assassins were coming closer and closer. It was not long before he entrusted the unscrupulous Lang to receive all his correspondence, even from the Archdukes and Electors, and to act as his go-between with the outside world. Lang even controlled military and civil appointments.

Despite his melancholy, Rudolf still played with his dream of forming a grand alliance of Spain, the Italian States, Poland, Russia and eventually England to break the power of the Ottoman Empire once and for all. He had not given up his vision of East and West shaking hands above the Mediterranean and destroying the Turks. To this end, he continued to court Persia, which had recently had some success against their common enemy. When a Persian ambassador came to Prague, the Emperor received him with an unusual display of splendour. Rudolf refused to let him kiss his feet and offered his hand instead. But when his servants advanced on their knees at great speed to do the same, 'This way of showing reverence made his Majesty laugh, something which has not been seen for twenty years.'[8] Needless to say, Rudolf was unable to realise his great project as individual nations were too concerned with following their own interests. Rudolf was hardly capable of uniting his own army, let alone Christendom.

Rudolf could, however, still be decisive and intransigent when it came to the troubled lands of Transylvania and Hungary, constantly threatened by the Turks and torn apart by religious conflict. Protestant rebellions in Transylvania and Hungary at the beginning of the new century soon turned the region into a battleground between the main religious factions. In 1604, matters came to a head when the imperial army led by Italian Catholic generals mistreated the Protestant people of Transylvania and Hungary by pillaging and terrorising them. The Hungarian parliament, supported by

Matthias for his own ends, made repeated protests against the persecution of Protestants. Rudolf refused any religious compromise and confirmed the edicts against the Protestants; it would seem that his rivalry with Matthias got the better of his judgement. But the measures only incited a revolt by Hungarian Protestant nobles led by István Bocskay, who signed a treaty with the Sultan of the Ottoman Empire and proclaimed himself prince sovereign of Transylvania and Hungary. His light cavalry devastated Moravia. In the ensuing turmoil the Turks seized the most important cities in Hungary. Vienna itself was under threat.

Maximilian called a meeting of his fellow Archdukes at Linz and proceeded to Prague where they urged Rudolf to give the government of Hungary to Matthias and to choose a successor. After keeping them waiting and then offering only a short audience, he refused their proposal outright. For the time being his prestige as Holy Roman Emperor was still sufficient for them to go no further. Nevertheless, Ferdinand of Styria wrote that privately the 'Archdukes are resolved to tear from him the sceptre and the crown'.[9] The noose around Rudolf's neck was beginning to tighten.

Suddenly, though, he roused himself from his torpor and had the Catholic Count Barbiano de Belgioioso arrested as responsible for the defeat. He had his best and most loyal general, the Saxon Protestant Baron Hermann Christoph Graf von Russwurm, make the accusation. It split the leadership of the imperial army which was directed by German-speaking commanders, whose council was represented by Russwurm, and by an Italian group, which included Belgioioso.

This development displeased Rudolf's favoured assistant, his former valet and now chamberlain Philip Lang, who considered Russwurm, the charismatic hero of the Turkish front, a potential rival for the Emperor's attention. He therefore told Rudolf that the general was playing a double game: while suggesting to him that he should assassinate the Archdukes, the general's real intention was to put Maximilian on the throne. Rudolf found it difficult to believe; he was thrown further into depression. In the meantime, the general attempted to reform the chaotic imperial army into a permanent force but had insufficient funds from Rudolf to pay off the mercenaries.

Despite Russwurm's efforts, the Turks took Gran fortress in Hungary after a long siege on 8 October 1605. The imperial mercenaries even sold their weapons to the enemy. The last straw was when Rudolf heard that Russwurm had been wounded in a duel with the recently freed Belgioioso who was shot dead by one of his party. Rudolf had recently made fighting duels in Prague a capital offence and to see the heads of the imperial army acting in this way was the last straw. Russwurm was arrested. Far from expressing remorse, he boasted that he had killed fifteen men with his sword and would do the same again. Paid by the Archdukes, Lang persuaded Rudolf to sign the death warrant for his most reliable general, insinuating that his very authority was being tested.

Not long after, in a sudden panic, Rudolf bitterly regretted his decision. He sent a reprieve but it arrived an hour too late. Russwurm's head had already been cut off. On the scaffold, his last words had been: 'I cannot hope that misfortune will spare a prince who has his best servants put to death without having listened to them.'[10]

Rudolf would pay the price; he had thrown away the only shield that would protect him. Magic would prove insufficient when it came to the final onslaught against his authority.

To make matters worse, an *Apology* appeared in Hamburg in 1605 written by the daughter of the arch Catholic Jiří Popel of Lobkovic, the former High Steward of Bohemia, whom Rudolf had incarcerated in 1593 for seeking the support of the Czech Estates in his bid for the post of Burgrave. The document, possibly inspired by the Jesuits, accused the Emperor of being an unjust monarch and the persecutor of innocents. Under hard questioning, Lobkovic refused to renounce his right to criticise the crimes of his sovereign and died in the royal dungeons two years later in 1607.

While usually humane and generous, Rudolf was becoming increasingly frustrated with the mutinies within his empire and the rumours of plots and assassinations at court. He insisted on the absolute obedience of his ministers; indeed, he considered them 'servants' rather than respected 'officials', lower even than his alchemists, astronomers and artists whom he frequently elevated to the nobility. Rudolf always had an intense desire to rule directly himself and would brook no opposition; he could be ruthless if checked or slighted.

In the worsening situation, the agents of the Vatican renewed their pressure at Rudolf's court as part of their wider campaign against Protestantism. They continually harried the Emperor about the lack of an agreed successor. They remained convinced, despite Pistorius's measured views, that Rudolf was bewitched. With the arrival of the new Pope Paul V, the hated Spinelli was recalled to Rome. The new nuncio Giovanni Stefano Ferreri duly reported on 4 April 1605 to Rome a remark allegedly made by Rudolf to Philip Lang: 'I know that I am dead and damned; I am a man possessed by the devil.'[11] It only confirmed the Vatican's worst fears.

As the storm clouds grew about him, Rudolf increasingly withdrew from the magical theatre of the world he had created around him. He retreated even from his gardens and beloved Belvedere to live within the security of the castle walls. He lived a life of solitude in a hushed palace, surrounded by his paintings and statues of beautiful women in alluring poses. In the satirical novel *Euphormionis Lusinini* written by the Scot John Barclay in 1607, he appears sitting at a table surrounded by astrological books and terrestrial and celestial globes. Close at hand is an alchemical laboratory in which he pursues the elixir of life and the Philosopher's Stone.[12]

The only people Rudolf now trusted were his artists, adepts and valets, some of whom were the most untrustworthy people of all. Beyond the castle walls, the erstwhile 'Good Master of Prague' was now called the 'Recluse of Prague'. He became so withdrawn from public life that it was even rumoured he had died.

THE LABYRINTH OF THE WORLD

They refuse to swim until the water is up to their mouths, and by then
it will be too late . . . In short, I think that the Babylonian confusion
can scarcely have been as great as this.

                              The Elector Ernst of Cologne (1610)

Rudolf's ambitious and Machiavellian younger brother Archduke
Matthias was being kept well informed of developments at Prague
Castle. One of his secret agents reported that the valets, painters,
alchemists and such people ruled the country and had the Emperor's ear. At
the same time, Rudolf did not shrink from his reputation as an *adeptus*; indeed
in 1606, he authorised the issue of a thaler which depicted him as an
alchemist, with various magical symbols on his coat. On seeing the silver
coin, the Pope sent a message via the nuncio in Prague warning Rudolf
against advertising his involvement with the forces of the 'inferior world' in
such a blatant manner.

Realising that Rudolf by now was a lost cause, the Vatican began to
support Matthias, a blunt soldier and staunch Catholic, as his successor.
Matthias's mentor and guide, Cardinal Melchior Khlesl, Bishop of Wiener
Neustadt and Vienna, counselled that the people of the empire would not be
united until Matthias took Rudolf's place.

Matthias had long been a scheming and sinister figure in Rudolf's life and
was jealous of his inherited power. They had grown up separately and there
had never been any love between them. Their first major dispute took place
as early as 1577 when Matthias on his own initiative and without informing
his brother attempted to take over the government of the Netherlands at the
request of some local nobles, an act Rudolf saw as a direct threat to his rule.

On the other hand, when Matthias fell out with their uncle Philip II in 1587, Rudolf had diplomatically tried to reconcile them. But Matthias's grasping ambition soon became all too apparent and from the late eighties they had only a few frosty meetings. After 1600 the two brothers were in open opposition to each other.

In April 1606, Matthias, in secret talks in Vienna to his fellow Archdukes Maximilian, Ferdinand II and Maximilian Ernst of Graz, presented a list of revengeful Propositions in which he condemned his brother outright. His criticism was devastating. He claimed that Rudolf had not only abandoned Catholicism altogether but hated and cursed all those who attended religious services.

> His Majesty has now reached the stage of abandoning God entirely; he will neither hear nor speak of Him, nor suffer any sign of Him. Not only does he refuse to attend any sermon, public service, procession or the like, but he hates and curses all who participate in them, being never more impatient of God and every good work on such holy occasions.

He then went on to insist that Rudolf's neglect of the affairs of empire was due to his deepening interest in magic and the Hermetic secrets, 'in wizards, alchemists, Cabbalists and the like'.[1]

Matthias appealed to his fellow Archdukes' interest by reminding them of the Turkish threat to Austria and the growing religious conflict in their lands. He eventually persuaded them that he was the only one able to negotiate a peace with the Turks and hold the empire together. In a momentous decision, they recognised him as head of the House of Habsburg and unaminously nominated him as their candidate as the future king of the Romans, but they rejected the idea that the Emperor should be forcibly removed from the throne. When Rudolf was informed of their decision, he was incensed and deeply hurt; now that Ernst was dead, his whole family had turned against him.

For the time being, Rudolf could still count on his subsidies from Rome, by now his only source of income apart from the tributes from the Bohemian Estates. In 1606, the nuncio wrote that the Emperor was battered by melancholy. He was further concerned that Rudolf's confessor Father Pistorius had on Easter Day put his hand on his head when giving absolution of his sins. Could it mean that he considered the Emperor to be possessed by the Devil? In the warm spring, it was reported that when the Emperor saw three flies on the table before him, he remarked: 'Ah! There are the Pope, the King of Spain and Archduke Matthias!'[2] He had correctly identified his principal enemies.

Matthias saw his fellow Archdukes' approval as a powerful endorsement of his policy and increasingly took affairs into his own hands. Brother stood against brother.

As governor of Hungary, he negotiated the Vienna Treaty on 23 June 1606 with Bocskay following the Hungarian-Transylvanian uprising of 1604. As military commander, on 11 November 1606 Matthias further negotiated the Zsitva-Torok Treaty with the Ottoman Turks to bide time and direct his forces from the eastern boundary of the empire to focus on Bohemia. It was agreed that the frontiers would rest as they were at the time, reducing the territory of Hungary by three-quarters. A handsome tribute of 200,000 guilders of silver, gold and other precious objects was also exacted. The Sultan swore to see in the Emperor a second father and the Emperor to accept the Sultan as his son. It was not an empty formula: it was the first time that the Ottoman Empire and the Holy Roman Empire had recognised each other in such terms.

Rudolf felt Matthias had betrayed him and was reluctant to sign either treaty. He still wanted to pursue the war against the Turks, recognising in them a constant threat to Europe and was shown to be right in 1683 when Vienna almost fell to them and was only saved by a pan-European coalition of forces. He was also still convinced that the Regensburg Reichstag would provide him the necessary funds to wage war against the Turks until they were completely defeated. His grand imperial vision had nothing to do with the *realpolitik* of his brother.[3] And Matthias was far from being qualified to be an emperor. His intervention in the Low Countries had been disastrous. He had, at a stroke, lost the war against the Turks and signed a dishonourable treaty purely in order to further his designs on the imperial crown.

On 8 March 1608 the Moravians elected Karel of Žerotín at the Landtag as the Supreme Land Captain. He and the Moravian leader Karl of Liechtenstein threw their weight behind Matthias against his brother. Events began to move swiftly. Rudolf called a sitting of the Landtag in Bohemia from

10–17 March which, against all expectations, temporarily strengthened his position. The only two individuals who made no secret of their support for Matthias were Václav Budovec of Budov, the leader of the Czech Brethren and former Court Master at the Imperial Embassy at Constantinople, and the Bohemian aristocrat Petr Vok Rožmberk, who had converted to their cause under the influence of his wife. Both Matthias and Rudolf were now courting the support of the Protestants, much to the fury of the Vatican.

Having refused to abdicate voluntarily and to cede the right of succession to Matthias, Rudolf made one final attempt to reassert his authority in April 1608. Despite being refused funds for the Turkish Wars by the Reichstag of Regensburg and never having been so weak and ineffectual, Rudolf still had unswerving faith in his imperial mission. He had always lived on the borders of fantasy but was now entering its unreal world.

On the advice of the Spanish envoy Don Guillén de San Clemente and the papal nuncio Antonio Caetano, Rudolf reluctantly agreed to ratify the peace treaty with the Turks. But it was not enough to halt Matthias's momentum. He arrived at the Bohemian border on 3 May with 20,000 men under his command. Although the Bohemian nobility refused to support Matthias, Rudolf could only muster 4,500 poorly equipped men. He was obliged to concede sole governorship of Hungary and Austria to Matthias and allow his brother's claim to the crown of Bohemia. Still Matthias was not satisfied; he wanted it there and then.

With enemy troops only 25 kilometres from the Castle, Rudolf called a meeting of the Landtag of the Bohemian Estates on 23 May 1608. It was the first time that he had appeared in public for years. The ranked delegates were stupefied as they contemplated the Emperor shuffle into the vast hall, walking with his eyes lowered behind his Chamberlain Johann von Waldstein, who carried his unsheathed sword. It was particularly shocking for those who had attended his coronations to see the 56-year-old Rudolf so bowed by his troubles. He looked like an old man with a skeletal frame, stooping shoulders, grey hair and a deathly pallor. On gaining his throne, he thanked in a feeble voice all for coming and apologised for not being able to conduct the debates. He then retired. Though marked by age and illness, the dignity of his comportment won the respect of the delegates. The Bohemian Estates decided to back him against his brother.

Rudolf refused to see his brother face to face. After another meeting between envoys, Rudolf finally agreed to sign the so-called Peace of Libeň on 25 June 1608 which handed over the kingdom of Hungary and the Archdukedoms of Austria and Moravia and granted Matthias succession rights in Bohemia. Unable to raise a substantial army, he had no choice. Two days later Matthias, still outside the castle walls, had himself crowned King of Hungary, taking the title and realm from his brother. Rudolf remained Emperor in title if not in reality. The former *Dominus Mundi* was now left with only a rump of his empire – the administration of Bohemia, Silesia and Lusatia.

If that was not bad enough, Rudolf's melancholy was further deepened by the news of his favourite son Don Giulio. Banished to Krumlov Castle, he had spent his days in hunting and debauchery. One day he went too far: he seized, raped and held captive a barber's daughter called Maruška from the local village. When after a month, she ran away he threatened to kill her father if she did not come back. On 17 February 1608, the day after her return, servants forced the door to Don Giulio's apartment to find the girl hacked to pieces with a hunting knife, her eyes gouged out, her teeth broken and her ears cut off. The Holy Roman Emperor's oldest and favourite son, naked and covered in excrement, was embracing his victim. He was confined to a chamber with barred windows. Four months later, he died like his cousin Don Carlos in mysterious circumstances.

With the Emperor now laid so low by his brother and son, the Protestant Estates pressed their advantage. Their representative Václav Budovec put forward a twenty-five-point declaration on behalf of the Protestant nobility in Bohemia calling for far-reaching religious and political freedoms. But the Catholics in his entourage urged Rudolf at all costs to postpone the discussion to a later date. Rudolf indicated to the Estates that the declaration would be granted but any final decisions on the matter of religion should be left to the next Landtag. In the meantime, it was agreed that all religious persecution would be forbidden in Bohemia.

Rudolf then signed the celebrated 'Letter of Majesty' on 9 July 1609 which assured complete religious freedom to the people of Bohemia, including the peasants. Although Rudolf's Catholic Chancellor Zdeněk Popel of Lobkovic refused to sign it, it confirmed at last in writing the *Confessio Bohemica* which Maximilian had promised shortly before he died and which had been embodied in the treaty of 1575. This was Rudolf's last great political act, albeit undertaken reluctantly, and it proved to be the greatest of his reign. It was the culmination of Rudolf's lifelong liberal attitude to religion and advocacy of tolerance. As even a hostile critic recalled: 'While he was monarch the inhabitants of this kingdom were for many years not hindered at all in their various religious deviations; each man thought and believed whatever suited him best . . .'[4]

The immediate result in Prague was that the Protestants could once again elect 'defenders' to the Consistory, completely independent of imperial authority, who would ensure that all religious groups would respect each other's rituals, possessions and claims. Prague University was again in their hands; it would be administered by the Estates who would be responsible for all appointments. New schools and churches could be built without restraint. The sealed document was taken to the Town Hall in the Old Town where for several days the people of Prague filed passed it as if it were a relic. The Charter of Tolerance, as it came to be known, recognised that the State could not dictate the religion of its citizens and was the most democratic religious law in Europe at the time.

Despite his abject loss of power, Rudolf still had his court artists paint him for posterity. Von Aachen painted from 1606–8 the most famous portrait of Rudolf from this period. Fitting the conventions of contemporary state portraits, it shows the Emperor in a black gold-buttoned tunic and a black bejewelled cap with a grey feather. Around his neck he has a stiff ruff and the symbol of the Order of the Golden Fleece hanging from a gold chain. His jutting chin, fleshy ears and bulbous nose are realistically portrayed as is the finely painted hair of his sparse beard and flowing moustache that reaches down over his thick protruding lower lip. The spectator's attention is drawn to the weary, hooded eyes with their puffy lower lids, dark irises and inflamed corners. It is the face of an ageing and melancholy man looking out from his own darkness.

Although quite incapable of making a decision in matters of the heart, Rudolf still went through the motions of seeking an empress among Europe's royalty. There were continual rumours of new marriage plans. Even as late as 1608, he was sending von Aachen to paint the daughters of the Italian dukes as possible matches. Johann Ruprecht Hegenmüller told Rudolf's sinister adviser Andreas Hannewaldt on 22 November 1608:

Yesterday His Majesty ordered me to write that you should make diligent and secret enquiries what sort of nubile princesses, or even high ranking countesses are available; Lorraine has had some good-looking females in its time and they say that Baden has something Catholic on offer.[5]

Rudolf still had Adriaen de Vries make heroic bronze busts of himself. One in 1607 shows him with the emblem of the Order of the Golden Fleece while another in 1609 associates him with the lion-killer Hercules. In the latter, a large lion mask was placed over the shoulder piece of his armour which implied that he was not only capable of overpowering such a creature but is

The most famous portrait of the mature Rudolf, painted by his court artist Hans von Aachen (1606–8)

himself the human equivalent of the king of the jungle. It was made at the nadir of Rudolf's power but was typical of the kind of imperial apotheosis which the court artists indulged in to earn their patronage. It was clearly intended for posterity, supposedly revealing the Emperor's real character stripped of his all-too-human failure, weakness and cowardice.

Not everyone was writing Rudolf off though. Some of his former glory, however faded, still impressed. The diplomat Daniel Eremita, who came to Prague accompanying the Tuscan embassy in 1609, observed that the Emperor clung to the dress and manners of earlier times and had withdrawn into himself: 'Disturbed in his mind by some ailment of melancholy, he has begun to love solitude and shut himself off in his Palace as if behind the bars of a prison.'

Eremita, who was irritated by being kept waiting, further lamented how Rudolf had abandoned the affairs of state for the study of art and nature and preferred to spend his time in his alchemists' laboratories, artists' studios and clockmakers' workshops. He has so delighted, he wrote,

> in the investigations of natural matters and the ornaments of painting, that he has even given up the cares of the empire and the business of princes for the study of the arts . . . For he himself tries alchemical experiments, and he himself is busily engaged in making clocks, which is against the decorum of a prince. He transformed his seat from the imperial throne to the workshop stool.[6]

On the other hand, he felt obliged to recognise the strength of Rudolf's mind and character:

> The Emperor's amazing knowledge of all things, ripe judgement, and skill have made him famous, while his friendliness, steadfastness in religion, and moral integrity have won him popularity; these were the principles of his outstanding and remarkable reign which gained the plaudits of the whole world.[7]

Apart from visiting his studios and workshops, Rudolf still called regularly on Johannes Kepler although the imperial mathematician now preferred to offer his advice in the form of short essays. He was very wary of giving Rudolf any astrological predictions for fear of offering him false hope and encouraging him to make rash decisions.

The heavens might have been turning regularly but administration of the House of Habsburg was in chaos. Rudolf's empire was collapsing and his brother's machinations were becoming more insolent and threatening by the day.

Throughout Europe fanaticism was growing and the forces of the Catholic Counter Reformation were on the move. For ten years there had been a cold war between France and the House of Austria. At the Edict of Nantes in 1608, Henri IV had secured the liberty of conscience for the Protestants. A dispute over the successors of the Duchies of Clèves and Juliers on the Dutch border threatened to precipitate a war between the two major powers. But on 14 May 1610 an apparent miracle took place: Henri IV was assassinated by the Catholic fanatic François Ravaillac. This deflected the impending war but it also made Rudolf shudder with fear. Had not Tycho Brahe predicted that the Holy Roman Emperor would be killed by the hand of a monk?

Matthias was still not satisfied without the crown of Bohemia and left Vienna with an army to wrest the last vestige of Rudolf's power. Desperate to check his advance, Rudolf made a serious error when he decided to ally himself with his ambitious young cousin Archduke Leopold V, Bishop of Passau, who suggested bringing a mercenary army to Bohemia. Although he had no military or political experience, the real motive of the twenty-three-year-old was to seize the crown of Bohemia for himself. Having lost his favourite son, Rudolf was easily seduced by his charm. Leopold claimed that only by force could Matthias and his Protestant allies in Bohemia be defeated. Despite the advice of his loyal counsellor and fellow adept Heinrich Julius, Duke of Brunswick, Rudolf agreed.

Leopold's ill-disciplined band of ten thousand mercenaries led by Colonel La Ramée arrived and camped on the White Mountain outside Prague on 30 January 1611 and two weeks later occupied the right bank of the river. Rudolf had no money left in his coffers to pay them. Rather than being his shield, they were to prove his downfall.

The Vatican was more cautious. Aware of the negative reaction of Prague citizens to the aggressive and brutal behaviour of the mercenaries, the Pope's envoy and the Spanish ambassador arranged a meeting with Leopold in a Capuchin monastery. They insisted that his forces be disbanded. But it was already too late. La Ramée occupied the Lesser Town and threatened to burn the Old Town but his troops were prevented from crossing the main stone bridge. Protestant defenders attacked many Catholic churches and monasteries, including the Jesuit College of St Clement and the Franciscans of St Mary of the Snow. Stories were told of Italian residents shooting at Protestants from windows. The Jewish Town was invaded and plundered.

With his band of mercenaries, Rudolf had finally alienated both the Catholics and Protestants of Bohemia. The papal nuncio and the ambassador of Spain left Prague and went over to Matthias's side.

As a precondition of the prompt departure of the Passau Army, Petr Vok Rožmberk agreed to pay off the mercenaries – a decision which cost him his entire family fortune. They left on 8 March 1611, followed two days later by the Archduke Leopold, Bishop of Passau.

Rudolf at last realised that it was the end. Despairing of ever regaining his power he locked himself away in his darkened rooms. Drinking heavily, he could be heard at night running down the corridors, crying out nonsense such as his back and stomach had changed places.

He could no longer trust his administrators and valets; his artists, alchemists and astrologers were his only consolation. Having failed with natural means, it was rumoured that he resorted to necromancy. Living increasingly in a fantasy world, Rudolf became convinced that his brother was trying to bewitch him.

Matthias and his forces were welcomed in Moravia and he entered Prague on 24 March 1611, accompanied by members of the Hungarian, Moravian and Bohemian nobility. Rudolf was forced to resign for neglecting the affairs of state. On 12 April, at a hastily called Landtag, the Bohemian Estates voted in favour of the usurper as long as he respected Rudolf's 'Letter of Majesty' guaranteeing religious freedom.

Rudolf had thought that he could at least rely on the Bohemian Estates who had so benefited from his benign rule. On hearing the news of their change of heart, he ran to the window of his palace in the Castle in a state of shock and looked across the steeples and roofs of the city which had seen so much change in his reign. He then uttered the terrible curse:

Prague, ungrateful Prague, I have made you famous but now you are driving me, your benefactor, out. Let revenge come upon you and damnation befall you and the whole Czech nation![8]

Rudolf's curse was a tragic ending to his idealistic project. The Philosopher's Stone had been for him a symbol of the harmony he had hoped to spread throughout the world. But Rudolf was not emotionally strong enough to realise his ideal and too gullible to distinguish between truth and falsehood. The weaker he grew politically, the more he came to rely on magic to achieve his ends. The final dreadful curse on the city he had loved showed how far he had fallen both morally and spiritually: Rudolf's Faustian yearning for all the knowledge and experience of the world ended in his personal downfall as a man and emperor.

With the full support of the Catholic and Protestant Estates, Matthias was declared King of Bohemia at Whitsun on 23 May 1611 in St Vitus cathedral where Rudolf had received the crown of St Wenceslas thirty-six years before. Not long after, he married the Archduchess Anne of Tyrol whom Rudolf had once thought of making his Empress.

Rudolf was allowed to live in Hradčany Castle with an income of one hundred thousand thalers a year and remain Emperor until he died. He was virtually a prisoner in his own palace and a real prisoner of his melancholy. He was so depressed that he could not even bring himself to walk in the Castle gardens where sweet music had once emerged from the carefully groomed groves.

Matthias's new regime imposed its presence by a dreadful cacophony. Guards let off their rifles to signal his comings and goings. Military bands replaced the court musicians, some of the best in Europe. Having all his life hated harsh noise, the rude sound of his brother's military entourage only made Rudolf's captivity all the more execrable.

For his part, Matthias tried to demonise his usurped brother. He wrote to Archduke Maximilian that terrible things intended to make him die a horrible death had been found in Rudolf's chambers. Legend has it that in his bouts of depression Rudolf was persuaded by one of his more dubious conjurors to participate in black magic rites. The alchemist-magician Christopher Hauser was said to have practised black magic on Matthias's clothes so that they would harm him. An imperial chaplain was accused of having baptised a dog in Matthias's name and then killed it in the hope that a similar fate would befall his namesake. Rudolf was reported to have witnessed ritual sex on an altar in a magic circle in order to countervail the supposedly destructive influences of his brother.

At the lowest point in a distressed life, the Holy Roman Emperor had become little more than Faust's conjuror but without his magical powers. Rather than sustaining him, the world around him was acting like a poison, slowly killing him.

Rudolf was a broken man. He hardly left his private rooms. His magic theatre of the world, which had drawn like a magnet so many great artists, philosophers and scientists, had become a prison. At one stage he even thought of going to live in Regensburg but Kepler did not want to leave his observatory nor Hans von Aachen his studio. They were his only solace now.

His hatred of his brother did not diminish. Whenever ambassadors or visitors would come, he was often heard to groan: 'He's snatched my crowns from me, one after the other!'[9]

Yet Rudolf still did not give up. He continued to intrigue about the succession – anything to avoid the mantle of Holy Roman Emperor passing to Matthias. He considered marrying a Protestant, either the sister of the Duke of Brunswick or the widow of the Elector of the Palatinate. He began to court the Evangelical Union who represented the Protestants and were calling for an interregnum. The Pope was alerted and wrote despairingly: 'Caesar turns towards apostasy.'[10] As one modern historian has observed: 'Though Rudolf cared much more for his thaumaturgic sovereignty than for any revealed religion, it was the Catholic temple which shook from his Samson-like orgy of self-destruction.'[11]

Despite desperate attempts to delay the inevitable, a final audience in the Landtag was arranged on 16 November 1611 to discuss the succession. It had all the appearance of a funeral. Rudolf wore a black velvet costume with a short and pointed collar, a black hat in the Spanish style, a black velvet cloak, black stockings and white shoes. As he stood on the last step of his throne, the great Caesar seemed like a shadow of his former self. On a table in front of him were placed two objects, a golden sword and a silver clock. One represented his imperial power, which was disappearing fast, while the other symbolised his passion for science and the passage of time, which was rapidly running out for him. A representative of the Electors declared that it was imperative to choose a new king of the Romans. Rudolf graciously thanked them for coming and said he would give his decision later.

Exhausted by the effort, he told his chamberlain Pruskovský afterwards: 'They have delivered my funeral oration! One would have said that they had taken counsel with God to decide that I will die this year!'[12]

There was one more altruistic mission Rudolf tried to get off the ground before it was too late. The Czech philosopher Jan Amos Comenius claimed after Rudolf's death that having achieved harmony in Bohemia by his 'Letter of Majesty', he wished at the end of his reign in 1610 to establish 'an Order or an Apprenticeship for defending the freedom of conscience'. The aim was to unite sympathetic Protestant and Catholic rulers and princes, about forty in number. He chose two Protestant nobles who had been persecuted for their beliefs, Jan Eusebius of Kahn of Austria and Jan Šmíd na Kunštátě, to head the mission but they failed to win over any converts. As an old man in 1626, Šmíd showed Comenius a golden chain Rudolf had given him as the badge of the 'Society of Peace' and said: 'This jewel of peace was made by his holiness the emperor with his own hands', adding, 'the curse of the God-fearing Emperor upon us who were ungrateful to him has now struck us'.[13]

The 'Society of Peace' was probably the same brotherhood that Rudolf tried to set up to reward those of his inner circle who had remained loyal. He called it the 'Order of the Knights of Peace', intended for those who had contributed to the maintenance of freedom of worship. The symbol of his Order was a gold arm band and its motto: 'Not I, only God'. The initiation of his old friend and fellow adept Heinrich Julius, Duke of Brunswick, into the Order was Rudolf's last physical act.

All this feverish activity undermined Rudolf's health which had long been fragile at the best of times. He caught bronchitis and, soon after, his legs began to swell. Contrary to the advice of his physicians, he insisted on putting on his shoes each morning to go and see his treasures in the *Kunstkammer*, his only lingering pleasure. Because of the pain he left his shoes on for two days, and when they were finally taken off, his legs showed the unmistakable signs of gangrene. His lungs were seriously damaged and his liver inflamed. But he refused to take the medicine of his physicians or let them wash his wounds. Instead, he took a potion from the Scottish alchemist Seton which contained amber and finely ground bezoar (gallstones from various animals). Although he had helped launch the new science, he still relied on the old. It was to no avail. In keeping with Tycho Brahe's astrological prediction, the erstwhile temporal ruler of Christendom died three days after the death of his favourite lion at seven o'clock in the morning on 20 January 1612.

During his short illness, Rudolf regretted that his oldest brother Ferdinand had died as an infant; if he had lived, he mused, he could have supported the weight of the crowns that destroyed him. But then he grew serene. His mind drifted back to his childhood. He told his chamberlains Barwitz and Pruskovský: 'My dear friends, when my father recalled me from Spain so that I could come back to my country, I was seized with such a joy that the following night I could not sleep. Why should I be sad at present, why should I not be more joyful since I begin my voyage towards my celestial home where there is no separation, no change and no evil.'[14]

To the end, he rejected, like his father, the last sacraments. He refused to confess to a priest and showed no sign of contrition. 'We would only want a priest if one could find one of our own kind', he was reported to have said to his servants.[14] This was later taken to mean that he wanted to die a Protestant or by some that he no longer considered himself a Christian.

Rudolf died alone with his two chamberlains, supported by no wife, no children, no family, no friends and no members of his court. Those who had been so obsequious and demanding during his life abandoned him in his death. The Caesar who had ruled half of Europe had been left to fight his demons of melancholy and face his death alone. His courtiers had left him for another rising star.

When the news of his death finally reached the people outside the castle walls, there was widespread and deep-felt mourning. They forgot the 'Recluse of Prague' and remembered the 'Good Lord' who had brought them years of peace and prosperity and had transformed their town into a great European city.

Rudolf was not buried as expected in the mausoleum of his father Maximilian in St Vitus cathedral within the walls of Prague Castle. Instead, his earthly remains were sealed in a lead sarcophagus – the first substance of the alchemists being also associated with Saturn – and placed deep inside the crypt under the mausoleum of his ancestors next to the coffin of Charles IV. It was a fitting place for a man who had spent most of his life searching for the Philosopher's Stone.

At the funeral, Matthias seemed to have feared the presence of his brother's spirit. He refused to give his respects to the corpse, which was dressed in an elegant cloak made in the Eastern fashion. His brain and heart were extracted and placed in separate visceral vessels and remain in Prague Castle, a common practice with the Habsburgs. Only Matthias's new wife,

Anne of Tyrol, whom Rudolf had nearly married, prayed passionately at the feet of the dead Emperor.

The labyrinth, a symbol of process and goal, of voyage and arrival, of pilgrimage and alienation, was a perfect symbol of Rudolf's spiritual, intellectual and artistic quest. Like Comenius, he had sought a *Centrum Securitatis*, a centre of peace, an inner paradise. As a pilgrim, he passed through the 'Labyrinth of the World', with its ultimately meaningless institutions and ideals, in search of the 'Paradise of the Heart', with its divine wisdom and peace.[15] Tragically, he lost his way before reaching the celestial city.

It was the world rather than Rudolf that was upside down. He was searching for reality in a world of illusions. His theatre of the world became a masked play in which the audience vacated the seats before the performance was over. By looking at the extraordinary and the extreme, he hoped to catch a glimpse of the real. His main interest was in finding the key to the riddle of existence and a way out of the labyrinth. But there was no Ariadne to lead him to the noonday sunshine of enlightenment and wholeness.

EPILOGUE

There are more things in heaven and earth, Horatio,
Than are dreamt of in your philosophy.

Shakespeare, *Hamlet* (c.1601)

On becoming Emperor, Matthias sent most of Rudolf's artists, alchemists and astrologers packing. Kepler was reconfirmed as Imperial Mathematician and asked to complete the *Rudolfine Tables* for the glory of the House of Habsburg. He left Prague to live in Linz, salvaging Brahe's astronomical data just before the Jesuits seized his instruments and papers in order to suppress any evidence for the Copernican system.

Roelandt Savery stayed on in Prague to complete some of his greatest paintings of natural harmony inspired by Rudolf's wonderful collection of exotic animals and birds. In his *Garden of Eden* (1618) and *Orpheus with Beasts and Birds* (1622) the creatures are in a state of quiet repose; predators ignore prey nearby. The peace in the natural world was undoubtedly intended to echo Rudolf's vision of universal harmony in the human sphere.

The power-seeking and unscrupulous Matthias was primarily motivated by territorial ambitions rather than seeking the good of the House of Habsburg, or that of the people in its dominions. The bluff soldier was no connoisseur but he fully realised the propagandist value of a good portrait. He therefore commissioned Rudolf's official court painter and close confidant Hans von Aachen to paint him around 1611 in his favourite clothes as King of Hungary: his right hand is placed on his hip in a show of triumph, while his left hand lies firmly on the Crown of St Wenceslas. He also got von Aachen to portray him as King of Bohemia between 1613 and 1614 to impress his subjects.

Roelandt Savery's Orpheus with Beasts and Birds *(1622), inspired by the creatures in Rudolf's menageries. It depicts Rudolf's vision of a harmonious world while Europe was engulfed in the Thirty Years' War*

Matthias did not linger in Prague and soon moved the imperial court back to Vienna. He found the Hofburg palace there much more congenial than the imposing castle with its dark and labyrinthine corridors haunted by his dead brother. The curtains of Rudolf's magic theatre of the world were drawn once and for all. The Rudolfine era, which had seen Prague become the artistic and scientific centre of Europe, was no more.

The early death of his wife Anne of Tyrol in 1618 meant that Matthias had no heir. Indeed, the House of Habsburg seemed predestined to sterility: neither Maximilian nor Albrecht had any offspring either. As a result, the fanatical Catholic Ferdinand II of Styria, brought up by the Jesuits, was recognised as the future king of Bohemia.

It was not a time for Christian love and forgiveness. Religious conflict, long checked by Rudolf's policy of compromise and procrastination, was increasing throughout Central Europe. The Prague Catholics began to counter-attack and violate Rudolf's 'Letter of Majesty', the self-rule of the Bohemian towns was abolished by decree and the Protestants were deprived of traditional offices. The levelling of two recently built Protestant churches on land belonging to the Benedictine monastery was particularly provocative.

A congress of the Bohemian Protestant nobility was convened in the spring of 1618 but was banned by the new sovereign. An angry group led by Václav Budovec, who represented the Czech Brethren, and Count Matthias Thurn, a military officer, marched up to the Castle on 23 May 1618 to the centre of the administration in the Old Royal Palace. In the dispute that followed three leading Catholic officials, including the supreme judge Jaroslav Bořita of Martinice and Vilém Slavata of Chlum, were thrown out of the windows to the gardens below. They survived the fall; Protestants saying that they fell on a dung hill; Catholics, that the Virgin Mary had miraculously spread out her mantle to break the fall. When the news of the Defenestration, as it came to be known, reached the town, citizens attacked churches and monasteries and plundered the Jewish Town once again. The Bohemian Estates elected thirty directors to form a government. It marked the beginning of the Thirty Years' War.

Hans von Aachen's portrait of
Rudolf's brother Matthias as King
of Bohemia (1613–14)

The childless Matthias, still pondering how to react to the turn of events, died on 20 March 1619. His death confirmed the famous prediction of Kepler for the year, the so-called horoscope of the seven M's: *'Magnus Monarcha Mundi Medio Mense Martio Morietur'* ('A great monarch of this world will die in the middle of the month of March).

Ferdinand II took over as King of Bohemia. But following a new constitution which separated Bohemia into a confederation of lands with equal rights, he was deposed by the Bohemian Estates in August. They were supported by the Estates of the other countries of the Bohemian Crown (Silesia, Lusatia, Moravia), Lower and Upper Austria and Hungary. Jesuits, the constant allies of Spain, were expelled from Prague and Catholic property was confiscated. The Calvinist Palatine Elector, Frederick V, known as the Palsgrave, the leader of the Union of the German Protestant Estates, was then elected as King of Bohemia by the rebel government of thirty members who gave power to the assembly of supreme land officials. The Hungarian Prince of Transylvania marched on Vienna.

Being situated on the middle section of the Rhine, the Protestant Palatinate had long been a serious threat to Spain's communications from its Italian dominions to the Netherlands, particularly as the routes through France and the Channel had been cut after the rout of the Armada. At the time of Frederick's election, the deposed Ferdinand achieved a considerable diplomatic coup by being crowned Holy Roman Emperor. He could count on the support of Spain and the Vatican as well as Maximilian, Duke of Bavaria, the leader of the Catholic Estates of Germany.

Rudolf's former entourage had taken heart when the wedding occurred in 1613 between Frederick V, the Elector of the Palatinate, and the poetess Elizabeth, daughter of James I of England. Francis Bacon and Sir Philip Sidney attended the celebrations in London. For many it seemed to anticipate the 'Chemical Wedding' of Sol and Luna described in the Rosicrucian manifesto which appeared two years later. It was hoped that at last Paracelsus's vision of universal harmony was about to be realised and the new Messiah 'Elias Artista' was about to return to bring about an alchemical trans-formation of the world and inaugurate a new 'golden age'.[1]

Well-educated and dashing, Frederick, however, was totally inexperienced at diplomacy and ignorant of war. His wife, a well-groomed beauty celebrated by the English poets John Donne and Sir Henry Wotton, was principally

Alchemists sought the Chemical Wedding of Sol and Luna, representing Sulphur and Mercury, in order to produce the Philosopher's Stone and to bring about universal harmony. Michael Maier, Atalanta fugiens (1618)

interested in court entertainments when not too pregnant.

When the 23-year-old Frederick was elected King of Bohemia in 1619 it was widely hoped that the new Protestant regime would be based on the principles of religious tolerance and freedom of thought and expression so espoused by Rudolf. Such hopes were tragically short-lived.

In 1620, a Spanish army marched from the Spanish Netherlands and occupied the Palatinate. Maximilian of Bavaria, on behalf of the recently elected German Emperor Ferdinand II, then marched on Prague with the support of troops of the Catholic League. Although outnumbered (about 20,000 to 26,000), Frederick's forces had the advantage on a desolate plateau on White Mountain just outside the city. But fog descended and they quickly fell into disarray. The infantry division commanded by Count Matthias Thurn fled as soon as the enemy came into range and a retreat rapidly turned into a stampede. Within two hours the battle was over. The Protestant nobles made a serious error in not arming the peasants as in the old Hussite days and Frederick himself did not even attend the battle. According to one legend, the Moravian infantry fought to the last man, but in fact they were mostly mercenaries who did not understand their German orders to retreat. The majority of the mercenaries surrendered; their leader even went over to the winning side. It seems that only Christian of Anhalt the Younger, son of the Supreme Commander, put up a spirited fight.

After the Battle of White Mountain and the unconditional surrender of Prague, a commission was set up by Ferdinand II to ask the question: How to punish the rebels in order that 'by the deed of the wholesome terror of the entire country they be led into obedience of the Emperor?'[2] In reply the commission arrested, tortured and ordered the execution of twenty-seven Bohemian and Moravian nobles and burghers (including one Catholic) in front of the Old Town Hall on 21 June 1621. Among them was the 74-year-old Vacláv Budovec, patriarch of the Czech Brethren and hero of the Defenestration, and Kryštof Harant of Polžice, musician and artillery commander. Rudolf's last physician, the anatomist Jesenský, who had given the address at Brahe's funeral and supported Kepler, was singled out. Because he had negotiated on behalf of the Estates, the new Emperor insisted that his tongue be cut off before he was beheaded and quartered rather than the other way round. His head was stuck on a pike with those of ten others on the tower of Charles Bridge as a warning. They were allowed to rot there for twelve years before their final remains fell into the swirling waters of the Vltava River or on to the heads of passers-by.

As for Frederick the Palsgrave, the 'Winter King', his life was spared but he lost his hereditary lands and went into exile with his wife and wagons the day after losing the battle. He spent the rest of his life in The Hague where he continued to call himself King of Bohemia. His daughter Sophia eventually became mother of George I of Great Britain.

Ferdinand II is said personally to have cut in two, with a pair of scissors, Rudolf's 'Letter of Majesty' guaranteeing religious freedom. He also had erected two obelisks at the spot where Martinice and Slavata fell from the window of the Old Royal Palace during the Defenestration. There was a swift take-over of the dominant positions in Bohemia by the Catholics. For the next two years, large-scale expropriations were carried out and land redistributed to Catholic loyalists.

The first decrees of the Counter Reformation of 1621 were aimed at the Czech Brethren, the Lutherans and the Calvinists. In the new constitution of 1624 all faiths were forbidden apart from Catholicism. The Jews, whose financial support was still needed, were allowed to remain in their own quarter. The Jesuits took over all the schools and printing presses and imposed rigid censorship. The new constitution further declared that Bohemia was a dominion of the House of Habsburg to be ruled not by election as before but by direct inheritance; it proved the end of Bohemian and Moravian independence for three centuries.

With the defeat of the 'Winter King' on White Mountain, Bohemian Protestantism, the oldest and among the most radical in Europe, was destroyed. The despairing philosopher Comenius went into exile with his community of Czech Brethren and many other Protestants. The dream of an alchemical revolution had disappeared in a puff of smoke. The extraordinarily creative era of humanist culture and religious toleration encouraged by Maximilian and Rudolf was over.

The Thirty Years' War officially began in Bohemia and Germany in 1618. Spain, still smarting from the rout of its Armada and jealous of the growing power of Holland and Venice, was more than willing to go to war.[3] The ensuing conflict between Catholics and Protestants devastated Europe. Bohemia alone lost almost a third of its population. Germany lost more than a third of its people and suffered from such famine that many resorted to cannibalism. When the Peace of Westphalia was signed in 1648 between Sweden and the Habsburgs, it was out of exhaustion of all the parties involved. There were no winners.

The great pillaging of Rudolf's unique and priceless collections began soon after his death; Matthias took many paintings to Vienna with him; Bohemian rebels sold his jewels to Nuremberg merchants to pay for their rebellion against Vienna; following the Battle of the White Mountain, Maximilian of Bavaria left with 1,500 wagons of booty which became part of Munich's now renowned art collections.

During the Thirty Years' War, Protestants and Catholics equalled each other in ruthlessness. When the Saxons occupied Prague for a few weeks in 1631, they left for Dresden with fifty wagons of precious loot. A few days before the Peace of Westphalia was signed in 1648, the Swedish chancellor gave orders for the occupying forces to seize what remained of the collections in Hradčany Castle. They tortured Dionisio Miseroni, Rudolf's aged guardian of the *Kunstkammer*, to give up the keys. They systematically drew up an inventory, dated 31 August 1648, and carted off in convoys for Queen Christina most of the precious works of art that had not already been taken.

Finally, Emperor Joseph II of the illustrious Habsburg dynasty appointed a commission in 1781 to itemise and sell off what was left so that he could turn the Castle into an artillery barracks. Dürer's *The Feast of the Rosary*, so coveted by Rudolf, went for one gold piece and 18 kreutzers. It is extraordinary that some works still remain in the Castle.

But not all of Rudolf's heritage was lost. His patronage had given considerable impetus to the Rosicrucian movement which emerged shortly after his death. The symbol of the Rosicrucian Brotherhood, also known as the 'Fraternity of the Rosy Cross', was a rose blossoming on a cross. A shadowy organisation, its symbolism first appeared in Heidelberg in 1600 although its main texts were not published until 1614–16. Its exact support remains uncertain – some have questioned its very existence – but three widely influential tracts were published which expressed the strongly Hermetic and alchemical ideas which had circulated in Rudolfine Prague. They aroused curiosity and speculation throughout Europe.

By his own admission, Valentin Andreae wrote the allegorical romance called *The Chymical Wedding of Christian Rosenkreutz* in 1604 although it was not published until 1616. The anonymous *Fama Fraternitas* typically presented the Brotherhood as an intellectual elite who had recovered a secret store of ancient wisdom and possessed occult powers through alchemical knowledge. It called for all men of learning to join in the moral and spiritual regeneration of society and its practice involved curing the sick and helping lost souls. The ideas and language echoed those of the Hermetic reformers who had gathered at Rudolf's court: Khunrath, Maier, Dee and Bruno. Maier in particular defended the movement in his *Verum inventum* (1619) which he dedicated to Christian of Anhalt and to the Brotherhood. Moreover, the Rosicrucian movement shared the *fin de siècle* atmosphere of prophecy, doom and revelation that prevailed at Rudolf's court.[4] In a debased form, it is still in existence with a wide, if discreet, following.

Even the great mystical philosopher Jacob Boehme, from Gorlitz, Silesia, was attracted to the lingering magical atmosphere of Prague and lived in the city between 1619 and 1620. He had served an apprenticeship as a cobbler but came under the influence of Paracelsus. In 1598, he had a mystical experience in which he felt he was surrounded by divine light for several days and became convinced that he had seen the light at the centre of 'The Book of Nature'. Then again in 1600 while examining the lustre of a pewter dish in the sun, he suddenly felt that the veil of nature was lifted and that he saw to the heart of matter. He wrote up his vision in *Red Sky at Morning* and, in this and other works, he stressed the divinity of the human soul and the importance of free will. Like Rudolf's adepts, Boehme's philosophy dealt with 'Alchemy in the cosmos: its first Matter and its Three Principles; Alchemical work in Man: the threefold life in him; The Eternal Essence and the Tincture in Man and Nature'.[5] Rudolf would have fully appreciated his faith in gnosis, the illumination of the soul through Hermetic knowledge.

Comenius, perhaps more than any other, best represented the currents of thought and mood at Rudolf's court.[6] In *The Labyrinth of the World and the Paradise of the Heart* (1623), he attempted to show how the celestial city could be built on earth through love. In *The Forerunner of Complete Wisdom* (1639), he further presented a method of continuous education based on the correspondences between words and things. It combined philosophy, alchemy and natural science in a millenarian vision of a new society. At the heart of Comenius's pansophy was an 'Academy of Wisdom' formed of an educated elite, very similar to that of the Rosicrucian movement. But Comenius was born too late, and, in exile and at the centre of the maelstrom of the Thirty Years' War, he looked back to Rudolf's reign as a golden age of peace and prosperity.

After Matthias's appointment of Kepler as Imperial Mathematician, it was finally agreed with the Brahe family that he could take custody of all his old master's celestial observations. He moved to Linz where he carefully selected one woman from eleven potential candidates to become the mother of his two children. His final choice was Susanna, the twenty-four-year-old daughter of a cabinet maker, only a year older than his stepdaughter. The only bar to his new-found happiness was that in 1615 his mother Katharina was accused of witchcraft, being alleged to have produced a 'witch's drink' for a prostitute recovering from an abortion and to have used a 'witch's grip' when brushing past a group of girls in a lane. Kepler devoted himself to her defence and it was only her eloquent refusal to admit guilt when shown the instruments of torture that brought her acquittal. Even while Kepler was laying the foundations of the Scientific Revolution, the baneful superstitions of the Middle Ages were still clearly very much alive.

To supplement his income, Kepler began to produce astrological calendars once again in 1616 which he described as 'a little more honourable than begging'. From 1618, he also produced an annual *Ephemeris* with tables giving the position of each planet for every day of the year, invaluable to astrologers and navigators alike. It was not his favourite work; in a letter explaining the delay with the publication of the *Rudolfine Tables*, he wrote: 'Some like the Tables and Nativities; I prefer the flower of astronomy, the artful structure of the movements.'[7] From 1615–21, he also published seven volumes of *The Epitome of Copernican Astronomy* which was to be his longest and one of his most influential books.

Despite his enormous contribution to practical and theoretical astronomy, Kepler remained a metaphysician to the end. He was both a visionary and a scientist. 'The astronomers', he believed, 'are priests of the highest god.' He considered his best work to be the *Harmony of the World* (1618), partly inspired by a work called *Harmony* by Ptolemy, which attempted to demonstrate that mathematical harmonies among the planetary orbits, speeds and distances from the Sun are linked on a deep level with music. By seeking to interpret and explain the universe in terms of celestial harmony and number, Kepler composed a reinterpretation of the ancient concept of the Music of the Spheres. True to his sense of religious enlightenment, he included a prayer near the end of the book:

O You who by the light of nature arouse in us a longing for the light of grace, so that by means of that You can transport us into the light of glory: I give thanks to You, Lord Creator, because You have lured me into the enjoyment of Your work . . . I have shown the glory of Your works to men . . . for my mind was made for the most perfect philosophising . . .[8]

As he was finishing the book, Kepler discovered his third law of planetary motion, the so-called 'harmonic law'. He was ecstatic and experienced a 'sacred frenzy' when he realised its import. It describes the mathematical relationship between the distances of the planets and the times they take to complete their orbits. It states that the ratio of the squares of the orbital periods of the two planets is equal to the ratio of the cubes of their average distances from the Sun. Taken together, Kepler's three laws form the foundation of the modern system of astronomy.

With Rudolf in the grave, Kepler dedicated the five volumes of his *Harmony of the World* to King James I of England in the hope that he would mirror the glorious harmony of God's Creation by bringing peace to the churches and nations of the earth. Only four days after Kepler completed the book and wrote the dedication, Protestant Bohemia rose and triggered the Thirty Years' War.

For all his savagery after the Battle of White Mountain, Ferdinand II confirmed Kepler's position as Imperial Mathematician. He went on to produce the *Rudolfine Tables* in 1624 which included Brahe's catalogue of a thousand stars, the latitudes and longitudes of many cities and logarithm tables. Kepler in a gesture of generosity gives Brahe's name on the title page as the primary author. The tables were the crowning achievement of Brahe's and Kepler's lives and would probably have never seen the light without the patronage of Rudolf.

To illustrate his concept of the history and nature of astronomy, Kepler had an ornate frontispiece designed for the *Rudolfine Tables*. It depicts a pavilion with twelve columns. At the back, a Babylonion astronomer stands using his fingers to make an observation. Nearer the front are Hipparchus and Ptolemy and then in the foreground sits Copernicus by an Ionic column. Tycho Brahe stands by a Corinthian column with some of his instruments hanging from it. Kepler himself is sitting at a desk to the right of Brahe, burning the midnight oil with a banner of his major books above him. Six goddesses represent the muses who helped Kepler in different ways: Magnetica, Stathmica (Weighing), Geometrica, Logarithmica, and one goddess holding a telescope and another with a globe. On the central panel at the base of the pavilion is a map of the island of Hven where Brahe built his Uraniburg, his City of the Heavens. At the top of the whole flies the Habsburg eagle. Coins fall from its beak, but, noticeably, very few over the author.

Kepler's last work *Somnium* was a whimsical twenty-eight-page story (with fifty pages of notes) and diagrams which has been called the first work of science fiction. The narrator visits Uraniburg but most of the action takes place on the Moon and is intended to show how the Earth and the heavens appear for the inhabitants living there. If only Rudolf had been able to take such a perspective on the intrigues at his court.

Kepler died on 15 November 1630 in Regensburg. He was in the position of professional astrologer to the wealthy general Albrecht von Wallenstein, Duke of Friedland and Mecklenburg, in his duchy of Sagan. He was still in thrall to the wanton daughter of astronomy. The general had commissioned anonymously a horoscope from Kepler in 1608 which predicted that in March 1634 there would be 'dreadful disorders over the land'. The general was assassinated on 25 February of that year by Irish and Scottish officers in his retinue.

On the evening of Kepler's death a meteor shower fell, as if marking the passing of a man who had revolutionised astronomy and retained his faith in God. Kepler was buried in the Protestant cemetery in Regensburg, although his grave is now lost, with his own epitaph:

> I measured the heavens; now the earth's shadow I measure.
> Skybound, my mind; Earthbound, my body rests.

As Einstein made clear, Kepler solved two fundamental problems in astronomy: the true movements of the planets as they would look to an observer on the nearest fixed star and the mathematical laws governing those movements. He also argued that Kepler's remarks on astrology show that 'the inner enemy, conquered and rendered innocuous, was not yet completely dead'.[9] Yet, like Einstein, Kepler hated the idea of an accidentally arranged universe. For all his concern for observation and experience and his careful mathematical theorising, Kepler was never able to free himself entirely from the way of thinking that he had inherited from his 'masters' Pythagoras and Plato. His ecstatic discovery of the elliptical orbits of the planets was seen as a confirmation of their theory of the Music of the Spheres.

There can be no doubt that, in his own words, Kepler 'cleansed the Augean stables' of the traditional geocentric cosmology. At the same time, he echoed the old Hermetic philosophers and anticipated the modern theory of Gaia by comparing the Earth to an enormous living being. He likened the tides to waves passing through the gills of a vast sea creature and suggested that the effects of the Sun and the Moon on tides result from their alternate states of sleeping and being awake.

Nevertheless, for all his deep religious faith and indebtedness to the sacred science of the ancients, Kepler made clear that his mathematics were not based on mystical intuitions but quantitative measurements. He wrote to the English mystic Robert Fludd that if a comparison is to be made between their works on harmony, 'I shall transmit the substance of mathematics in a mathematical manner, while you do so in a Hermetic manner.'[10]

The uneasy collaboration between Brahe and Kepler at Rudolf's court led to a huge leap forward in the understanding of astronomy and marked a watershed in the history of science. The Copernican Revolution began with Copernicus and ended with Newton but Rudolf's two imperial mathematicians played a central role. The Copernican Revolution not only transformed astronomy but brought about fundamental conceptual changes in cosmology, physics, philosophy and religion. And if Rudolf had not brought Brahe and Kepler together in his court – indeed, if he had not continually offered his imperial protection to scientists as well as to artists – it is probable that it would have been considerably delayed.

Newton acknowledged Brahe and Kepler as giants on whose shoulders he stood and while adopting the new Copernican cosmology he was, like them, steeped in the Hermetic tradition. He spent much of his life at Cambridge writing biblical prophecies and practising alchemy. Even his notion of gravity assumes occult forces at work in the universe. Furthermore, he held that there was an extremely subtle aether linking the Earth with the cosmos which had strong echoes of the *spiritus* of the Hermetic thinkers. And while he believed like Kepler that the underlying structure of the universe was mathematical, his conviction that the same laws operate throughout the cosmos echoed the ancient alchemical, astrological and magical belief: as above, so below. Newton has been correctly described by Maynard Keynes as the 'last of the Sumerians'; indeed, he was the 'Ultimate Magus'.[11]

Nevertheless, Newton completed the new orientation of the sciences developed by Brahe and Kepler. By making science more mathematical, the emphasis shifted from the symbolic qualities of numbers to quantitative criteria. By arguing that mechanical laws of nature operate throughout the universe, he began the long process of separating science from religion. No longer were phenomena explained through analogy, but causally. Newton's science led to rationalism and mechanical physics, to the notion of a physically determined and mathematically measurable world. By draining the universe of its animism, by replacing the psychic life of nature with the laws of inertia and gravity, by removing the subjective from the scientific method, Newton helped create the brave new model of nature as a machine governed by universal laws. The Alchemist-Creator, associated with the miracle-working magus, was thereby transformed into the Great Architect and ultimately into the Blind Watchmaker.

*

If Newton was the father of modern science, then René Descartes was the father of modern philosophy. By an extraordinary coincidence, he was serving as an artillery surveyor in the army of Maximilian, Duke of Bavaria, when Frederick was crowned king of Bohemia. He spent the winter of 1619 during the campaign which led to the Battle of White Mountain 'sitting in a stove', trying to place the edifice of his thought on a firm foundation. By doubting everything, he realised that the only certainty left was the very process of doubting. From this, he inferred the most famous principle in the history of Western philosophy – *cogito ergo sum* ('I think, therefore I am'). His first rule in his *Discourse on Method* (1639) was to accept only what presented itself to his mind 'so clearly and distinctly' that he had no occasion to doubt it.

Ironically, Descartes was interested in the Rosicrucians but his philosophical approach swept away the uncritical acceptance of occult learning as surely as Ferdinand's cannon cut through the Palgrave's troops. Only the existence of God and the truths of mathematics survived Descartes's devastating method of universal doubt. He went on to develop a mechanistic philosophy of nature and to envisage a universal science based on self-evident truths which rigidly separated the mind from the body and humans from the rest of the natural world. The creatures in Savery's paintings were reduced to unconscious automata. The *anima mundi* of the alchemists became a mathematical machine extended in space. There was simply no room for magic in Descartes's mechanical world. He saw pure mathematics as the only safe tool for objective enquiry. By doing so, he ensured that the Enlightenment of the eighteenth century would be based on analytical reasoning rather than the kind of spiritual illumination which had prevailed at the court of the Holy Roman Emperor at the turn of the seventeenth century. In the age of Reason, Newton and Descartes triumphed, and the Rosicrucian movement and all that it stood for retreated into the shades from its blinding light.

To the modern pragmatist, Rudolf's theatre of the world might seem like a theatre of the absurd, made up of superstitions, dreams and fantasies. But late Renaissance humanists who acted on its stage helped lay the foundations of the modern world. Moreover, the world view that prevailed in Rudolf's magic circle finds echoes today when the notion of inevitable progress of the Enlightenment is being questioned and the model of the world as a machine seems increasingly limited. As the historian Hugh Trevor-Roper has written: 'The Rudolfine age, like the Elizabethan age, is an age in itself; it had its own philosophy, its own inner springs; and that philosophy is perhaps more intelligible to us, who live in a world of ideological tensions and ecumenical aspirations, than to our predecessors . . .'[12]

Rather than being the first of the moderns, the alchemists, astrologers and thinkers who gathered in Prague during Rudolf's reign were in many important ways the last of the ancients. On the cusp of modernity, they were the products of the medieval and ancient world view which, ironically, is being recovered at the cutting edge of physics and ecology today. Not only has the Newtonian view of a mechanical world governed by universal laws been replaced by the uncertainties of quantum physics and chaos theory but the ancient Hermetic notion of nature as an organic, interdependent being has been resurrected in the Gaia theory of the Earth as a living organism.

Rudolf's support for magic, alchemy, astrology and occult philosophy had far-reaching consequences. By bringing together artists, scientists, artisans and philosophers from different fields in a convivial and supportive environment, he encouraged the creative exploration of correspondences across the arts and the sciences. This had profound implications for the development of both.

Rudolf's death is often seen as a critical turning point in the seventeenth century, heralding the decline of magic and the rise of science. But the picture is by no means clear-cut. The alleged 'follies' of alchemy and astrology at his court were more than just 'barnacles to a ship's bottom'; without Rudolf's encouragement of them, modern chemistry, medicine, pharmacy and astronomy would not have developed so quickly.[13] The history of Western civilisation is not simply a process of clear-sighted rationalists and empiricists replacing confused mystics and conjurors. The natural magic of Dee and Bruno, the astrology of Kepler and Brahe, the alchemy of Sendivogius and Croll did not forestall the coming of the Scientific Revolution of the seventeenth century but provided the context for it to take place.

The case of Rudolfine Prague shows that it would have been virtually impossible for many thinkers to make headway in their subject without the medieval world view and the Renaissance recovery of ancient learning. While espousing the new heliocentrism, Bruno wished to restore the *prima theologia* of the ancient Egyptians and Hebrews. Kepler could not have developed his cosmology without his Neoplatonic and Pythagorean philosophy. Both Brahe's and Kepler's acceptance of the Hermetic philosophy on which their astrology was based was not the 'inner enemy' to conquer, as Einstein argued, but the creative and imaginative fountain of their astronomical innovations.

Rudolf has been called the most ineffectual of the Habsburg rulers and there can be no doubt that he was flawed in many ways.[14] His failure to act as an emperor had disastrous personal, social and political consequences. His grand plan for lasting and universal peace proved a mirage. As a spiritual pilgrim, he failed to find a way through the labyrinth of the world to the paradise of the heart. Compared to the imperial glory of his contemporary monarchs Philip II of Spain, Henri IV of France and Elizabeth I of England, Rudolf cut a poor figure. But none of these had such an influence on the cultural and intellectual history of Europe. Rudolf may not have changed the political face of the earth, but he transformed the heavens. One of the last magi, he helped lay the foundations of the modern world.

As a man, his manic possessiveness, which found expression in his obsessive collecting, was far from attractive. He seemed incapable of love and had few close relationships. As a sensualist, he had little discernment. In many ways, he was a lost soul, not because he was possessed by the Devil, but because he found no real direction in his life beyond collecting. Although his mind did not collapse into madness, his paranoia and melancholy were real and he suffered at least two nervous breakdowns. His grand ambitions came to nothing.

Nevertheless, his was a heroic failure. On the day of his funeral, the Calvinist Saxon scholar Melchior Goldast, the last man to see the body of the Emperor, wrote in his diary: 'The Emperor Rudolf was, they say, a most intelligent and sagacious Prince who long maintained a wise peace in the Empire; he was cast in the heroic mould and contemned all vulgar things, loving only the rare and miraculous. His rule was happy, peaceful and secure until the four years before his death.'[15] It was largely true. Rudolf had not only refused to expand his empire but postponed the religious conflicts throughout his reign for thirty years until they finally broke out in the Thirty Years' War. Through his patronage of the arts and sciences, he had helped change the perspectives of humanity at a crucial stage in their history. In an extraordinary flowering of the late Renaissance, his theatre of the world had offered a stage to launch the new science and astronomy. He provided the stepping stone between the medieval world view and the modern outlook.

For all his absolutist tendencies and love of the mystique of the House of Habsburg, Rudolf, like James I of England, tried to follow a middle path in his policies. He hated the extremes of religion and war and sought in Europe a balance of power by trying to arbitrate between rival forces. In his view, harmony between Protestants and Catholics within Christendom was essential in order to deal with the Islamic threat of the Ottoman Empire. As a Christian, he advocated religious tolerance, and as a seeker after truth, he defended freedom of enquiry and expression. Compared to the other intransigent and fanatical rulers at the time, Rudolf appears four centuries later as almost an enlightened, liberal monarch.

Rudolf's greatest achievement was to have created a positive and tolerant environment and then to have had the wisdom to let things happen. He provided just the catalyst required to fixate the boiling crucible of ideas that was lighting up Europe. Under his patronage, he turned Prague into the principal cultural and intellectual centre of the West.

The result was a remarkable synergy which provided fertile ground for the flowering of late Renaissance art and science. Rudolf's artists developed a truly European school of art and imaginatively stretched Mannerism to its limits before it gave way to the excesses of the Baroque. Out of the ashes of his alchemical experiment emerged the phoenix of the new cosmology and the ideals of the Enlightenment. His tortured search for miraculous knowledge and his active support for some of the greatest and most daring thinkers of the late Renaissance made a profound contribution to the history of Western civilisation.

For all his high artistic and scientific endeavours, the Holy Roman Emperor died a broken, lonely and dispirited man, but with his comrades in the pursuit of truth he helped create a cultural revolution in Renaissance Prague which is still reverberating today.

Notes

CHAPTER 1

1   See R.J.W. Evans, *Rudolf II and his World: A Study in Intellectual History 1576–1672* (London, 1997), p.10

2   Hugh Trevor-Roper, *Princes and Artists: Patronage and Ideology at Four Habsburg Courts, 1517–1633* (London, 1976), p.88

3   In Philippe Erlanger, *L'Empereur insolite: Rodolphe II de Habsbourg (1552–1612)* (Paris, 1971), p.43

4   In Robert B. Vurm, *Rudolf II and his Prague: Mysteries and Curiosities of Rudolfine Prague* (Prague, 1997), pp.27–8

5   See Paula Sutter Fichtner, *Emperor Maximilan II* (New Haven and London, 2001), pp.1, 4

CHAPTER 2

1   Andrew Wheatcroft, *The Habsburgs: Embodying Empire* (Harmondsworth, 1996), p.142

2   Erlanger, *L'Empereur insolite*, p.48

3   Wheatcroft, *The Habsburgs*, p.140

4   Ian Robertson, *Spain* (London and New York, 1993), p.303

5   Erlanger, *L'Empereur insolite*, p.51

6   Ibid., p.52

7   Ibid., p.58

8   Ivan Muchka, 'Architectural Styles in the Reign of Rudolf II: Italian and Hispanic Influences', *Rudolf II and Prague: The Court and the City*, ed. Eliška Fučíková *et al* (London, 1997), pp.93–4

9   Evans, *Rudolf II and his World*, p.50 n

10 Erlanger, *L'Empereur insolite*, p.59. See Wheatcroft, *The Habsburgs*, p.176

CHAPTER 3

1   André Breton, *L'Amour fou* (Paris, 1935)

2   For the designs, see Arcimboldo's sketchbook dedicated to Rudolf in 1585, in Werner Kriegeskorte, *Giuseppe Arcimboldo (1527–1593)* (Köln, 2000), pp.72–6. See also T. DaCosta Kaufmann, *Variations on the Imperial Theme in the Age of Maximilian II and Rudolf II* (New York and London, 1978), pp.33–40

3   See Lars Olof Larrson, 'Portraits of Emperor Rudolf II', *Rudolf II and Prague*, p.122

4   Erlanger, *L'Empereur insolite*, pp.62–3

5   See Peter Brock, *The Political and Social Doctrines of the Unity of the Czech Brethren in the Fifteenth and Early Sixteenth Centuries* (Gravenhage, 1957)

6   Erlanger, *L'Empereur insolite*, p.67

7   Ibid., p.72

8   See Evans, *The Making of the Habsburg Monarchy 1550–1700: An Interpretation* (London, 1973), pp. 95–6

9   Sir Philip Sidney to Francis Walsingham, 22 March 1576[–7]; Sidney to Walsingham, 3 May 1577, *Works*, vol.3, ed. Albert Feuillerat (Cambridge, 1923), pp.107, 111

10 Erlanger, *L'Empereur insolite*, p.78. Cf. Evans, *Rudolf II*, p.59

11 See Evans, *Rudolf II and his World*, p. 42, n. 1. No diaries exist and in the Habsburgs' correspondence which has survived in Vienna Rudolf is notably absent. The only printed collection of Rudolf's letters consists almost entirely of official communications limited to the years 1589–92.

12 Erlanger, *L'Empereur insolite*, p.86

13 Ibid., p.91

CHAPTER 4

1   Erlanger, *L'Empereur insolite*, p.97

2   See Peter Demetz, *Prague in Black and Gold: The History of a City* (London, 1998), pp.4–5

3   See Vurm, *Rudolf II and his Prague*, p.50

4   David Gans, *Zemah David*, 95b, in André Neher, *Jewish Thought and the Scientific Revolution of the Sixteenth Century: David Gans (1546–1613) and his Times* (Oxford, 1986), pp.21–2

5   Fynes Morison, *An Itenerary* (London, 1617; Amsterdam,1971), Pt.1, Bk.1, ch.2, p.14

6   See Wheatcroft, *The Habsburgs*, pp.105–110

7   Pierre Bergeron, from the report of his travels (1603) in Eliška Fučíková, Petre Chotěbor and Zdeněk Lukeš, *Prague Castle Gallery: A Guide to the Collections* (Prague,1998)

8   See DaCosta Kaufmann, 'Perspective on Prague: Rudolfine Stylistics Reviewed', *Rudolf II and Prague*, p.100

9   In Eliška Fučíková, 'Prague Castle under Rudolf II, his Predecessors and Successors', *Rudolf II and Prague*, p.14

CHAPTER 5

1   Demetz, *Prague in Black and Gold*, p.219

2   D.J. Jansen, in *Leids Kunsthistorisch Jaarboek* 1 (1982), pp.57–69, has suggested that Rudolf's mistress was Ottavio Strada's illegitimate daughter called Anna Maria

3   John Barclay, *Euphormionis Lusinini sive Ioannis Barclii Satyricon* (Frankfurt, 1623)

4   In Fučíková, *Prague Castle Gallery*, prelims

5   In Lubomír Konečný, 'Picturing the Artist in Rudolfine Prague', *Rudolf II and Prague*, p.107. See also DaCosta Kaufmann, *The School of Prague: Paintings at the Court of Rudolf II* (Chicago and London, 1988)

6   See DaCosta Kaufmann, *Court, Cloister and City: The Art and Culture of Central Europe: 1450–1800* (Chicago, 1995), p.193

7   See Thea Vignau-Wilberg, '*Pictor Doctus*: Drawing and the Theory of Art around 1600', *Rudolf II and Prague*, p.185

8   See Angelo Maria Ripellino, *Magic Prague* (1973), tr. D.N Marinelli, ed. M.H. Heim (London, 1994), pp.80–3

9   Roland Barthes, *Arcimboldo* (Palma, 1978), pp.15–16, 51

10 See Lee Hendrix, 'Natural History Illustration at the Court of Rudolf II', *Rudolf II and Prague*, p.158

11 See Kriegeskorte, *Giuseppe Arcimboldo*, p.48

12 See DaCosta Kaufmann, *The Court and the Cloister*, p.191

13 Kriegeskorte, *Giuseppe Arcimboldo*, p.45

14 Evans, *Rudolf II and Prague*, p.163

15 In Fučíková, *Prague Castle Gallery*, p.19

16 Barclay, *Euphormionis Lusinini*. See also Demetz, *Prague in Black and Gold*, p.183

17 See Joaneath Spicer, 'Roelandt Savery and the "Discovery" of the

Alpine Waterfall', *Rudolf II and Prague*, pp.146–55

18   Paula Findlen, 'Cabinets, Collecting and Natural Philosopy', *Rudolf II and Prague*, p.211

19   See DaCosta Kaufmann, 'The Problem of Stylistics of Rudolfine Prague', *Rudolf II and his Court, Leids Kunsthistorisch Jaarboek,* (Delft, 1982), pp.119–22; *The School of Prague*, p.115

CHAPTER 6

1   Evans, *Rudolf II and his World*, p.162

2   See DaCosta Kaufmann, *Court, Cloister and City*, p.181

3   In Findlen, 'Cabinets, Collecting and Natural Philosophy', *Rudolf II and Prague*, p.216. For a catalogue of some of the items in Rudolf's *Kunstkammer*, see *Rudolf II and Prague*, pp.473–541

4   See Beket Bukovinská, 'The *Kunstkammer* of Rudolf II: Where it Was and What it Looked Like', *Rudolf II and Prague*, pp.199–200

5   Barthes, *Arcimboldo*, p. 66

6   In Findlen, 'Cabinets, Collecting and Natural Philosophy', *Rudolf II and Prague*, p.215

7   In Evans, *Rudolf II and his World*, p.196

8   In Hendrik, 'Natural History Illustration at the Court of Rudolf II', *Rudolf II and Prague*, p.162

9   Ibid., p.166

10   See Lee Hendrix and Thea Vignau-Wilberg, eds., *Mira calligraphiae monumenta: A Complete Facsimile of Europe's Last Great Illustrated Manuscript* (London, 1992); *The Art of the Pen: Calligraphy from the Court of Emperor Rudolf II* (Los Angeles, 2003)

11   See Kaufmann, *Variations on The Imperial Theme*, pp.105–13

12   In Findlen, 'Cabinets, Collecting and Natural Philosophy', *Rudolf II and Prague*, p.212

13   In Erlanger, *L'Empereur insolite*, p.110

14   Ripellino, *Magic Prague*, p.77

CHAPTER 7

1   In Evans, *Rudolf II and his World*, p.33

2   See Nicolette Mout, 'The Court of Rudolf II and Humanist Culture', *Rudolf II and Prague*, p.220

3   In Evans, *Rudolf II and his World*, p.196

4   Plato, *Timaeus*, tr. H.D.P. Lee (Harmondsworth, 1965), pp.44–5

5   'Asclepius', *Hermetica*, tr. Brian Copenhaver (Cambridge, 1995), p.69

6   Osw. Crollius, *Discovering the Great and Deep Mysteries of Nature* in *Philosophy Reformed and Improved*, tr. H. Pinnell (London, 1657), p.24

7   Sir Walter Raleigh, *History of the World* (London, 1614), preface

8   See B.L Sherwin, *Mystical Theology and Social Dissent: The Life and Work of Judah Loew of Prague* (London and Toronto, 1982), p.15

9   Ibid., pp.28–9

10   In Demetz, *Prague in Black and Gold*, p.209

11   See Jirina Šedinová, 'The Jewish Town in Prague', *Rudolf II and Prague*, p.307

12   See Sherwin, *Mystical Theology and Social Dissent*, p.25

13   See Rabbi Ben Zion Bokser, *From the World of the Cabbalah: The Philosophy of the Rabbi Judah Loew of Prague* (London, 1957), pp.192–3

14   Judah Loew, *Tiphereth Yisrael*, ch.6, in F. Thieberger, *The Great Rabbi Loew of Prague* (London, 1955), p.109

15   Loew, *Tiphereth Yisrael*, ch.13, ibid., p.46

16   See Sherwin, *Mystical Theology and Social Dissent*, pp. 124–41

17   David Gans, *Zemah David* (Prague, 1592), in Neher, *Jewish Thought and the Scientific Revolution of the Sixteenth Century*, p.33

18   In Sherwin, *Mystical Theology and Social Dissent*, p.15

CHAPTER 8

1   See D.B. Ruderman, *Kabbalah, Magic and Science* (Cambridge, MA, and London, 1988) and Penelope Gouk, 'Natural Philosophy and Natural Magic', *Rudolf II and Prague*, pp.233–4

2   In Erlanger, *L'Empereur insolite*, p.102

3   Giovanni Pico della Mirandola, *Apologia* in Eugenio Garin, *Astrology in the Renaissance: The Zodiac of Life*, tr. C. Jackson and J. Allen (London, 1990), p.91

4   See Peter Marshall, *The Philosopher's Stone: A Quest for the Secrets of Alchemy* (London, 2001), pp.292–3

5   Johann Trithemius, *Steganographia* (Frankfurt, 1606)

6   H.C. Agrippa, *Of the Vanitie and Uncertaintie of Artes and Sciences*, tr. James Sandford (London, 1656), fol.54r

7   See A.G. Debus, *The Chemical Dream of the Renaissance* (Cambridge, 1968), pp.31–2

8   Daniel Stoltzius von Stolzenberg, *A Chemical Pleasure-Garden* (Frankfurt, 1624)

9   See Trevor-Roper, 'The Paracelsian Movement', *Renaissance Essays* (London, 1986) p.181

10 In Marshall, *The Philosopher's Stone*, pp.352, 349

11 Galileo Galilei to Johannes Kepler, 4 August 1597, in J.M Ross and M.M. McLaughlin, eds., *The Portable Renaissance Reader* (Harmondsworth, 1985), p.597

CHAPTER 9

1   See Frances A. Yates, *The Occult Philosophy in the Elizabethan Age* (London, 1979), p.160. See also J.P. French, *John Dee: The World of an Elizabethan Magus* (London, 1972)

2   In Evans, *Rudolf II and his World*, p.219, n. 3.

3   C.H. Josten, 'A Translation of John Dee's "Monas Hieroglyphica"', *Ambix*, XII, 2, 3 (1964), p.137

4   See Susan Bassnett, 'Revising a Biography: A New Interpretation of the Life of Elizabeth Jane Weston (Westonia)', *Cahiers Elisabéthains*, 37(1990), pp.1–8

5   Dee to Rudolf, 17 August 1584, Dee, *A True and Faithful Relation of what passed between Dr John Dee and some Spirits* (London, 1659), p.218

6   Ibid., p.212

7   In Benjamin Woolley, *The Queen's Conjuror: The Life and Magic of Dr Dee* (London, 2002), p.246

8   Dee, *A True and Faithful Relation*, pp.215–17

9   In Woolley, *The Queen's Conjuror*, p.249

10 Ibid., p.251

11 Dee, *A True and Faithful Relation*, pp.230–1

12 Ibid.

13 Dee, 6 October 1584, *The Diaries of John Dee*, ed. Edward Fenton (Charlbury, 1998)

14 In C.H. Josten, 'An Unknown Chapter in the Life of John Dee', *Journal of the Warburg and Courtauld Institutes*, 28 (1965), pp. 223–57

15 In Evans, *Rudolf II and his World*, p.224

16 Ibid., p.103

17 In Woolley, *The Queen's Conjuror*, p.265

18 In Evans, *Rudolf II and his World*, p. 223

19 In Woolley, *The Queen's Conjuror*, p.271

20 In Evans, *Rudolf II and his World*, pp.103–4

21 Ibid., p.226

22 Ibid., p.226, n.7

23 Edward Kelley, 'The Theatre of Terrestrial Astronomy', in R. Grossinger, ed., *Alchemy* (California, 1979)

24 In Evans, *Rudolf II and his World*, p.226

25 In H.C. Bolton, *The Follies of Science at the Court of Rudolph II 1576–1612* (Milwaukee, 1904), pp.48–9

26 Ibid., p.49

CHAPTER 10

1 Oswald Croll, 'Admonitory Preface', *Basilica chymica*, translated as *Philosophy Reformed & Improved in Four Profound Tractates. The I. Discovering the Great and Deep Mysteries of Nature: by OSW. Crollius*, tr. H. Pinnell (London, 1657)

2 In Marshall, *The Philosopher's Stone*, p.390

3 Croll, 'Admonitory Preface'

4 Ibid.

5 Croll in *The Occult in Early Modern Europe: A Documentary History*, ed. and tr. P.G. Maxwell-Stuart (London, 1999), pp.127–8

6 Robert Burton, *The Anatomy of Melancholy* (London, 1621)

7 See Vurm, *Rudolf II and his Prague*, p.88

8 See J.B. Craven, *Count Michael Maier* (Kirkwall, 1910)

9 Michael Maier, 'A Subtle Allegory concerning the Secret of Secrets', *Musaeum Hermeticum Reformatum et Amplificatum* (Frankfurt, 1677), tr. A.E. Waite as *The Hermetic Museum Restored and Enlarged* (London, 1893), pp.220–1

10 Maier, *Atalanta fugiens* (Oppenheim, 1618) in Stanislas Klossowski de Rola, *The Golden Game: Alchemical Engravings of the Seventeenth Century* (London, 1998), p.97

11 In Evans, *Rudolf II and his World*, pp.214–15

12 Heinrich Khunrath, *Ampitheatrum sapientiae aeternae* (1602) in Klossowski, *The Golden Game*, p.29

13 For the full text, see Marshall, *The Philosopher's Stone*, pp.250–3

14 See John Bossy, *Giordano Bruno and the Embassy Affair* (New Haven, 1991)

15 Giordano Bruno, *La Cena de la Ceneri* (1584), dialogue 2, in Yates, *Giordano Bruno and the Hermetic Tradition* (London, 2002), pp. 316–17

16 Bruno, *Spaccio de la bestia trionfante* (1584) in ibid., p.227

17 In Woolley, *The Queen's Conjuror*, p.210

18 Asclepius, *Hermetica*, ed. Copenhaver, p.69

19 Bruno, *Spaccio*, dedication; dialogue 3, in Yates, *Giordano Bruno*, p.243

20 Bruno, *De la causa, principio, et uno*, dialogue 1, in Yates, *Giordano Bruno*, p.281

21 In Evans, *Rudolf II and his World*, p.233. See also Yates, *The Art of Memory* (London, 1966), pp.287–93

22 Bruno, *De magia*, in Yates, *Giordano Bruno*, p.289

23 See D. Berti, *La Vita di Giordano Bruno da Nola* (Florence, 1867)

24 Father Joseph Pittau, in conversation with the author, *The Philosopher's Stone*, p.335

25 In Bolton, *Follies of Science*, p.126

26 Sendivogius, 'New Chemical Light', in *The Hermetic Museum*

27 Ibid.

28 Ibid.

29 See Richard Brezinski and Zbigniew Szydlo, 'Michael Sendivogius', *History Today* (May, 1997)

30 In Evans, *Rudolf II and His World*, p.205

31 Martin Ruland, *A Lexicon of Alchemy or Alchemical Dictionary* (Frankfurt, 1612), p.199

32 Evans, *Rudolf II and his World*, p.210

33 See Demetz, *Prague in Black and Gold*, p.196

CHAPTER 11

1 See Pierre Brind'Amour, *Nostradamus astrophile* (Ottawa, n.d.), pp.377–80, 452. The German manuscript of Rudolf's horoscope, completed in 1564, is held at the Kungliga Biblioteke, Stockholm, v., J.1695

2 In Vurm, *Rudolf II and his Prague*, p.13. See also C.D. Hellman, *The Comet of 1577: Its Place in the History of Astronomy* (New York, 1944)

3 Evans, *Rudolf II and his World*, p.137

4   In György E. Szönyi, 'Scientific and Magical Humanism at the Court of Rudolf II', *Rudolf II and Prague*, p.224

5   See Brahe, *De stella nova* (1573) in *The Portable Renaissance Reader*, p.594

6   In Kitty Ferguson, *The Nobleman and his Housedog. Tycho Brahe and Johannes Kepler: The Strange Partnership that Revolutionised Science* (London, 2002), p.47

7   Brahe, *De Disciplinis mathematicis oratio* (1574) in *The Occult in Early Modern Europe*, pp.84–5. See also Marshall, *World Astrology: The Astrologer's Quest to Understand the Human Character*, (London, 2004), pp.335–6

8   Nicolaus Copernicus, *De revolutionibus orbium caelestiu* (1543)

9   In Ferguson, *The Nobleman and his Housedog*, p.98

10 See Victor E. Thoren, *The Lord of Uraniborg: A Biography of Tycho Brahe* (Cambridge, 1990), p.210

11 In John Allyne Gade, *The Life and Times of Tycho Brahe* (New York, 1947), p.122

12 In J.L.E. Dryer, *Tycho Brahe: A Picture of Scientific Life and Work in the Sixteeenth Century* (1890)(New York, 1963), p.130

13 In Erlanger, *L'Empereur insolite*, p.126

14 In Ferguson, *The Nobleman and his Housedog*, p.216

15 Ibid., p.217

16 Ibid., pp.193, 219

17 Ibid., p.235

18 Brahe to Holger Rosenkratz, 30 Aug 1599, in Thoren, *The Lord of Uraniborg*, p.413

19 Ibid.

20 In Gade, *The Life and Times of Tycho Brahe*, pp.178, 172

21 David Gans, *Nechmad ve-N'maim* ('Nice and Pleasant') (Jesenice, 1743), in Neher, *Jewish Thought and the Scientific Revolution of the Sixteenth Century*, pp.25–6

22 In Gade, *The Life and Times of Tycho Brahe*, pp.179–80. The translation wrongly describes the Capuchins as Carthusians.

CHAPTER 12

1   In Ferguson, *The Nobleman and his Housedog*, p.103

2   Ibid., p.190

3   Kepler to Galileo, 4 August 1597, in *The Portable Renaissance Reader*, pp.597–9

4   Kepler to Johann Herwart, 16 March 1598, ibid., pp.602–4

5   Brahe to Kepler, 26 January 1600, in Ferguson, *The Nobleman and his Housedog*, p.247

6   In ibid., p.251

7   Kepler to Michael Mästlin, 1600, ibid., p.274

8   Max Caspar, *Kepler*, tr. Doris Hellman (London and New York, 1959), p.149

9   In Ferguson, *The Nobleman and his Housedog*, pp.279–80

10   Kepler to Herwart, April 1599, in *Renaissance Reader*, pp.606–7

11   In Caspar, *Kepler*, p.108

12   Kepler to Mästlin, 1598, in Louis MacNeice, *Astrology* (London, 1964), p.156

13   In Ferguson, *The Nobleman and his Housedog*, p.181

14   In Caspar, *Kepler*, p.152

15   In Marshall, *World Astrology*, p.337

16   Kepler, *De stella nova*, ch.28. See also John Anthony West, *The Case for Astrology* (New York, 1991), pp. 105–6

17   In Arthur Koestler, *The Watershed: A Biography of Johann Kepler* (New York, 1960), p.39

18   In Carola Baumgardt, *Johannes Kepler: Life and Letters* (New York and London, 1952), p.99

19   In Koestler, *The Watershed*, p.204

20   In MacNeice, *Astrology*, p.156. See also W. Pauli, 'The Influence of Archetypal Ideas on the Scientific Theories of Kepler', in C.G. Jung and W. Pauli, *The Interpretation of Nature and the Psyche*, tr. Priscilla Silz (London, 1955)

21   Kepler to Mästlin, 5 March 1605, in Baumgardt, *Johannes Kepler*, p.91

22   Kepler, *De stella nova in pede Serpentarii* (Prague, 1606) in Garin, *Astrology in the Renaissance*, p.9

23   In Bolton, *The Follies of Science*, p.87

24   In Baumgardt, *Johannes Kepler*, pp.76–7

25   Galileo to Kepler, July 1610, in Ferguson, *The Nobleman and his Housedog*, p.326

26   Kepler to Galileo, 9 August 1610, in Baumgardt, *Johannes Kepler*, pp.84–5

27   In Ferguson, *The Nobleman and his Housedog*, p.329

CHAPTER 13

1   Evans, *Rudolf II and his World*, p.35
2   In Erlanger, *L'Empereur insolite*, p.118
3   Ibid., p.121
2   See Ivana Čornejová, 'The Religious Situation in Rudolfine Prague', *Rudolf II and Prague*, pp.310–22
5   Sir Henry Wotton to Lord Zouche, 17 April 1591, in L. Pearsall Smith, *The Life and Letters of Sir Henry Wotton* (Oxford, 1907), vol.1, pp.251, 268
6   Erlanger, *L'Empereur insolite*, p.95
7   In Evans, *Rudolf II and his World*, p.71
8   In *L'Empereur insolite*, p.146
9   Ibid., p.163
10 In Caspar, *Kepler*, p.151
11 Filippo Spinelli to Pope Clement VIII, in Hans Holzer, *The Alchemist* (New York, 1985), pp.85, 91
12 Archduke Albrecht to Rudolf, ibid., p.86
13 Wolf von Unverzagt to Ferdinand of Styria, in Erlanger, *L'Empereur insolite*, p.168
14 In Čornejová, 'The Religious Situation in Rudolfine Prague', *Rudolf II and Prague*, p.317
15 In Evans, *Rudolf II and his World*, p.91
16 In Erlanger, *L'Empereur insolite*, p.175

CHAPTER 14

1   Evans, *Rudolf II and his World*, p.49
2   Ibid., p.80
3   Yates, *The Occult Philosophy in the Elizabethan Age*, p.51
4   See Trevor-Roper, 'Robert Burton and *The Anatomy of Melancholy*', *Renaissance Essays*, p.257
5   See Demetz, *Prague in Black and Gold*, pp.219–20; Evans, *Rudolf II and his World* p.58, n.1
6   See Kaufmann, *The School of Prague*, pp.22–3
7   In Erlanger, *L'Empereur insolite*, pp.182–3
8   Ibid., p.198
9   Ibid., p.202
10 Ibid., p.201

11 In Evans, *Rudolf II and his World*, p.198
12 See Barclay, *Euphormionis Lusinini*, Pt II.

CHAPTER 15

1 In Evans, *Rudolf II and his World*, pp.84, 196
2 In Erlanger, *L'Empereur insolite*, p.203
3 See Herbert Haupt, 'From Feuding Brothers to a Nation at War with Itself', *Rudolf II and Prague*, p.238
4 Vilém Slavata in Evans, *Rudolf II and his World*, p.33
5 Ibid., p.57
6 In Kaufmann, *School of Prague*, p.7
7 In Evans, *Rudolf II and his World*, pp.44–5
8 In Vurm, *Rudolf II and his Prague*, p 20
9 In Erlanger, *L'Empereur insolite*, p.246
10 Ibid., p.247
11 Evans, *The Making of the Habsburg Monarchy*, p.53
12 Erlanger, *L'Empereur insolite*, p.249
13 In Evans, *Rudolf II and his World*, pp.81–2, n.3
14 In Erlanger, *L'Empereur insolite*, p.252
15 See Johann Amos Comenius, *The Labyrinth of the World and the Paradise of the Heart* (1623), tr. M. Spinka (Michigan, 1972)

EPILOGUE

1 See Trevor-Roper, 'The Paracelsian Movement', *Renaissance Essays*, p.183
2 In Vurm, *Rudolf II and his Prague*, p.30
3 See Trevor-Roper, 'The Outbreak of the Thirty Years' War', *Renaissance Essays*, p. 289
4 See Yates, *The Rosicrucian Enlightenment* (London, 1972)
5 See Marshall, *The Philosopher's Stone*, p.387
6 See Evans, *Rudolf II and his World*, pp.283–4
7 Kepler to Vincenz Bianchi, 17 February 1618, in Baumgardt, *Johannes Kepler*, pp. 39–40
8 Kepler, *Harmony of the World* (1618) in Ferguson, *The Nobleman and his Housedog*, p.342
9 Einstein, Preface, Baumgardt, *Johannes Kepler*, p.13
10 See Yates, *Giordano Bruno and the Hermetic Tradition*, pp.479–81

11   See Marshall, *The Philosopher's Stone*, ch.45, 'The Ultimate Magus', pp. 398–409

12   Trevor–Roper, *Princes and Artists*, p.96

13   Bolton, *Follies of Science*, p.204

14   See Evans, *The Making of the Habsburg Monarchy*, p.95

15   In Evans, *Rudolf II and his World*, p.5

SELECT BIBLIOGRAPHY

TEXTS

Abecedarium: Illustrated Alphabet from the Court of Europe, Rudolf II, ed. Lee Hendrix, (New York, 1997)

Ashmole, Elias, *Theatrum chemicum Britannicum* (London, 1652)

Bacon, Francis, *New Atlantis* (London, 1627)

Barclay, John, *Euphormionis Lusinini sive Ioannis Barclii Satyricon* (Frankfurt, 1623)

Brahe, Tycho, *De stella nova* (1573)

——, *Astronomiae instauratae mechanica* (Nürnberg, 1602)

——, *De Disciplinis mathematicis oratio* (1574)

Bruno, Giordano, *De la causa, principio, et uno* (Venetia [in fact, London], 1584)

——, *De l'Infinito universo et mondi* (Venetia [in fact, London], 1584)

——, *La Cena de la Ceneri* (London, 1584)

——, *Spacio de la bestia triofante* (Parigi [in fact, London], 1584)

——, *One Hundred and Sixty Articles against Mathematicians and Philosophers* (Prague, 1588)

——, *On the Calculations and Combinations according to R. Lull* (Prague, 1588)

Burton, Robert, *The Anatomy of Melancholy* (London, 1621)

Comenius, Johann Amos, *The Labyrinth of the World and the Paradise of the Heart* (1623), tr. M. Spinka (Michigan, 1972)

Confessio Fraternitatis (Cassel, 1615)

Croll, Oswald, *Basilica chymica* (Frankfurt, 1608)

Crollius, Osw[ald], *Philosophy Reformed & Improved in Four Profound Tractates*, tr. H. Pinnell (London, 1657)

Dee, Dr John, 'Mathematicall Praeface', *The Elements of Geometrie, Euclid*, tr.

H. Billingsley (London, 1570)

——, The *Private Diary of Dr John Dee and the Catalogue of his Library of Manuscripts*, ed. J.O. Halliwell (London, 1842)

——, A *True and Faithful Relation of what passed for many years between Dr. John Dee . . . and some spirits*, ed. Meric Causabon (London, 1659)

——, 'A Translation of John Dee's "Monas Hieroglyphica"', tr. C.H. Josten, *Ambix*, XII, 2, 3 (1964), pp.88–221

——, The *Diaries of John Dee*, ed. Edward Fenton (Charlbury, 1998)

Fama Fraternitatis (Cassel, 1614)

'*Fama Fraternitatis and Confessio Fraternitatis*': *The Fame and Confession of Fraternity of R.C.: Commonly of the Rosie Cross*, tr. Eugenius Philalethes (London, 1652)

Fludd, Robert, *Utriusque cosmi, maioris scilicet et minoris* (Frankfurt, 1617–19)

Hermetica, tr. and ed., Brian P. Copenhaver (Cambridge,1995)

Kelley, Edward, *The Englishman's Two Excellent Treatises on the Philosopher's Stone* (Hamburg, 1676)

——,*The Alchemical Writings of Edward Kelley*, tr. A. E. Waite (London, 1893)

——,'The Theatre of Terrestrial Astronomy', in R. Grossinger, ed., *Alchemy* (California,1979)

Kepler, Johannes, *Prodromus dissertationum cosmographicum* (1596)

——, *De fundamentis astrologiae certioribis* (Prague, 1602)

——, *Astronomiae pars optica* (1604)

——, *De stella nova in pede Serpentarii* (1606)

——, *Astronomia nova* (Prague, 1609)

——, *Dissertatio cum nuncio sidereo* (1610)

——, *Dioptrice* (1611)

——, *Harmonice mundi* (1618)

——, *Rudolfine Tables* (1624)

——, *Epitome astronomiae Copernicae*, 7 vols., (1615–21)

Khunrath, Heinrich, *Amphitheatrum Sapientiae Aeternae* (Hanau, 1609)

——, *The Amphitheatre Engravings of Heinrich Khunrath*, ed. Adam McLean, tr. Patricia Tahil (Grand Rapids, MI, n.d.)

Lull, Ramón, *Doctor Illuminatus: A Ramon Lull Reader*, ed. and tr. Anthony Bonner (Princeton, N.J., c.1993)

Maier, Michael, *Arcana arcanissima* (London, 1614)

——, *Symbola aureae mensae* (Frankfurt, 1617)

——, *Atalanta fugiens* (Oppenheim, 1618)

——, *Tripus aureus* (Frankfurt, 1618)

——, *Viatorium* (Oppenheim, 1618)

——, 'The Subtle Allegory concerning the Secrets of Alchemy', in *The Hermetic Museum Restored and Enlarged*, tr. A.E. Waite (London, 1893)

Mira Calligraphiae Monumenta: From the Library of Emperor Rudolf II. A Complete Facsimile of Europe's Last Great Manuscript, eds. L. Hendrix and T. Vignau-Wilberg (London, 1992)

Morison, Fynes, *An Itenerary* (London, 1617); facsimile (Amsterdam, 1971)

Musaeum Hermeticum Reformatum et Amplificatum (Frankfurt, 1677), tr. A.E. Waite as *The Hermetic Museum Restored and Enlarged* (London, 1893)

Nature Illuminated: Flora and Fauna from the Court of Rudolf II, ed. Lee Hendrix (San Marino, 1997)

Paracelsus, *Paracelsus on the Secrets of Alchemy*, tr. R. Turner (London, 1656)

——, *The Hermetic and Alchemical Writings of Aureolus Philippus Theophrastus Bombast Paracelsus*, tr. A.E. Waite, 2 vols. (London, 1894)

Pico della Mirandola, 'Oration on the dignity of man' (1486), in *The Portable Renaissance Reader*, trs. J. Ross and M.M. McLaughlin (Harmondsworth, 1977)

Plato, *Timaeus*, tr. H.D.P. Lee (Harmondsworth,1965)

Rulands, Martin, *A Lexicon of Alchemy or Alchemical Dictionary*, tr. A.E. Waite (London, 1892)

Sidney, Sir Philip, *Works*, vol.3, ed. Albert Feuillerat (Cambridge, 1923)

Sendivogius, Michael, *Novum lumen Chemycum* (Frankfurt and Prague, 1604)

——, *The New Chemical Light, drawn from the Fountain of Nature and of Manual Experience*, in *The Hermetic Museum Restored and Enlarged*, tr. A.E. Waite (London, 1893)

Trithemius (of Sponheim), Johannes, *Steganographia* (Frankfurt, 1606)

Zetzner, Lazarus, *Theatrum Chemicum*, vols.1–3 (Ursel, 1610), vol.4 (Strasbourg, 1613), vol.5 (1662–4), reprinted 6 vols. (1659–61)

GENERAL

Armitage, Angus, *The World of Copernicus* (New York, 1954)

Arnold, Paul, *Histoire des Rose-Croix et les origines de la Franc-Maçonnerie* (Paris, 1955)

Barthes, Roland, *Arcimboldo* (Milan, 1978)

Bassnett, Susan, 'Revising a Biography: A New Interpretation of the Life of Elizabeth Jane Weston (Westonia)', *Cahiers Elisabéthains*, 37(1990), pp.1–8

Bauer, Rotrand and Herbert Haupt, 'Das Kunstkammerinventar Kaiser Rudolfs II', 1607–1611', *Jahrbuch der Kunsthistorischen Sammlungen in Wien*, 72 (1976)

Baumgardt, Carola, *Johannes Kepler: Life and Letters* (New York and London, 1952)

Berti, D., *La Vita di Giordano Bruno da Nola* (Florence, 1867)

Bibl, Victor, *Maximilian II, der rätselhafte Kaiser* (Vienna, 1929)

Blau, J.L., *Christian Interpretation of the Cabala in the Renaissance* (New York, 1944)

Bokser, Ben Zion, *From the World of the Cabbalah: The Philosophy of Rabbi Judah Loew of Prague* (London, 1957)

Bolton, Henry Carrington, *The Follies of Science at the Court of Rudolph II. 1576–1612* (Milwaukee, 1904)

Bor, D. Ž., *Na prahu Vznešena (Pokus o poetu císař Rudolfu II)* (Prague, 1997)

Bossy, John, *Giordano Bruno and the Embassy Affair* (New Haven, 1991)

Brind'Amour, Pierre, *Nostradamus astrophile: les astres et l'astrologie dans la vie et l'oeuvre de Nostradamus* (Ottawa, n.d.)

Brock, Peter, *The Political and Social Doctrines of the Unity of Czech Brethren in the Fifteenth and Early Sixteenth Centuries* (Gravenhage, 1957)

Brod, Max, *Tycho Brahes Weg zu Gott* (Leipzig, 1916)

Brodrick, James, *Galileo: The Man, his Work, his Misfortunes* (London, 1964)

Burtt, E.A., *The Metaphysical Foundations of Modern Physical Science* (London, 1932)

Čapek, Karel, *Věc Makropulos* (Prague, 1922)

Caspar, Max, *Kepler*, tr. Doris Hellman (London and New York, 1959)

Clark, George, *Early Modern Europe* (Oxford, 1957)

Clulee, N.H., *John Dee's Natural Philosophy: Between Science and Religion* (London, 1988)

Craven, J.B., *Count Michael Maier* (Kirkwall, 1910)

Dauxois, Jacqueline, *Der Alchimist von Prag: Rudolf II von Habsburg* (Erschienen, 1999)

Debus, A.G., *The Chemical Dream of the Renaissance* (Cambridge, 1968)

Dehio, Ludwig, *The Precarious Balance: The Politics of Power in Europe 1494–1945* (London, 1963)

Demetz, Peter, *Prague in Black and Gold: The History of a City* (London, 1997)

Denis, Ernest, *Fin de l'indépendance Bohème* (Paris, 1930)

Dillon, Kenneth, *Kings and Estates in the Bohemian Lands* (Brussels, 1976)

Dreyer, J.L.E., *Tycho Brahe: A Picture of Scientific Life and Work in the Sixteeenth Century* (Edinburgh, 1890; New York, 1963)

Dudák, Vladislav, *Prague Castle Hradčany* (Prague, 1998)

Elliott, J.H., *Imperial Spain 1469–1716* (London, 1963)

Erlanger, Philippe, *L'Empereur insolite: Rodophe II de Habsbourg (1552–1612)* (Paris, 1971)

Evans, R.J.W., *The Making of the Habsburg Monarchy 1550–1700: An Interpretation* (Oxford, 1979)

——, *Rudolf II and his World: A Study in Intellectual History 1576–1612* (1973) (London, 1997)

Faivre, Antoine, *The Eternal Hermes: From Greek God to Alchemical Magus* (York Beach, ME, 1995)

Ferguson, Kitty, *The Nobleman and his Housedog. Tycho Brahe and Johannes Kepler: The Stange Partnership that Revolutionised Science* (London, 2002)

Fichtner, P.S., *Emperor Maximilian II* (London and New Haven, 2001)

French, Peter J. *John Dee: The World of an Elizabethan Magus* (London, 1972)

Fučíková, Eliška, Petre Chotěbor and Zdeněk Lukeš, *Prague Castle Gallery: A Guide to the Collections* (Prague, 1998)

Gade, John Allyne, *The Life and Times of Tycho Brahe* (New York, 1947)

Garin, Eugenio, *Astrology in the Renaissance: The Zodiac of Life*, tr. Carolyn Jackson and June Allen (London, 1990)

Gindely, A., *Rudolf II und seine Zeit*, 2 vols. (Prague, 1862–5)

Girtanner, Christoph, *Charakteristik der Kaisers Rudolph von Habsburg* (Leipzig, 1817)

Hausenblavosá, Jaroslava and Michel Sronek, *Das Rudolfinische Prag* (Druck, 1997)

Hauser, Arnold, *Mannerism*, 2 vols. (London, 1965)

Hellman, C.D., *The Comet of 1577: Its Place in the History of Astronomy* (New York, 1944)

Hendrix, Lee and Thea Vignau–Wilberg, *The Art of the Pen: Calligraphy from the Court of Emperor Rudolf II* (Los Angeles, 2003)

Holzer, Hans, *The Alchemist* (New York, 1974)

Janáček, Josef, *Rudolf II. a jeho doba* (Prague, 1987)

Josten, C.H., 'An Unknown Chapter in the Life of John Dee', *Journal of the Warburg and Courtauld Institutes*, 28 (1965), pp.253–88

——, *Elias Ashmole* (1617–92), 2 vols. (Oxford, 1966)

Karpenko, Vladimir, 'Bohemian Nobility and Alchemy in the Second Half of the 16th Century', *Cauda Pavonis*, 15, 2 (1966), pp.14–18

Kaufmann, T. DaCosta, *Variations on the Imperial Theme in the Age of Maximilian II and Rudolf II* (New York and London, 1978)

——, *The School of Prague: Paintings at the Court of Rudolf II* (Chicago and London, 1988)

——, *Court, Cloister and City: The Art and Culture of Central Europe: 1450–1800* (Chicago, 1995)

——, 'The Problem of the Stylistics of Rudolfine Prague', in *Rudolf II and his Court, Leids Kunsthistorisch Jaarboek 1982* (Delft, 1982)

Kinross, Lord (John Balfour), *The Ottoman Centuries: The Rise and Fall of the Turkish Empire* (London, 1977)

Klossowski de Rola, Stanislas, *The Golden Game: Alchemical Engravings of the Seventeenth Century* (London, 1998)

Koestler, Arthur, *The Sleepwalkers* (London, 1959)

——, *The Watershed: A Biography of Johann Kepler* (New York, 1960)

Konečný, Labomír with Beket Bukouviská and Ivan Muchka, *Rudolf II, Prague and the World: Papers of the International Conference, Prague, 2–4 September 1997* (Prague, 1998)

Köslerova, Diana, *The Parnassus of the Arts* (Cranford, c.1987)

Koyré, A, *La révolution astronomique* (Paris, 1961)

Kriegeskorte, Werner, *Giuseppe Arcimboldo (1527–1593)* (Köln, 2000)

Kuhn, Thomas, *The Copernican Revolution: Planetary Astronomy in the Development of Western Thought* (Cambridge, Mass., 1957)

Lynch, John, *Spain under the Habsburgs*, 2 vols. (Oxford, 1965–9)

MacNeice, Louis, *Astrology* (London, 1964)

Marshall, Peter, *The Philosopher's Stone: A Quest for the Secrets of Alchemy* (London, 2001)

——, *World Astrology: The Astrologer's Quest to Understand the Human Character* (London, 2004)

Matthews, W. H., *Mazes and Labyrinths* (London, 1922)

Maxwell-Stuart, P.G., ed., *The Occult in Early Modern Europe: A Documentary History* (London, 1999)

Mout, M.E.H.N., 'Hermes Trismegistos Germanicus: Rudolf II en der arcane wetenschappen', *Rudolf II and his Court, Leids Kunsthistorisch Jaarboek 1982* (Delft, 1982)

Muneles, Otto, ed., *The Prague Ghetto in the Renaissance Period* (Prague, 1965)

Neher, André, *Jewish Thought and the Scientific Revolution of the Sixteenth Century: David Gans (1546–1613) and his Times* (Oxford, 1986)

Novák, J.B., *Rudolf II. a jeho pád* (Prague, 1931)

Pauli, W., 'The Influence of Archetypal Ideas on the Scientific Theories of Kepler', in C.G. Jung and W. Pauli, *The Interpretation of Nature and the Psyche*, tr. Priscilla Silz, (London, 1955)

Read, John, *Prelude to Chemistry* (London, 1936)

Ripellino, Angelo Maria, *Magic Prague* (1973), tr. D.N Marinelli, ed. M.H. Heim (London, 1994)

Rose, J., *The Winter Queen: The Story of Elizabeth Stuart* (New York, 1979)

Ross, J.M and M.M. McLaughlin, eds., *The Portable Renaissance Reader* (Harmondsworth, 1985)

Ruderman, D.B., *Kaballah, Magic and Science* (Cambridge, MA, 1988)

Rudolf II and his Court, Leids Kunsthistorisch Jaarboek 1982 (Delft, 1982)

Rudolf II and Prague: The Court and City, ed., Eliška Fučíková *et al.*, (London, 1997)

Sargent, R.M., *At the Court of Queen Elizabeth: The Life and Lyrics of Sir Edward Dyer* (Oxford, 1935)

Scholem, Gershom G., *Major Trends in Jewish Mysticism* (New York, 1941)

——, *On the Kabbalah and its Symbolism* (London, 1965)

Schwarzenfeld, Gertrude von, *Rudolf II: Der saturnische Kaiser* (Munich, 1961)

Sherwin, B.L., *Mystical Theology and Social Dissent: The Life and Work of Judah Loew of Prague* (Rutherford, N.J., 1982)

Sherwood, Frances, *The Book of Splendor* (New York, 2002)

Shumaker, W., *The Occult Sciences in the Renaissance* (Berkeley, 1972)

——, *Renaissance Curiosa* (New York, 1982)

Singer, D.W., *Giordano Bruno: His Life and Thought* (New York, 1950)

Smith, L.P., *The Life and Letters of Sir Henry Wotton*, 2 vols. (Oxford, 1907)

Strathern, Paul, *Mendeleyev's Dream: The Quest for the Elements* (London, 2000)

Sviták, Ivan, *Sir Edward Kelly: cesky rytr, 1555–1598* (Prague, 1994)

——, 'John Dee and Edward Kelly', 5, *Kosmos* (1986)

Thieberger, F., *The Great Rabbi Loew of Prague* (London, 1955)

Thomas, Keith V., *Religion and the Decline of Magic* (London, 1971)

Thoren, Victor E., *The Lord of Uraniborg: A Biography of Tycho Brahe* (Cambridge, 1990)

Thorndike, Lyn, A History of Magic and Experimental Science, vols.5–7 (New York, 1941–8)

Tillyard, E.M.W., The Elizabethan World Picture (London, 1963)

Trevor-Roper, Hugh R., Princes and Artists: Patronage and Ideology at Four Habsburg Courts, 1517–1633 (London, 1976)

——, Renaissance Essays (London, 1985)

Trunz, Erich, Wissenschaft und Kunst im Kreise Kaiser Rudolfs II, 1576–1612 (Neumünster, 1992)

Vickers, B., ed., Occult and Scientific Mentalities in the Renaissance (Cambridge, 1989)

Vocelka, Karl, Rudolf II und seine Zeit (Vienna and Cologne, 1985)

Vurm, Bohumil, The Beauties and Secrets of the Czech Republic: History, Symbols, Personalities in the European Context (Prague, 2004)

Vurm, Robert B., Rudolf II and his Prague: Mysteries and Curiosities of Rudolfine Prague (Prague, 1997)

Waite, A.E., Lives of the Alchemystical Philosophers (London, 1888)

——, The Brotherhood of the Rosy Cross (London,1924)

——,The Secret Tradition in Alchemy (London, 1926)

Walker, Susan, Spiritual and Demonic Magic from Ficino to Campanella (London, 1958)

Webster, Charles, From Paracelsus to Newton: Magic and the Making of Modern Science (Cambridge, 1982)

West, John Antony, The Case for Astrology (New York, 1991)

Wheatcroft, Andrew, The Habsburgs: Embodying Empire (Harmondsworth, 1996)

White, M., Isaac Newton: The Last Sorcerer (London, 1997)

——, The Pope and the Heretic: The True Story of Courage and Murder at the Hands of the Inquisition (London, 2002)

Whitefield, Peter, Astrology: A History (London, 2001)

Wilding, Michael, Raising Spirits, Making Gold and Swapping Wives (Beeston, 1999)

——,'Edward Kelley: A Life', Cauda Pavonis, 18, 1–2 (1999), pp.1–26

Woolley, Benjamin, The Queen's Conjuror: The Life and Magic of Dr Dee (London, 2002)

Yates, Frances A., Giordano Bruno and the Hermetic Tradition (London, 1964)

——, The Art of Memory (London, 1966)

——, The Rosicrucian Enlightenment (London, 1972)

——, The Occult Philosophy in the Elizabethan Age (London, 1979)

Index